NOBODY SEES THIS

UNSEEN REALM

HOW TO UNLOCK BIBLE MYSTERIES

PAUL RENFROE

PARADIGM LIGHTHOUSE

Destin, Florida, United States of America

© 2022 Paul Renfroe

All rights reserved. No part of this publication may be reproduced in any form without written permission from publisher.

Published by Paradigm Lighthouse, PO Box 48, Freeport FL 32439 www.ParadigmLighthouse.com

Nobody Sees This Unseen Realm: How to Unlock Bible Mysteries
by Paul Renfroe

ISBN 979-8-9853944-2-9 paperback; 979-8-9853944-3-6 hardcover

LCCN 2022910303

BISAC: REL012120, RELIGION, Christian Living, Spiritual Growth

REL095000, RELIGION, Christian Education, Adult

REL006700, RELIGION, Biblical Studies, Bible Studies

REL074000, RELIGION, Christian Ministry, Pastoral Resources

Cover Design by Hannah Linder

Editing by Kay Coulter

Interior Design by Michael Williams

Publication Consulting by Susan Neal

Except where indicated, Scripture quotations are from the New King James Version®. Copyright © 1982 by Thomas Nelson. Used by permission. All rights reserved.

Greek words and phrases are from the Aland/Black *et al* 3rd edition of the Greek New Testament, published in USA by American Bible Society, New York NY

This book is for informational purposes only. While every precaution has been taken in the preparation of the book, neither the author nor the publisher shall have any liability to any person or entity with respect to any loss or damage caused by the content of this book.

Printed in the United States of America
First Edition

IN THE *UNSEEN* SERIES:

Book 1

Nobody Sees This You: How to Live as a Spirit in the Unseen Realm

Book 2

Nobody Sees This Unseen Realm: How to Unlock Bible Mysteries

Book 3

Nobody Sees This Creation: The Origin of the Devil and His Replacements

Book 4

Nobody Sees These Enemies: How to Discern and Disarm Unseen Tempters

Book 5

Nobody Sees This Israel: God's Vanguard Against Darkness

Book 6

Nobody Sees This Warrior: God's Secret Ambush

Book 7

Nobody Sees This Church: Resisting Darkness

Book 8

Nobody Sees These Friends: Partners in the Unseen

Book 9

Nobody Sees This Victory, Yet: Defeating Darkness

OTHER BOOKS BY PAUL RENFROE:

Christian, What Are You? Removing the Blindfolds (2013)
Inadequacy (2015)
The Pains of the Christian: Desire, Glory, Joy (2015)

"If anyone loves me, he will keep my word, and my Father will love him, and we will come to him and make our home with him." (John 14:23)

FREE GIFT TO READERS
The above 11x17 full color poster summarizes this
Book Two of the Unseen Series. Each book has such a poster.
You can get yours for free. Post it to encourage yourself,
as well as all who see and ask about it.
Learn how you can receive one for free at *ParadigmLighthouse.com*.

CONTENTS

Introduction   1
  The Great Explainer   2
  Not Normal   3
  Safety   4
  About Capitalization   5
  Housekeeping   5

Chapter One: *War Engaged*   7

Chapter Two: *Danger*   15

Chapter Three: *Word, Spirit, Love*   37

Chapter Four: *Baselines*   43

Chapter Five: *Advanced Bible Logic*   65

Chapter Six: *Coder and Code, Decoder and Key*   89

Chapter Seven: *God's Words*   109

Chapter Eight: *Time Travel*   129

Chapter Nine: *Explanatory Power*   147

Chapter Ten: *Puzzles and Mysteries*   167

Resources   175
  About The *UNSEEN* Series   177
  Works Referenced   185
  Topical Listing of Books for Your Spirit   187
  Reader Engagement Resources   191
  Sample Study: Esther   193

FOREWORD

Paul and Diane Renfroe have a long history of intense hunger for spiritual growth. Paul's love for the Bible is evident to all who know him. He has done the work and paid the price to learn it well.

With their leadership gifts, they have served in many churches. We have ordained them as ministers, acknowledging a clear love for people in both their past ministry and their writing. It is well-known that Paul and Diane have sought to be conformed to the image of Jesus Christ.

That's the subject of my book titled *Your Highest Calling*. I founded Christian International in 1968. For over fifty years, we have activated Christians globally in spiritual gifts, including prophetic ministry.

Paul learned about us in 2006, and quickly recognized Christian International as a welcoming home for their spiritual hunger. They attended our schools in Indiana and Florida. In 2011, they became local residents so they could participate in our headquarters church, Vision Church at Christian International.

What Paul has produced in *Nobody Sees This Unseen Realm*—Book Two of the nine-book *Unseen Series*—will enable any spiritually hungry reader to replicate his own discovery process. The subtitle, *How to Unlock Bible Mysteries*, captures the essential protective skill you need to advance truthfully.

Your church background gives you a foundation to build upon, and if you seek more, this is the book for you. Few churches pretend they can provide everything that a hungry Christian seeks. Every church and group of any kind has people who are on the forward edges, seeking more and not knowing where to look. You may be one such person.

The Bible habits and techniques that Paul Renfroe describes in this book will equip you to satisfy many unsolved curiosities. I strongly encourage you to adopt Paul's Bible reading attitudes. You will advance your spiritual maturity in ways you never thought possible.

Bishop Bill Hamon
Bishop: Christian International Apostolic-Global Network
Author: *Who Am I & Why Am I Here; The Eternal Church; Prophets & Personal Prophecy; Prophets & the Prophetic Movement; Prophets, Pitfalls, & Principles; Apostles/Prophets & the Coming Moves of God; The Day of the Saints; The Final Reformation & Great Awaking; 70 Reasons for Speaking in Tongues; God's Weapons of War; Your Highest Calling; and How Can These Things Be?*

To The Reader

The test readers have asked me about my audience. It's you: curious, growing, unsatisfied, inquisitive, or charged to help such people. Like you, many now sense the unseen realm. The nine-book *Unseen* Series offers Christian explanations of that perception. Your own process of testing will reveal if these explanations are satisfying to you.

You are holding the second book of the series: *Nobody Sees This Unseen Realm: How to Unlock Bible Mysteries*. The Bible explains the unseen influences on your life and on this world. This series is based on the Bible. Please see *About the Unseen Series* at the end of this book.

Many fields and authors attempt to explain the influences on people: philosophy, comparative religion, astrophysics, economics, history, ancient writings, and Christian literature. The explanatory power of the *Unseen* series unveils the origins of unseen forces and entities. **The series purpose is to equip readers for righteous and effective function among unseen spirits.**

You might experience the same relief and delight of understanding. I say "might," because it is conditional upon responding to the King of the Unseen as He desires. It's possible that you don't think of yourself as a Christian, but that you are closer than someone who does. *About the Unseen Series* at the end of the book describes the protocol for becoming a living spirit and maturing.

Prior to publication, test readers from various age groups and walks of life reviewed and improved this book. Though unknown to you, their contribution has curbed or eliminated potential misunderstandings. Many thanks are due to them.

A private online discussion group awaits you at ParadigmLighthouse. com. There, you and other readers can discuss our discoveries about life as spirits. Each reader can request log-in credentials on that website.

INTRODUCTION

This book is the second installment in the *Unseen* Series: *Nobody Sees This Unseen Realm: How to Unlock Bible Mysteries.*

Unseen influences are pressing into our field of view. Invisible entities are causing more effects. These spiritual agents are immune to our scientific experimentation, resistant to our control, and undetectable by our five senses.

The *Unseen* Series offers Christian explanations, tested by millions for centuries. You and your friends can test them for yourselves. The world's dearest values today originate in the Bible; billions of people know God as their Father from it. Yet more billions read the Bible who are not Christians. You may be in either group. In both, people often embark upon its pages and find nothing—possibly you as well. Wherever your starting point, I wrote the *Unseen* Series to unlock the Bible and transform it for you—from an ancient book into the daily speech of your Father. By intimacy with the King of unseen kings, and Lord of unseen lords, we can effectively function in this bulge of the unseen world. After all, He created the unseen, and gave us spirit birth. Know it or not, the Christian spirit lives there—in the unseen.

Possibly, you don't consider yourself a Christian, but you might be closer than someone who does. One evidence: the hunger that brought your eyes to this page. In the Resources appendix, *About the Unseen Series* describes God's protocol to become a living spirit.

Book One of the *Unseen* Series is *Nobody Sees This You: How to Live as a Spirit in the Unseen Realm.* Start the series with any volume. Full benefit comes by reading them in order, because the discoveries are cumulative—each building upon the previous. This Book Two assumes the reader's familiarity with living as a spirit in the unseen realm. Feeling lost in what follows may signal the need to read Book One, where life as a spirit is covered in depth.

Your spirit's effectiveness can grow. Like visiting a foreign country, you can pick up the language. This Book Two improves your engagement with the Bible, where God reveals the seen and unseen realms. These habits of engagement help us know the Bible, thus the subtitle: *How to Unlock Bible Mysteries.*

"Improves:" many readers have made a life's passion of Bible study, as I have. If so, you will find in the following pages principles and techniques which I have never heard from anyone nor seen in print. Please join in the forum at ParadigmLighthouse.com to share your responses. If I am wrong at some point, in today's world it can be corrected and reprinted.

However, Bible reading principles of any kind may be new to you. The payoff is a new power for explaining life. I cannot overvalue or overstate the resulting security. In the Bible, God reveals the grid behind all our brushes with the unseen—the structures of the unseen realm. Understanding *why* and *how* things happen is very satisfying. Encounters with God's unseen world can be unsettling and frightening, and that's my personal testimony. Just because you have such encounters does not make you a weirdo.

THE GREAT EXPLAINER

Whether they occupy an hour of study or a passing thought, words in the Bible are not normal. We can hear or read them; we can feel them in Braille or see sign language. In any format, printed, audio, or digital, its sentences and paragraphs are packages of the unseen. The Bible is the Great Explainer.

That's certainly my testimony. God blessed me with an insatiable hunger to be His friend. In me, He placed an unconventional and unashamed curiosity about the Bible. Many are like me. I didn't qualify for these implants. I just asked Him. Any reader can ask Him to amplify that inner hunger and curiosity. You can ask Him right now.

In the unseen world are invisible murderers. They hate God and His created mankind. These unseen enemies are known by their effects and by the obstacles they erect against God's friendships. There's plenty of help from humanity itself, with all our systems to dismiss or control God. The combined effect is to obscure the Bible, and to obstruct intimacy with God.

> I can't blame others, though. Right inside me, closer than thought itself, is a willpower for my own way. You, reader, can relate to that. In fact, did we stop and ask God to

> make us hungry for Him? Did our enemies help us rush on past? Even if we only ask for help to ask, God's Holy Spirit will rush in and help us ask.
>
> Lord, I believe; help my unbelief! (Mark 9:24)

God helps us obey and trust Him; He desires moment-by-moment intimacy with each of us. Billions of people live that way with Him. I have found He never tires of helping us love Him, coaxing us further in and further up (*The Last Battle,* Book 7 of the Narnia Chronicles by C. S. Lewis).

For example, when this book and the *Unseen* series began pouring into me, He helped me obey Him—the first but not the only motive for this book. I also love improving our Bible reading. You have heard the adage: give someone a fish, feed them for a day, but teach them to fish, and feed them for a lifetime. A third motive is identifying our preconceived notions. Thinking we know enough or are mature enough sends the kingdom of darkness a text alert that we are vulnerable.

The Bible also makes sense of today's world, a fourth motive—which equips us for full, relevant function. People want a unified theory of reality. Albert Einstein's 1916 book on relativity offered an explanation. Physicist Stephen Hawking offered one in his 2006 book, *The Theory of Everything.* Likewise, God offers one: *The Explanation of Seen and Unseen Influences.* He had people write it over 1,400 years and compile it in the year 327. We know it as the Bible.

It is the Great Explainer. Making sense of the world with improved Bible reading helps our spirits mature. Recognizing heaven's present-day influence transforms our lives, our citizenship, our family, church, and community.

NOT NORMAL

One certainty: the unseen inhabitants are not going away. The good ones such as angels, we want. But the evil ones who steal, kill, and destroy are right at hand as well. The unseen enemies promote themselves as the source of happiness—just like a Venus flytrap promotes itself to flies. The unseen enemies' sneaky deceptiveness makes a formidable opponent for us. We are easily tricked by enemy spirits because we refuse to admit the poverty in spirit that Jesus blesses. The kingdom of darkness has age-old, global strategies and door-to-door tactics. With these, they control, torment, and oppress people, both individually and in groups.

The *Unseen* series unveils their origins and purposes and equips readers to cooperate with God in victory. Bible discoveries alone are the source. I have had no knowing or willing interaction with the unseen enemies of God. Any such curiosity in the reader is perverse and hazardous.

Let the reader be warned: the Bible is not a regular book. It holds both life and death. A person can't live with it because it convicts, and can't live without it because it nourishes. The key is how a reader responds to the Person in the Bible. God Almighty inspired its forty authors, oversaw its compilation, and superintends its translations into the languages of the world. He did this to talk with me and with you because He knows each of us and desires our friendship.

SAFETY

Such warm intimacy with Him makes it possible to be meek without fear: safely. Accepting God's call to our full function in His unseen creation can be scary. But He imparts safety to us. Tremble as we might, He created us for full spirit function in the unseen realms. Yes, you're correct: you and I are completely inadequate and humbly fearful. Our safety must be in His loyal love alone. Only His adequacy can enable our function in the unseen.

The Bible is the authoritative book of Christian faith—complete, unique, divinely inspired and entirely trustworthy. The *Unseen* series explains away nothing found in it but instead seeks the most plausible, effective explanation of its mysteries. What we are contemplating in the *Unseen* series is not conjecture.

God uses questions and puzzles to bring us closer to Him. To Job's protests, God responded with 150 questions, and the answers are absent. Likewise, the Bible incites many questions and not all the answers are available to us. But it does not have a "stay away" warning on any topic. A disciple asks and waits. As lovers of God our delight is in the Person loved, not the knowledge. If the answer comes forth or if it doesn't, our joy is the same: in Him.

Scripture reveals everything God wants us to discover, but not all is low-hanging fruit or instantly available. There is a barrier to entry: meekness is required. God's revelation in its pages awaits our maturity in meekness. Apostle Paul exemplifies such meekness in 1 Timothy 1:15, *"Christ Jesus came into the world to save sinners, of whom I am chief."*

ABOUT CAPITALIZATION

To disarm the formal religious awkwardness of certain words, and to properly reflect the identity of personal participants in the unseen world, we have adopted the following guides for each book in the *Unseen* series.

We capitalize the first letter of each pronoun referring to God or a person of the Trinity. Current style guidelines regard this as archaic; I regard it as respectful. It also helps us keep the characters straight as we talk about the many spirits in the unseen world.

Because capitalization indicates honor, I've chosen not to use an upper case first letter for the devil. The word *satan* means accuser in the Bible, a functional description and not capitalized. Originally created as a cherub, Lucifer does have a first letter cap as his given name prior to falling.

You'll learn that there are active personal entities that can't be seen but not completely revealed in the Bible, and when I refer to them, it is with an upper case first letter. Examples are Creation, Sin, and Earth. When they are lower case first letter, the reference is to the acts of creating and sinning, or to land, dirt, or acreage.

HOUSEKEEPING

I cite the Scriptures discussed right in these pages, using the New King James translation of 1982. With a digital or printed Bible of your own, you can test these principles for yourself. To dig deep is its own reward; what you can find is friendship with God. There are many books offering spiritual benefit; the Bible is the only book to deliver the ultimate prize.

As with Book One, "beta readers" from various age groups and walks of life reviewed and improved this Book Two. One test reader said, "I expected that I would learn how to fight evil, and instead it was about reading the Bible." I report this interchange for your protection. For your safety, it is absolutely necessary to be a lifelong student of the Word of God. Though unknown to you, such test readers earned all our gratitude, because their catches eliminated potential misunderstandings and added much clarity to my writing.

Churches often have study groups for books like this one that help us know and apply the Bible. Please help me publicize this *Unseen* Series for the benefit of many; the appendix includes Reader Engagement Resources. Also there: discussion and reflection starters, as well as a sample study of Esther.

A private forum for the *Unseen* series awaits you at ParadigmLighthouse.com. Each reader can request log-in credentials on that website. There, you and other readers can discuss our Bible discoveries about life as spirits. Turn the page, and never look back again.

No one, having put his hand to the plow, and looking back, is fit for the kingdom of God (Luke 9:62).

CHAPTER ONE

WAR ENGAGED

To fully benefit from the Bible, we want to read it twice. You want to read the lines, and you want to read *between* the lines. It's simple to say and do, like bathwater safe for a baby. You'll get a life of unending exploration, deep enough never to hit the bottom. The pages of your Bible explain everything from war to peace, birth to death, intimacy to ferocity.

A BOOK FOR UNSEEN WAR

The battle of light and dark is intensifying in the early twenty-first century. The Church of living spirits represents God against His violent enemies. We wage unseen war in tandem with Him. All around the world, today's prophets are discerning: it's time for conflict. The war of light and darkness is evident in our civil governments and courts. Churches are no longer permitted neutrality; they enlist in God's unseen army, or they wither. A major shaking and rearranging are occurring.

Everywhere Christians are realizing there is no turning back. You'll need a new Bible reading mindset to fight in this conflict of the unseen worlds. The kingdom of darkness is looking for people who are dim-witted about the unseen realm, to serve as unwitting cannon fodder. That's not what we want to be. By capable engagement with God's written Word, that battle will not catch us flat-footed. The full reading of the Bible protects us. Even better: we become God's effective army in the unseen realms.

We are obeying our Lord's deployment. For years we have longed for His return, which is definitely closer than when we first believed (Romans 13:11). We are the Army of Revelation 19:11–16, our first study.

Now I saw heaven opened, and behold, a white horse. And He who sat on him was called Faithful and True, and in righteousness He judges and makes war. His eyes were like a flame of fire, and on His head were many crowns. He had a name written that no one knew except Himself. He was clothed with a robe dipped in blood, and His name is called The Word of God. And the armies in heaven, clothed in fine linen, white and clean, followed Him on white horses. Now out of His mouth goes a sharp sword, that with it He should strike the nations. And He Himself will rule them with a rod of iron. He Himself treads the winepress of the fierceness and wrath of Almighty God. And He has on His robe and on His thigh a name written:
KING OF KINGS
AND LORD OF LORDS.

THE WAY THE WRITER INTENDED

We zoom out first from the passage at hand and we identify the book and its purpose. Apostle John wrote Revelation as his eyewitness account of a visit with the ascended Jesus (1:1, 10–11). He was not the first to see Jesus after His ascension; many had, such as Apostle Paul. Nearly one hundred years old, John was on the isle of Patmos, in the Aegean Sea; Roman persecution evidently exiled him there (1:9). The book is 22 chapters long and contains 394 allusions or references to the Old Testament—the most of any New Testament book.

Next we identify the literary genre of Revelation: apocalyptic. What are the rules for understanding apocalyptic literature? Do we take it like a Terminator movie—as total fiction? Or is Revelation literal, like Jesus teaching the disciples in Matthew 24 about the end of Jerusalem? Opinions vary among people. Right in the pages of Revelation, God says some things are symbolic—but which ones? If not clearly stated, how should we take each symbol—as figurative or literal? Here is your answer, one which applies to all Bible literature: **we take it the way the writer intended.** John clearly intends us to read this chapter 19 vision as his literal eyewitness account: *"Now I saw."*

> The vast majority receive Revelation as Apostle John clearly intended: God's preparatory warning that He will end the world and bring all things under judgment, and His invitation for everyone to follow Him. A minority disputes that Revelation is inspired by God. Some even

argue that Apostle John was not the author of Revelation. At the core of such theories always lurks an unprovable preconceived notion: that the Bible is not trustworthy. But that notion was decided by their heart, not their mind. *The heart chooses, and the mind excuses*, as the saying goes. How can you spot such theories? The telltale sign: they measure the unseen realm by the reason and science of the seen world. This handicap pervades their entire view of reality. They explain away miracles, for instance. Within seminaries for pastors and priests, this handicap has flourished. As a result, many congregations hear the Bible dismissed or diluted by their church leaders. If that is you, think for yourself: can citizens of the seen world mentally perceive the unseen world? They love reason, but how rational is it to rely on reason and science for the unseen world? A meek repentance recognizes the necessity of divine revelation of the unseen world. The invisible world of spirit can only be revealed by God Himself, whatever "scholars" might believe.

JESUS' SWORD

From Jesus' mouth John saw a sharp sword proceeding—but how close was John? What signaled that the sword was sharp? He didn't report touching it. Did John just know? This happens to us living spirits frequently: things we know, without knowing *how* we know. John told Christians how, in 1 John 2:27.

> But the anointing which you have received from Him abides in you, and you do not need that anyone teach you; but as the same anointing teaches you concerning all things, and is true, and is not a lie, and just as it has taught you, you will abide in Him.

Before reporting Jesus' sharp sword, John describes the armies of heaven behind Him—clearly a very large number. From this perspective of distance, seeing so many multitudes, there would be only one way to perceive the sword's sharp edges, by their visible glistening. Dull swords are oxidized like weathered metal, and do not shine.

He also had a close-up of the sword in Jesus' mouth previously and it was sharp (1:16). Jesus Himself spoke to John about the sword from His mouth, when dictating His letter to the church in Pergamum (1:12, 16).

There are practical questions about a sword in someone's mouth. This is not like a sword-swallowing act at a carnival: point in first, sheathing the business end with the mouth and merely a trick. Jesus' sword is useful; its business end is pointing out, unsheathed. It doesn't prevent His resurrection body from talking (1:17ff). The conclusion can only be this: a resurrected body can do much more than the ones we have now. I wonder what it will be like.

> Identifying such details are not a waste of time. Questions about details can open the door to further understanding. In 1978, James W. Sire (then editor of InterVarsity Press) wrote *How to Read Slowly*. The title expresses the hallmark of genuine receptivity. We betray our immaturity by reading the Bible in a hurry. When we rush a new dating friend because we want that feeling of intimacy, we are using them. When we habitually rush through the Bible, we may be using God. By lingering in study, prayer and reflection on Bible passages, we develop true intimacy with Him.

THE BIBLE WEAPON

Forcing a Bible passage to be either literal or figurative is a sure way to miss both. In the unseen world we are not bound to physical reality, as reviewed in Book One, *Nobody Sees This You: How to Live as a Spirit in the Unseen Realm*. Jesus' sword is literal, eye-witnessed by John, and it is also symbolic. In fact, the sword has long been used to represent the words God speaks.

Jesus told His disciples in Matthew 10:34 that He came to bring a sword on Earth. The writer of Hebrews identified the sword as the word of God, and Apostle Paul clearly defined the Bible as the sword in Ephesians 6:17.

Do not think that I came to bring peace on earth. I did not come to bring peace but a sword. Matthew 10:34

For the word of God is living and powerful, and sharper than any two-edged sword. Hebrews 4:12

And take the helmet of salvation, and the sword of the Spirit, which is the word of God. Ephesians 6:17

The sword from the resurrected Jesus' mouth is the Word of God. When seeing it, John knew its purpose: *"Now out of His mouth goes a sharp sword, that with it He should strike the nations"* (19:15).

JESUS' ARMY

As Jesus' army, we no longer limit the Bible to hearing God ourselves. We all desire peace and take reasonable actions to have security. But as with any army, God projects force through us—the force of His Word, the sword in Jesus' mouth. To shrink from God's battle is unbecoming for us whom He saved; it betrays our enlistment. Apostle Paul didn't shrink; some of his letters were written as he sat in chains. Hebrews 10:36–39 warns us not to shrink back..

For you have need of endurance, so that after you have done the will of God, you may receive the promise:

"For yet a little while, And He who is coming will come and will not tarry. Now the just shall live by faith; But if anyone draws back, My soul has no pleasure in him."

But we are not of those who draw back to perdition, but of those who believe to the saving of the soul.

Following Him loyally puts us on the front line in His unseen war. He has filled us with His Spirit and His home is in us (John 14:23). He has given us our primary weapon: the Scripture, His sword. His Word is sharp against God's unseen enemies,. Everyone deceived into complicity with them is cut by that sword—and we wield it as His partners in the effort.

And the rest were killed with the sword which proceeded from the mouth of Him who sat on the horse. And all the birds were filled with their flesh. (Revelation 19:21)

He is providing books like this Book Two so His Church can use His Word as He intends. The King of kings wants to equip your church and mine for conflict. Any reader can call upon His supply to receive His bravery.

THE CLOCK FOR WAR

As we follow Him, we can match the Bible's statements and prophecies to the events of our time. It serves as our clock and calendar, for discerning our times. By His Word we can identify what is happening in the unseen realm. In the coming pages we devote attention to the relationship of the Bible and our timeline.

VISIBLE DARKNESS

In our exciting times, the veil of the unseen is becoming more transparent. Twenty-first century people recognize: the kingdom of darkness is playing its long-hidden hand.

We see it not only in government and the courts of law, but also in our churches, families, and communities. Media big and small gleefully report violent discontent and excuse wrongdoing while ridiculing us who love freedom, righteousness, and prosperity. Terrorists destabilize security in every country; despots suck the blood of their nations and threaten their peace-loving neighbors. A Communist economic power blackmails smaller nations and those with less backbone, while it tortures all dissenters and persecutes all who refuse its idols. Amid this flood, the America which shed its blood for righteousness is now playing games with computers and elections.

Deep darkness is covering the earth.

We desire to preserve the great advances of our society. It's very easy to fret and worry about this new darkness. The threat to our peaceful lives is palpable. But by mature engagement with God's Bible, we will see much more than threats alone—we see opportunity, and our expectation mounts. We recognize that satan and his kingdom are overplaying their hand. Our God is preparing an ambush as He did outside the gates of Ai (Joshua 8). He delights in surprise attacks, ambushes, and feints as we will see in Chapter Six, *Coder and Code, Decoder and Key*. Thorough exploration awaits the reader in Book Six of the *Unseen* series, *Nobody Sees This Warrior: God's Secret Ambush*.

THE PEOPLE ARE COMING

Darkness seeks to spread its oppression against its hated enemy, God, and His image-creatures. Isaiah's prophecy in 60:1–5 shows how God reverses the effect of satan's actions.

Arise, shine;
For your light has come!
And the glory of the LORD is risen upon you.
For behold, the darkness shall cover the earth,
And deep darkness the people;
But the LORD will arise over you,
And His glory will be seen upon you.
The Gentiles shall come to your light,
And kings to the brightness of your rising.
Lift up your eyes all around, and see:
They all gather together, they come to you;
Your sons shall come from afar,
And your daughters shall be nursed at your side.
Then you shall see and become radiant,
And your heart shall swell with joy.

What did the writer intend? My word count: *come,* four times. *Glory, darkness,* and *light,* two times each. The idea of light and sunrise is captured in eight places with the implied visibility in three more places. Nor can we miss the repetition of large, diverse masses: *the earth, the people, the Gentiles, kings, all around, all gather, from afar.*

> By counting repeated words, phrases, and ideas, we see the writer's intent in a Bible passage. Those counts give the spine to which all the other statements are attached like ribs. What may feel juvenile is in fact a useful shoehorn. Any author identifies his unifying focus by the emphasis of repetition, and Bible authors are no exception.

In Isaiah's prophecy, God reveals what we can expect from this spreading darkness. The oppression that darkness deploys makes more people desire the light. Modern prophets describe the shaking now begun as the lead-up to a great worldwide awakening. Such an event is exactly what God showed Isaiah. They come to us Christians for light, as Apostle John wrote in John 1:4–5.

In Him was life, and the life was the light of men. And the light shines in the darkness, and the darkness did not comprehend it.

In the past, the unseen realm was more deeply veiled. We lived life as if the visible world was primary. But now darkness overplays its hand, and people worldwide are desiring relief. We living spirits are the only ones with the relief they seek: the gospel of Jesus Christ. Through this message alone can a person have intimacy with God as Father, forgiveness by faith in Jesus Christ, and the filling of God the Holy Spirit. These bounties, God offers only through the Bible.

CHAPTER TWO

DANGER

Our Christian Bible is life in a book. God inspired it for every person's benefit. Not everyone receives life from it, however.

The 1981 movie *Raiders of the Lost Ark* pits Indiana Jones and his friend Marion against an evil Nazi archaeologist, Belloq. The climax finds Indiana and Marion tied to a stake. Belloq prepares to open the ark of the covenant. Indiana yells to her,

> "Marion, don't look at it. Shut your eyes, Marion. Don't look at it, no matter what happens!"

The next scene finds only two people remaining—our protagonists. Using God's things without honor for God brought death to all others. Belloq melts instantly in his prideful falderal, but the honor shown by the wise pair protected them.

DATA INTO CONFLICT

Apostle Paul explained the conflict within a Christian to the Galatian church. The Bible word *flesh* has a comprehensive meaning, not only our bodies but also our souls with mind, will, and emotions. Flesh is the limit of human existence from birth. Your spirit is born by your loyal, obedient trust in Jesus. You become one of a new race, living human spirits in mortal bodies. You are both flesh and spirit. Galatians 5:17 says,

> For the flesh lusts against the Spirit, and the Spirit against the flesh; and these are contrary to one another, so that you do not do the things that you wish.

The Bible is a data input into the conflict between a Christian's living spirit and his or her flesh. Its words and paragraphs carry power to the superior contestant—but which is the stronger? Our flesh or our spirit? We have a choice. A Christian can read the Bible and come out nasty, mean, judgmental, and controlling. If we do, our long-practiced flesh has supremacy over our immature spirit. No finger-pointing—I have done that; maybe you have as well. But meek people repent and grow. Our spirit can mature out of such religious meanness.

The Bible produces goodness with its data input. From it, our full authority in the seen and unseen worlds grows. But there is a condition: meekness. Without it, the Bible lets us hide from the inner conflict of our flesh and our spirit. The choice is ours. Tolerating the superiority of our flesh, we can use the Bible for pretense. That was the choice of the greatest Bible students ever, the Pharisees of Jesus' day.

> You search the Scriptures, for in them you think you have eternal life; and these are they which testify of Me. But you are not willing to come to Me that you may have life.... You are of your father the devil, and the desires of your father you want to do. (John 5:39, 8:44)

DATA FOR SOCIETY

The Bible's data input affects not only individuals. Entire societies can welcome the Bible's data input. The structures of such societies can promote personal character. Christians and unbelievers benefit alike.

Such societies spread childhood education to develop human capital. Biblical standards protect the least and restrain the greatest. Frontiers yield to exploration. The cycle of challenge, solution, and advancement is continual. Manufacture grows. Research multiplies inventions. Humankind has flourished under the influence of Scripture.

The Bible's input blessed American society with our checks and balances system. Both the Protestant work ethic and our environmental stewardship come from Genesis 2.

Societies without the Bible input have corrupt, cruel leaders. Media, politicians, and the wealthy form the elites. Government runs on bribes and leaders pocket public money. The lives of their citizens are cheap, mere cannon fodder for the elites' loveless ambitions.

Nations can also willfully forsake Scripture. Significant advances won by past Christians can be lost. Scripture's fruit of character is not permanent. Societies can distort and misuse biblical values.

Good social structures then fall prey to evil manipulators. Hypocrisy fills the airwaves and spills out in print. Legal judgments favor the preferred. In place of brave public service, self-preservation drives elected officials.

The public's work ethic yields to convenience. Conscience runs on feelings. Everyone consumes and few produce. Churches and Christians offer social Band-Aids and call it healing.

The war is afoot. Seen and unseen are intermingling. The Bible is God's weapon. Each reader of God's Word has a contest, both inwardly and outwardly. Into that contest, the Sword from Jesus' mouth pierces. Scripture serves those who choose Him.

If people submit to His Word with meekness, then we grow to our full intended authority in both the unseen world and the seen.

In the beginning was the Word, and the Word was with God, and the Word was God. (John 1:1)

CONTEST FOR NORMAL

God's Word claims to reveal what is normal. But since we go our own way as a race, we have set up a competing normal. We do this as individuals, as a society, and as the human race. When we read the Bible, whose *normal* will win the contest? His or mine?

Establishing norms is common sense. Large numbers of people can operate in agreement with those norms. Consider a traffic norm: the yellow line that we agree to observe. Establishing this norm avoids head-on collisions. The law not to cross it does not prevent the collisions. Neither the line itself nor its yellow color erects a force field to keep cars apart. We agree upon the norm, and therefore, it works. Its power is agreement. Our lives are entrusted to total strangers. We go 50 miles an hour within two feet of another driver speeding in the opposite direction. The norm of the yellow line permits this trust.

God's fixed Word is like the natural laws governing collisions. The Bible reveals His unchanging norms and promotes their desirability. Using words like righteousness, He identifies the behaviors that bring prosperity. The Scripture supports intimacy between God and people.

Sometimes, the thought of reading the Bible comes with guilt or fear. It reveals my norms and yours. We know this and avoid that exposure.

As poor as we are, we still prefer the substandard norms we know over the pain of dying to ourselves and yielding to His norms. The following sections list just a few avoidance methods; you know your usual ones. Mine: "I am too busy right now."

Many influences compete to set the norms of our lives. A short list includes family, education, friends, childhood, health, and neighborhood. The most powerful norm-setter we fight is the kingdom of darkness. From birth, they trick us into feeling unsafe with God, just as satan tricked Eve. We agree with them and begin our lives by going our own way. I fall into an argument with the norms of my Father, and live as if His enemies are right.

The Bible is a searchlight that will expose your agreements with the kingdom of darkness. In the hands of the Holy Spirit, this torch will illuminate every argument with God. Your reading of the Bible always leaves you with a normative choice. God's? or yours?

Deliverance is the ministry of expelling demonic influence from our lives. *"Deliver us from evil,"* Jesus told us to pray. Receiving deliverance ministry restores our agreement with God. When we cooperate with the Holy Spirit that way, we turn the exposing spotlight onto darkness. Our past norms can fall away, and our Father's norms can prosper us.

Dear Holy Spirit, please spare no effort to help me agree with Father's norms.

MAGIC MELTING TALISMAN

Like Belloq, Hitler, and the Nazis in the movie, people lust for the unseen. Sorcery and witchcraft are efforts to participate with spirits, and have spirit power, without submitting to God. We can even consider the Bible as a way into that realm. Leveraging God's Word to get something more desirable is just like those dark arts.

With Bible verses, we can attempt to manipulate God, people, and creation. If we use the Bible rather than honor it, we insult Him and invite wrath. It's using the Bible when we love its gifts more than its Giver. We turn Scripture into a talisman.

God honors His Word. He reveals Himself to people through its words.

The fictional Belloq melted instantly. Real people who use God's Word melt gradually, indiscernibly. The Bible boils us from within when we use Him, like the proverbial frog in hot water. Many Christians provide evidence of this. Without judging them, let every Christian resolve: I will read the Bible because I love God, and I live with Him.

18

USING THE BIBLE

We can use the Bible and simultaneously refuse to submit to it. We pick and choose what we like in it. This limits its influence to the boundaries of our comfort zones. Such efforts reveal awful pride. We fall victim to our inner conflict. Using the Bible makes people into pawns of unseen God-haters.

In Matthew 23, Jesus prophesied woes for two specific groups of Jewish leaders, the scribes and the Pharisees. They built their entire lives around the Scripture. Why not the priests or the Sadducees, the other two groups who focused on Temple liturgy? The scribes and the Pharisees only used the Bible to support their priorities. They did not submit to God or His Word. Jesus identified them as users.

In relationships, using other people is bad. It's even worse to use God's Word for our own gain. James' letter describes the consequence in verse 4:34.

> You ask and do not receive, because you ask amiss, that you may spend it on your pleasures. Adulterers and adulteresses! Do you not know that friendship with the world is enmity with God? Whoever therefore wants to be a friend of the world makes himself an enemy of God.

John 5:39 is cited previously; it also describes many church people. I have no pleasure to write this. Like the Bible students who engineered Jesus' crucifixion, "believers" still use the Bible to crucify those who threaten them. You may have suffered at the hand of such immature Christians; I and my friends certainly have.

Our purpose here is not to judge them but to heed their warning example: do not be like them. Jesus will judge us all, and we all need His mercy that Day. So regardless of how others have hurt us with the Bible, we want to re-enter it healthily. Our spirits want more health, not less, from the Bible. We do not want to become negative, nasty people who give credence to the insult, "Bible-thumper."

TEACHABLE AND MEEK

Bible-thumpers happen—not because of a flaw in the Bible, but because of the flaws in us. **God designed the Bible to expose what hurts us, and promote what helps us.** We can love our pleasures, comforts, and habits more than we love Him. Thinking we know what the Bible means, we quickly satisfy ourselves that we have the best interpretation. Our heart chooses and our mind excuses. But the most cutting Book in the world exposes.

For the word of God is living and powerful, and sharper than any two-edged sword, piercing even to the division of soul and spirit, and of joints and marrow, and is a discerner of the thoughts and intents of the heart. (Hebrews 4:12)

That's why we must read it with meekness. A humble person comes to Scripture with receptivity. My mentors in ministry trained me to identify Christians with momentum. We used the acronym FAT—Faithful, Available, and Teachable. True humility makes us teachable and hungry for Him.

In contrast, we can read the Bible with pride and to our hurt. A man asked Jesus about the greatest commandments, and Jesus answered. But the man, standing in front of the Son of God, wanted to justify himself (Luke 10:29). This is the same pride that caused Lucifer's fall. It falsely disguises itself as humility and hunger. Christians can get stuck in never-learning, refusing to believe God's promises. False meekness prefers the comfort zone we know, even as bad as it is. People can actually choose to lie down with dogs—and use the Bible to excuse it.

This is the opposite of being teachable and meek. Maturing in spirit threatens us with changes. We justify our reluctance to advance in spirit. As a race, our fear of change spares us no misery to avoid it. We prefer the devil we know over the devil we don't.

Proud, closed minds can even treasure trials and sorrows. Such a pretended meekness protects our besetting problems from the God of solutions and advance. Such humility is false because it refuses obedience to Him who calls us forward. His path to our maturity lies through poverty of spirit, mourning, and meekness. We argue with our Savior, and agree with satan, just to avoid change.

We can even use the Word of God to oppose the work of God. Without meekness, we can use the Bible just like Jesus' crucifiers did. When our Bible study includes more pride than humility, repetitive patterns like the following arise.

WILLFUL BLINDNESS

Brand new drivers have much to learn. They have to operate between the lane lines. The idea of going off the road is scary. Fearing the ditch, they overcompensate by veering over to the center line.

We do that with God's written Word. After nearly five Christian decades, I can report: most people know the Bible is dangerous, and so they overcompensate. Most people respond to the Bible like new drivers; they veer to the center line of the road.

With the Scripture, veering to the center is more dangerous than the ditch. Feeling themselves to be safer, they instead fall in with traffic. It leads to willful blindness: "It can't mean that; no one else says that." A choice not to explore Scripture handicaps our spirits' maturing.

It's good to fear the ditch. We try not to steal and do not murder. Even if one of us must sin, we compulsively justify it, precisely because we fear the Bible judgment. In my observation, the vast majority of Americans are trying to avoid the Bible ditch of judgment. We are certainly appreciative, but by overcompensating, willful blindness sets in.

Avoiding the ditch would be adequate if the Bible were normal. It is not, as Hebrews 4:12 affirms. It testifies for billions of people.

> For the word of God is living and powerful, and sharper than any two-edged sword, piercing even to the division of soul and spirit, and of joints and marrow, and is a discerner of the thoughts and intents of the heart.

The Bible's piercing is individualized. I am pierced one way by it, and you, another way. Our flesh seeks to avoid all piercing. This divine scrutiny threatens us. Willful blindness means pretending we didn't see that. We know it exposes our thoughts and intents, and our flesh doesn't want that. So we control what we let in, and drift toward the center line with everyone else. Reading the Bible like everyone else, we feel safer.

So universal is this willful blindness, Hebrews 4:12 continues its testimony in 4:13:

> And there is no creature hidden from His sight, but all things are naked and open to the eyes of Him to whom we must give account.

Eventually, the maturing driver learns to avoid the ditch without overcompensating. Likewise, we learn to subject ourselves to the Bible's piercing. Where others place limits on the Bible, we sit right before it, open-eyed. Jesus used parables about eyes to highlight the danger of willful blindness, such as Matthew 6:23.

> If your eye is bad, your whole body will be full of darkness. If therefore the light that is in you is darkness, how great is that darkness!

After Jesus healed a man born blind, He warned the Pharisees of willful blindness.

> And Jesus said, "For judgment I have come into this world, that those who do not see may see, and that those who see may be made blind." Then some of the Pharisees who were with Him heard these words, and said to Him, "Are we blind also?" Jesus said to them, "If you were blind, you would have no sin; but now you say, 'We see.' Therefore your sin remains." (John 9:39–40)

FENCE-SITTING

We can limit the Bible's influence by sitting on the fence. Purposely ambivalent, we avoid uncontrolled engagement with it. Between ourselves and its accountability, we keep a manageable distance.

On one side, the Bible intimidates a fence-sitter. Uranium hums in movies, and God's Word has a menacing hum as well. It threatens our fears. People work hard to avoid change, and the Bible is change in a book. On the other side of the fence, the Bible magnetizes us. Deep within, we know: our race was made for more than we experience, much more. The Bible contains it, and we want it so badly.

In our time, God is tickling that deep knowledge to the surface. He is knocking at our door, as in Revelation 3:20. Yes, He knocks for our salvation, but that is only the beginning.

> Behold, I stand at the door and knock. If anyone hears My voice and opens the door, I will come in to him and dine with him, and he with Me.

He wants fellowship with us. Stewards that multiply His impartation are His desire. He wants us functional in His unseen world with Him. If we shrink back, our cowardice ranks with damnation, as in Hebrews 10:39 and Revelation 21:7–8.

> But we are not of those who draw back to perdition, but of those who believe to the saving of the soul.

> He who overcomes shall inherit all things, and I will be his God and he shall be My son. But the cowardly, unbelieving, abominable, murderers, sexually immoral, sorcerers, idolaters, and all liars shall have

their part in the lake which burns with fire and brimstone, which is the second death.

Fence-sitting takes several forms. A critical Christian may be on the fence. This was a past failing of mine, always ready with laments about today's Church. I knew the Bible and judged other Christians by it. Such attitudes can be a guise; they excuse the critic from following Jesus without others' approval. I repented and God gave me courage.

Christians enamored with the New Testament Church can also be on the fence. They watch church from a distance, uncommitted and complaining. "I would if I could, but I'm just one person. I'm not a leader." How easily we protest our spiritual innocence!

To sit on the fence requires willful blindness. How ready we are with defenses against God's Word! "I read the Bible all the way through, I study the Bible, my church preaches the Bible, I went to Sunday School, I have a daily devotion." We have ways to salvage some Christian pride, after all.

Some cats don't like to be picked up. Such self-protective measures—*I, I, I, I*—make us like that cat. We resist the Holy Spirit's affection, our legs extended to avoid unwelcome closeness. Like the reluctant cat, we can use the Bible to avoid being close to God. We can actually disdain Who wants to pick us up in His Word.

When you see this in yourself, stop what you are doing, no matter how Christian it is. Simply ask God to help you avoid stiff-arming Him, and receive Him in His Word.

Search me, O God, and know my heart;
Try me, and know my anxieties. (Psalm 139:23)

ARROGANCE

Many claim they understand the Bible. How hard could it be? The Bible is physical, tangible—words on a page. The Bible is the most well-studied book in human history, with thousands upon thousands of fantastic resources. No wonder we often hear a confident "what it really means." Such knowledgeable people can give us the certainty we lack.

But feeling safe with the Bible is a warning signal to each of us. God calls the Bible His hammer—like a hammer can build a house and also kill someone. How safe is the Bible?

"Is not My word like a fire?" says the Lord,
"And like a hammer that breaks the rock in pieces? (Jeremiah 23:29)

"Aslan is a lion—the Lion, the great Lion." "Ooh" said Susan. "I'd thought he was a man. Is he-quite safe? I shall feel rather nervous about meeting a lion."
"Safe?" said Mr. Beaver..." Who said anything about safe? 'Course he isn't safe. But he's good. He's the King, I tell you." (C. S. Lewis, *The Lion, the Witch & the Wardrobe*)

Like God who gave it, the Bible isn't safe—but it's good. The Scripture confirms the choices of its readers. For the readers who choose to love Him, the Bible produces life. For those readers who argue rather than agree with Him, the Bible produces judgment. Jesus identified this refusal in the Jewish leadership.

In John 5:38–40 above, Jesus exposed the religious leadership who searched the Scripture, but refused to come to Him. Later, Jesus raised a man to life four days after dying, and the news spread like wildfire. These same religious leaders demonstrate arrogance in John 11:47–50.

Then the chief priests and the Pharisees gathered a council and said, "What shall we do? For this man works many signs. If we let Him alone like this, everyone will believe in Him, and the Romans will come and take away both our place and nation."
    And one of them, Caiaphas, being high priest that year, said to them, "You know nothing at all, nor do you consider that it is expedient for us that one man should die for the people, and not that the whole nation should perish."

The nation's elites knew of Jesus' miracles. These Bible scholars knew that His works inspired faith. They actually called them signs because they recognized His works were signs of God's kingdom. But these Jewish leaders didn't like the many prophecies Jesus fulfilled.

They placed higher value on the prophecies concerning their nation. They thought they were obeying Scripture about Israel by crucifying Jesus. Would it surprise you to learn that their leadership positions depended on the prophecies about their homeland of Israel? Or that fulfillment of Messianic prophecies would leave them without power? Arrogantly, they decided what the Bible really meant. The overlap with their self-interest was predictable. Not even the Messiah could be allowed to challenge their hegemony. They show once again that the heart chooses, and the mind excuses.

Let all biblical Christians everywhere take warning. Like those religious influencers, we can study the Bible all life long, yet be unsaved. We can have favorite Scriptures all day long and yet fail in meekness. We decide what it means without teachability and meekness; the meaning we pick for a verse is the meaning that supports what we really want. That's how Jesus' crucifiers used the promises of God. For us, as for them, it is thinly veiled arrogance. As it blinded them, our self-will blinds us. Instead of recognizing our arrogance, we think we are faithful and obedient to the Bible.

Also like Jesus' crucifiers, we can think we are helping our church by Scriptural dogmatism. This gives our so-called love an arrogant, domineering quality. Pastors reveal this when they discourage unauthorized Bible questions. Do you know such a church leader? Regular Christians pursuing the Scripture's mysteries threaten their domineering power trip. In the name of protecting the flock, pastors and leaders can kill the very source of their church's life.

The opposite of their arrogance is meekness. Jesus said what is blessed: poverty of spirit, mourning, and meekness. Pastors and leaders can encourage members to love the Scripture and study its mysteries. When they do, their own meekness replicates throughout the congregation. But arrogance uses the Bible to avoid these blessed qualities, and makes someone like Jesus' persecutors. Whatever choice we make, the Bible will confirm it.

> To you who believe, He is precious; but to those who are disobedient,
> "The stone which the builders rejected
> Has become the chief cornerstone,"
> and
> "A stone of stumbling
> And a rock of offense." (1 Peter 2:7–8)

The Bible has an impact either way we choose. By yielding to God, we avoid its undesirable effects. If instead we avoid Him, the consequences resist control by any arrogance.

CHOOSINESS

The Bible helps people who choose to alienate themselves from God. A large corps of unseen enemies stands by to help. They even use the

Bible to help. Taking a verse by itself is a primary tactic. Choosing a verse we like may be sweet—on its face. It is also an excuse for not liking the whole Bible. Just because our favorite verse speaks to us doesn't mean it is God speaking. The devil quoted a sweet verse to Jesus (Matthew 4:6).

We defend ourselves against this enemy trick easily: by knowing and loving all of Scripture. That's how Jesus defended against the devil's Bible quote (Matthew 4:7).

Book One used pointillist paintings as an example. That style uses no brushstrokes, but only dots of paint. Seeing only dots, it's easy to think, "I can paint dots!" Before one famous painting, a person could focus on yellow dots and conclude it is a yellow painting of lights. But no one does that. Instead, they stand back and admire Van Gogh's *Starry Nights.* "What artistry!"

Same with the Bible: we can choose the dots, verses, and ideas we like. We choose what we can easily mimic—like the yellow dot viewer. Locking our attention onto the chosen Bible dots, we totally miss the entire Bible picture.

Yet more damaging: we only choose what gives us control. "I can do that!" We lose the benefits of inadequacy. Uninformed self-confidence persists because we only looked at the yellow Bible dots. The Holy Spirit then defends the Bible against *us*—not good.

Consider the Church, for an example. If you bring together a group of living human spirits, what do you get? You can choose joyous community from Acts 2:46. From Acts 4:29–30, you can focus on power evangelism. Perhaps you prefer authority like Matthew 16:19. *"Love one another"* is a good choice from 1 John.

But if you love all the Bible, you know the Church is God's intended ruling body for Earth. By choosing a well-understood Greek word, Jesus designated the spirit-born as that ruling body, *ekklesia.* (For a further discussion of the topic, see Book One's tenth chapter, "Church of Spirits.")

But how shall we rule, and whom? What legislation should we enact? What enforcement measures are available? The Bible holds the answers to such questions. However, by God's choice they are not in outline form. He didn't give us a rule book, a constitution, or His version of *Robert's Rules of Order.* He wants us to take in the entire Bible painting. We can choose a few dots of the painting, the verses we understand. Acting upon them, we reveal our immaturity.

We also justify our choosiness with verses we don't like. For example, Apostle Paul described a Church governing pattern in 2 Corinthians 10:4–6.

> For the weapons of our warfare are not carnal but mighty in God for pulling down strongholds, casting down arguments and every high thing that exalts itself against the knowledge of God, bringing every thought into captivity to the obedience of Christ, and being ready to punish all disobedience when your obedience is fulfilled.

This unambivalent assertion of authority over thoughts seems at odds with tolerance. The original American respect for individual freedom gave rise to tolerance ideology. Taken by itself, Paul's statement seems *1984*-ish: warfare against thoughts? punishing disobedience?

A person can choose to dislike the Bible over that, like refusing to look at any dots but yellow ones. But the fault is his own. Such a choice requires ignoring a different dot, in 1 Corinthians 5:12.

> For what have I to do with judging those also who are outside? Do you not judge those who are inside? But those who are outside, God judges.

The Church is just one example where the Bible's total picture tells who we are—but people who focus on dots will miss it. The whole counsel of God requires our respectful attentiveness to His voice, both in its pages and in our hearts—as the upcoming chapters instruct. Such love for His voice protects us against choosiness, an effective enemy tactic.

AVOIDANCE

We can choose which verses we like and highlight our favorite verses as long as we love all God's Word. But choosiness has a cousin: avoiding parts that are too challenging.

For example: Scripture describes the kingdom of darkness, but many desire to avoid that part. Tiptoeing around unseen enemies is a common attitude. Like not waking a sleeping baby, we try to avoid antagonizing the devil.

This timidity is beneath the Holy Spirit who lives in us. Delicate cowardice is clear in common sayings like these: *"Better the devil you know than the devil you don't." "New levels, new devils." "Satan will attack you!" "Don't pray for patience."* These warnings are accurate, but they are not true. Yes, opposition for darkness increases as we know the Lord and serve Him. But discouraging maturity because of these accurate warnings is untruthful. They are like satan's accuracy to Eve at the fateful tree—selectively chosen truths, packaged to inspire an untruthful response to God and His Word.

I began writing the *Unseen* series in November 2017 to expose the kingdom of darkness. Its working title was *The Rise and Fall of the Kingdom of Darkness*. Obstructions immediately arose, including reduced stamina and three fatal medical conditions. Treatments put me in bed for hours and days. My business suffered months of restricted cash flow. Government agencies hounded me. Everything easy took four times longer. I can testify: the kingdom of darkness can erect obstacles and obstructions.

But fearfully avoiding these enemies is an affront to Jesus' vision for us. Warnings to tiptoe around these powerful enemies are untruthful. By doing so, we are avoiding the doorway to our appointed rulership in God's kingdom. That doorway is our inadequacy. Jesus did not shrink from the Bible's hard things. He warned us not to avoid them.

I did not come to bring peace but a sword. (Matthew 10:34)

No one, having put his hand to the plow, and looking back, is fit for the kingdom of God. (Luke 9:62)

PRECONCEPTIONS

The Scripture blinds people who love their preconceived notions. The Jewish leaders knew the Scripture backwards and forwards, but were blind to the Messiah standing in front of them. And they didn't just miss Him—they killed Him. Their preconceived ideas blinded them to any Messiah who didn't line up.

What we think we know ain't necessarily so. When I was a child I loved the Christmas hymn, *We Three Kings of Orient Are*, and sang it constantly. They're also called the three wise men. Recall what you remember, then read Matthew 2:1–2 and see all the baggage we bring to the Bible. How did your preconceived notions match the actual record? Matthew doesn't say there were three men; he only reports three gifts. He does not identify them as kings or wise men but as magi. That sounds more like magic! We are only told they read stars. Astronomers catalog the stars and their movements scientifically; these men are not astronomers. They are astrologers who believed stars reveal the fate of men on earth. That's why they alone recognized "His star," and no one near Bethlehem.

If we are free from preconceptions, calling them wise looks way off. Herod's bloodthirsty climb to power was widely famed. Wise people would avoid Herod after a minimum reconnaissance. But unwisely, they actually consulted the current king to find the newborn King. These astrologers believed Herod's falsity and planned to tell him where Jesus was. Whatever wisdom they had was stupid about political power. Only a dream would prevent their disclosure to Herod; God could not lead them through their "wisdom."

Preconceptions blind us. The preventive is to submit them to the Bible regularly. Meekness is a major theme through the *Unseen* series—a primary requirement for understanding God's Word. If I already know what the Bible means, then that's all I will see. I'll be the person who only has a hammer; I'll only see nails.

If that principle is all you get from this book, you already have a great bargain for your money. Remember: knowing the Scripture doesn't mean you are saved. You are saved by following Jesus Christ as Savior and Lord (Matthew 7:21–23, John 5:39–40).

Paul wrote an oft-quoted statement to his protégé in 2 Timothy 3:16–17.

> All Scripture is given by inspiration of God, and is profitable for doc-
> trine, for reproof, for correction, for instruction in righteousness, that
> the man of God may be complete, thoroughly equipped for every
> good work.

Paul's description of Scripture includes some assumed requirements. For one, we must admit incompleteness. In humility we can be shamelessly candid about ourselves. Quite the opposite from *thoroughly equipped*, we still have so little. The Bible is useful for reproof and correction—and you must want it. If these required qualities are not in us, then the same Scripture confirms us as enemies. Preconceptions deaden our desire to be complete. As a result, the God-given resource lies untapped and unused. Instead of completing us, the unloved Bible testifies about our loveless-ness toward God.

Without meekness, we cannot submit to Scriptures outside our exist-ing explanations.

> **BACKFIRE!** In the *Unseen* series, you'll find sidebars
> titled Backfire! These highlight a repeated theme in God's
> dealings with darkness. The kingdom of darkness often
> enjoys success. Sometimes a strategy of darkness achieves
> 99.99% success. Yet God defeats them, in part by causing
> their own plan to backfire on them.

> The nations have sunk down in the pit which they made;
> In the net which they hid, their own foot is caught.
> The LORD is known by the judgment He executes;
> The wicked is snared in the work of his own hands.
> (Psalm 9:15–16.)

> Plans can backfire—both in the seen and the unseen. Preconceived notions are often the culprit. In Book Three, *Nobody Sees This Creation: The Origin of the Devil and His Replacements*, we'll explore Lucifer's preconceptions and backfires.

> Lucifer rebelled thinking that after replacing God, he would keep his exalted qualities. His preconceived idea was badly wrong! He mistook his God-given externals for his identity. Lucifer found quickly that God could take them away—a backfire of the greatest proportions.

Preconceptions signal that we understand the Bible well enough. When that happens, curiosity and maturing give way to spiritual sloth. God is gradually restoring all the Bible's truths to His Church, but not cheaply. He requires full engagement.

Our preconceived ideas are subtle. We may not recognize them in ourselves. Like corks in wine bottles, they keep out anything that differs. Peter rebuked Jesus in Matthew 16:22 for saying the Jewish leaders would reject Him. Peter and the disciples never heard Jesus' final phrase in all those warnings: *"and be raised the third day"* (16:21). They were certain the religious leaders must endorse Jesus. That preconception plugged their ears.

"Inspect what you expect" is a useful saying. Assess your Bible study habits occasionally. Do the methods only reinforce what you already know? Being satisfied requires a healthy self-assessment, *a.k.a.* pride.

Bible study is a necessity because so many ideas need correcting. None of us are finished Christians. Maturing requires our existing ideas to be corrected, and for new ideas to be deposited. And that cannot happen unless we are meek before God's Word.

Let the reader beware: only you can open yourself to the Holy Spirit's reproof and correction. John 16:13 makes it easy: *"When He, the Spirit of truth, has come, He will guide you into all truth."* We can ask Him. "Holy Spirit of God, You are welcome to guide me into all the truths of Jesus."

Such an invitation is best done frequently. A new anticipation explodes within as we join His adventure into all the truth.

DIVISIVENESS

Most people feel chagrin over the fractious nature of Christians and churches. The hundreds of Christian groups make it easy to question our sincerity. These Bible dangers originate much division.

Jesus prayed we would be one, as the Trinity itself is one (John 17:11–24). Sometimes, we must break unity in our Christian organizations. The purpose might be preserving Bible truths entrusted to us. In our times, Christians even disagree about obeying the Bible, requiring an organizational separation. This is within Jesus' prayer because He desired unity of love, rather than organization. But our divisiveness strikes at the love.

Prideful preconceptions presume that we know what the Bible means and need look no further. No listening to other points of view can add to what we know. These distort our watchful guard into cooperation with the kingdom of darkness. Whatever we protect through such a deceived pride has some poison DNA—Lucifer's.

Arrogant preconceptions always divide Christians. Satisfaction that we know enough makes people with more hunger look like threats. In place of meek love, we are defensive toward anyone who differs.

We are one body under one Head, and need each other. Disagreeing does not require dis-unifying. With meekness, we can each admit to our imbalances, whether in theology or in practice. Aren't such inadequacies to be expected? It is not threatening to admit this. But when we assume that it's everyone else who needs rebalancing, a serious red flag appears.

We might also think rightly but prioritize wrongly. Choosiness prefers some Scriptures over others. Proponents of differing views each line up their chosen proof-texts. Battle lines are drawn. Their minds excuse their heart's choice: to *dis*-unify.

The kingdom of darkness has used many weapons to resist the Church for two thousand years. They fear us most, us living human spirits. Division through arrogance is one of their best tactics, and includes the pressure to be right. Book Seven of the *Unseen* series is *Nobody Sees This Church: Resisting Darkness*. It reviews the pressure to be right in depth.

Darkness uses the pressure to be right against each of us. When we are one as Jesus imagined, it disarms the devil's pressure to be right. We surrender the divisive insistence that our existing explanations are the final ones. While listening to one another and reflecting joyously on our maturing process, we can resist the temptation to divide.

If you find the above statements chafing, it's a red flag designed to protect you. You may be a target of the pressure to be right.

TEMPTATION WITH THE BIBLE

We have all seen the Bible used in ungodly ways. The devil does it as well, and gladly uses the Bible to achieve evil. In Luke 4:9–11, satan cited Psalm 91:11–12 to tempt Jesus.

If You are the Son of God, throw Yourself down from here. For it is written:

"He shall give His angels charge over you,
To keep you,"
and
"In their hands they shall bear you up, lest you dash your foot against a stone."

Jesus refused the offer even though it was from the Bible. To rebuff satan's deceptive application of Psalm 91, Jesus replied with another Scripture, Deuteronomy 6:16. *"It has been said, 'You shall not tempt the Lord your God.'"*

The subtitle of this Book Two in the *Unseen* series is *How to Unlock Bible Mysteries.* For protection, we must be clear: our unseen enemies can trick us with the Bible. The kingdom of darkness knows our respect for the Bible. Using it, our unseen enemies try to alienate us from our Father.

Jesus resisted the trick by relying on the whole counsel of God. His tempter wanted Jesus to look at only at a few dots, but His love for the complete picture of the Bible protected Him.

Just as Jesus resisted the trick, we can as well. He was a living spirit and filled with the Holy Spirit, and so is everyone who follows Him in faith. God richly rewards our attention to His whole counsel in Scripture. Being teachable by the Bible is worth every meekness required.

KINGDOM BUILDING

We have a fig leaf addiction, ever since our first parent's disobedience. The exposure of our inadequacy is scary, and our instinct is to hide it. Among the cover-ups are power, fame, and money—motives strongly magnetized to the Bible. We actually use the Bible to feather our own nests, as Simon of Samaria illustrates in the eighth chapter of Acts. This summary is further explored in Book Seven, *Nobody Sees This Church: Resisting Darkness*. The sneaky evil of sorcery is not new.

Philip was one of the seven deacons chosen to administer the distribution of food for the widows in the Jerusalem church. He met the qualification in Acts 6:3, *"full of spirit and wisdom."* So full, in fact, Philip was quickly engaged in apostolic function. His powerful evangelism penetrated the territories of darkness, first Samaria and then Ethiopia.

In Simon's town, Philip did many miracles. He delivered Samaritans from demonic oppression. Through Philip, Jesus healed people with paralysis. Luke reports "there was great joy in that city."

Everyone was joyous but one: Simon, who enjoyed his public prominence. Townsmen called him "Simon the Great" because of his sorcery, which amazed them. But his personal ratings took a dive when Philip brought Jesus' gospel to Simon's city. He became "Simon the Has-Been."

Philip's ministry of Jesus' power and message eclipsed Simon's precious fame. Simon's once-sycophantic fans turned to Jesus. So, like them, Simon also believed the gospel. He was baptized, but his motives were mixed. He glommed onto Philip to see how he did it.

Philip's ministry in these apostolic capacities exceeded expectations. The apostles in Jerusalem visited to confirm Philip's ministry. They also baptized the new believers in the Holy Spirit. Simon was even more amazed when his former fans spoke in tongues. He glommed onto Apostle Peter, but would regret it after Acts 8:18–19.

> And when Simon saw that through the laying on of the apostles' hands the Holy Spirit was given, he offered them money, saying, "Give me this power also, that anyone on whom I lay hands may receive the Holy Spirit. But Peter said to him, "Your money perish with you, because you thought that the gift of God could be purchased with money!"

Simon was doing nothing out of the ordinary. Paying for sorcery scrolls was common practice. After Paul's ministry in Ephesus, believers valued the destroyed sorcery scrolls as a measure of their sacrifice for Jesus: today's

$4,000,000. Simon only did what he had always done: get power with money. Peter taught Simon that the Holy Spirit is not for sale, unlike the spirits and spells of a sorcerer.

Sadly, people misuse the Bible to build their personal kingdoms, like Simon the sorcerer. It is not a magic talisman, but we use it as one. We manipulate God as if He owes us what we want; we cite our favorite Scriptures to Him. A person skillful with the Bible can gain prominence and fame. We can harvest money by using the Bible. Leaders in family and church sometimes wield the Bible like their power tool to control others.

Like Simon of Samaria, we can use the Bible for modern-day idolatry and sorcery. To protect ourselves from this requires Beatitude qualities, a frequent topic in Book One. Meekness will be even more prominent in the pages to follow. It is the number one key for self-protection with this explosive Bible.

COMPLACENCY

Babies aren't born fully developed; they have baby thoughts and baby steps. The same is true of our Christian lives: we are not born again as mature Christians, but as baby ones. We must each endure a proving process which matures us.

Discomfort is constant during this maturing process. Just as our favorite old clothes may not fit our current bodies, our spirits outgrow our comfortable limits. As in the natural, so in the spiritual. Grow up! This is what the Scripture teaches us, as in Hebrews 5:13–14.

> For everyone who partakes only of milk is unskilled in the word of righteousness, for he is a babe. But solid food belongs to those who are of full age, that is, those who by reason of use have their senses exercised to discern both good and evil.

God's admonition to grow presumes our need to mature. Our understanding is not complete, our character is not perfect, and our final maturity awaits us. Our own stage of maturity limits each one of us.

Only meekness protects us from arrogance. Without that protection, we become like Jesus' crucifiers: certain we have solved the Bible, and confident of our correctness. Next thing you know, we are dividing Jesus' Church. We are killing our Christian brothers and sisters. It has happened many times in church history. Meekness before the Word of God is the only way to stay safe.

WHY NOT TO STUDY THE BIBLE

God empowered His Word to expose and confirm our choices. Therefore, we want to outgrow our immature Bible motives. He will leverage these motives for our good—up to a point.

My grandson likes rewards for chores because he is seven; I have a box of rewards hidden in the garage. When he is twenty years old, the same motive reveals immaturity. Likewise with us and the Bible: any motive is useful in our spiritual childhood, but we must leave some behind for maturity.

> When I was a child, I spoke as a child, I understood as a child, I thought as a child; but when I became a man, I put away childish things. (1 Corinthians 13:11)

Discussed above are the Bible-thumpers whose motive is imposing their interpretations upon others. Closely related are manipulators whose desire for power motivates their Bible reading. Self-promoters like Simon of Samaria above desire increased fame by using the Scripture.

Among Bible readers are contestants who distinguish themselves competitively, vanquishing other people's Bible knowledge. To remain quiet about what they know is a discipleship sacrifice.

Hummingbird readers want the Bible's sugar water. They don't land but hover; they flit away once it meets their felt needs. Spiritual feeding is good, but studying the Bible is beyond conception to the hummingbirds.

We can't neglect the dog fighters. They read the Bible to disprove it. They tear aggressively into anyone who dares assert its quality or authority.

Doubtless, there are more childish motives a reader could list, motives you see in those around you. Let's have mercy on them because we'll need mercy too. Don't be like them or use them as an excuse to do likewise. Instead, be exceptional: love the Word of God for itself.

> More to be desired are they than gold,
> Yea, than much fine gold;
> Sweeter also than honey and the honeycomb. (Psalm 19:10)

> I rejoice at Your word as one who finds great treasure. (Psalm 119:162)

Be diligent to present yourself approved to God, a worker who does not need to be ashamed, rightly dividing the word of truth. (2 Timothy 2:15)

So I wept much, because no one was found worthy to open and read the scroll, or to look at it. (Revelation 5:4)

CHAPTER THREE
WORD, SPIRIT, LOVE

God freely identified Himself as Word. *"For You have magnified Your word above all Your name"* (Psalm 138:2).

The Word became flesh to achieve our atonement, to die as our substitute. But following the resurrection, He left after only forty days. We might have stayed longer. His followers numbered 120. For us, a bigger organization would justify staying longer. We could wonder if it was a good plan to leave. The Church's history has been brutal. His physical presence might have prevented much loss, from our point of view.

But Jesus taught us it was better for Him to go. The presence of fakers and abusers did not surprise Him. Jesus also knew that some would choose the narrow way. For them, He left behind two resources: His Spirit and His Word.

> I tell you the truth. It is to your advantage that I go away; for if I do not go away, the Helper will not come to you; but if I depart, I will send Him to you. (John 16:7)

> 'He who believes in Me, as the Scripture has said, out of his heart will flow rivers of living water." But this He spoke concerning the Spirit, whom those believing in Him would receive. (John 7:38–39)

> You shall receive power when the Holy Spirit has come upon you. (Acts 1:8)

The spiritual birth of the believer was the wide-ranging subject of Book One in the *Unseen* series, titled *Nobody Sees This YOU: How to Live as a Spirit in the Unseen Realm*. Despite the breadth of Book One, it barely scratches the surface. Few Christians would claim they understand the

Spirit's filling, and fewer still would deny its power. But there's no escaping the obvious: Holy Spirit within us loves the Word of God.

RESCUE

Chapter 2, DANGER, listed repetitive patterns that hinder us with the Bible. Is there any hope for us? God says yes. He shows how He rescues us: the Holy Spirit.

In Romans 7 and 8, Apostle Paul writes autobiographically about fence-sitting in his own life. Since the day he penned these words in 7:21–8:2, they have been among the Bible's most dear. I cite them in full for our reassurance. Our Father rescues us.

> I find then a law, that evil is present with me, the one who wills to do good. For I delight in the law of God according to the inward man. But I see another law in my members, warring against the law of my mind, and bringing me into captivity to the law of sin which is in my members. O wretched man that I am! Who will deliver me from this body of death? I thank God—through Jesus Christ our Lord!
>
> So then, with the mind I myself serve the law of God, but with the flesh the law of sin.
>
> There is therefore now no condemnation to those who are in Christ Jesus, who do not walk according to the flesh, but according to the Spirit. For the law of the Spirit of life in Christ Jesus has made me free from the law of sin and death.

A reader stopping after that point, the end of Romans 7, has a belief and a hope. Only in the next chapter does Paul describe the how: the Holy Spirit rescues us. Our faith in Jesus gives us birth as spirit. The Holy Spirit fills us. Our rescue begins. Romans 8:5 and 9 are just two examples.

> For those who live according to the flesh set their minds on the things of the flesh, but those who live according to the Spirit, the things of the Spirit....
>
> So then, those who are in the flesh cannot please God. But you are not in the flesh but in the Spirit, if indeed the Spirit of God dwells in you.

THE BIRTH OF YOUR SPIRIT

How does living *"according to the Spirit"* rescue us? How does it help us engage with the Bible? Paul's statements above are based on the following

Bible summary, fully described in Book One of the *Unseen* Series, *Nobody Sees This You: How to Live as a Spirit in the Unseen Realm.* Scriptural citations there facilitate in-depth investigation if desired.

God created our first parents, Adam and Eve, in His image. God equipped them sexually to reproduce His image. He blessed them, and in them He also blessed you and me. We are unlike any other creature He created.

Being in His image, they each had a spirit, in a body, with a soul. But despite His warning, our parents disobeyed. Their consequence was tragic for all their descendants: their spirits died. All people ever since are born dead in spirit. Humanity is now defenseless against the devil and fallen angels exiled to Earth after rebellion against God.

With the fertility that God implanted in them, Adam and Eve reproduced and populated Earth. Their descendants—all of us—are born dead in spirit. People are born alive in soul and body only. This combination of a living soul and a body, the Bible names *our flesh.* It is everything we are, bereft of a living spirit.

Jesus was our substitute by His obedient self-sacrifice on His cross. We can become living spirits again by repenting and following Him. And the minute we do, a war starts—the war between our spirit and our flesh, described by Apostle Paul in Galatians 5:17,

> For the flesh lusts against the Spirit, and the Spirit against the flesh; and these are contrary to one another, so that you do not do the things that you wish.

Every person has internal conflicts, but only Christians have this war within themselves. This is the best kind of internal conflict to have; it leads to abundant life. Winning this conflict gives us intimacy with God Almighty as our Father. Only a living human spirit has this inward friction between flesh and spirit. Knowing this about yourself gives you an advantage with the Bible, as the Psalmist expressed in Psalm 42:7,

> Deep calls unto deep at the noise of Your waterfalls;
> All Your waves and billows have gone over me.

SPIRIT BIBLE

To read the Bible requires our mind. Appreciating it requires our emotions. To obey it involves us physically. But it is a deep book of spirit;

its depths calls to our depths. The Holy Spirit of God inspired it so He could communicate to our spirits, and ours with His. That's why Hebrews 4:12 identifies the level of its penetration: *the division of soul and spirit.*

A sign that we are misusing Scripture is when we prohibit God from engaging with our spirit. For a fuller understanding, see Book One of the *Unseen* series.

SPIRIT-RULE WITH SCRIPTURE

We can read the Bible as a living human spirit, made alive by faith in Jesus and the filling of His Holy Spirit. Resisting temptation is also much easier when we have stored up the Bible in our hearts and heads. When we determine that our spirit will rule our flesh, the Bible armors us for full spirit function. Paul described it in 1 Corinthians 10:6, 11.

> Now these things became our examples, to the intent that we should not lust after evil things as they also lusted.... Now all these things happened to them as examples, and they were written for our admonition, upon whom the ends of the ages have come.

Picture a gumball machine at the door of a store or restaurant. Put in your quarter, get a gumball—unless the machine is empty, neglected by its owner. People neglecting the Bible are like that neglected gumball machine. What if we decide to fill our empty containers with gumballs of Scripture? When our circumstance "quarters" enter the slot, we get the right Scripture "gumball" for that moment. King David used more poetic pictures in Psalms 119:9, 11. Pick any picture you want, and load up.

> How can a young man cleanse his way?
> By taking heed according to Your word.
> Your word I have hidden in my heart,
> That I might not sin against You.

MARTYRS

Throughout history, people have died for their faith in Jesus. Christians worldwide are dying right now because they refuse to compromise their love for Jesus. What can explain this sacrifice? Love.

Knowing mysteries is not the Bible's purpose. God didn't give it for our power or interaction with spirits. Those result, but Apostle Paul subordinated all those to a greater value, in 1 Corinthians 13:1–3.

> Though I speak with the tongues of men and of angels, but have not love, I have become sounding brass or a clanging cymbal. And though I have the gift of prophecy, and understand all mysteries and all knowledge, and though I have all faith, so that I could remove mountains, but have not love, I am nothing. And though I bestow all my goods to feed the poor, and though I give my body to be burned, but have not love, it profits me nothing.

When we respond to God, we engage with the Bible. There in its pages, intimacy with our Father grows. Our lives become full of abundance; we experience miracles, answered prayers, and fruitful influence on people we love. Our flesh—body and soul in combination—is superseded by our maturing spirit. With new senses for the unseen realms, we enjoy a functional citizenship there. Helen Lemmel described it in her 1922 hymn.

> Turn your eyes upon Jesus,
> Look full in His wonderful face,
> And the things of earth will grow strangely dim,
> In the light of His glory and grace.

MY BIBLE

Most Christians wear out Bibles periodically—one reason it is the best-selling book of all time. So many readers keep wearing it out and buying replacements. And like a Lay's potato chip, who can own just one? Or throw away old ones?

My grandmother was very superstitious about her Bible. At her age 78, Momma Ben still used her childhood Bible. A distinct memory is us reading her Bible together, wound together with five or six red rubber bands—stuffed with her prayer lists and special mementos. The first ritual was the gentle unwinding of her Bible. Those slow minutes were tough on an active little boy, but the memory is worth it.

Momma Ben didn't take notes in her Bible, and wouldn't ever let me set anything on it. In contrast, mine has curled pages where I excitedly press my pen too hard in the margins. My current Bible has lasted me about six years, an above average lifespan for mine. It has very wide margins for note-taking, so my notes don't overlap or obscure the Scriptures this time.

When we love the truth, we love it in any form. These days we can have the Bible on our phones, on the internet, on our wallpaper, and on our computers. Our cars and televisions now enable listening to Scripture. We can rapidly navigate from one distant verse to another. Quick sermon notes are easy on our devices. During later review, we can paste in the exact Scriptures.

Loving the truth is one way we love Jesus. He told Pilate, *"Everyone who is of the truth hears My voice"* (John 18:37). To the woman at the well, He said, *"Those who worship Him must worship in spirit and truth"* (4:24). Peter spoke for all the disciples when he told Jesus, *"You have the words of eternal life"* (6:68). A few hours before dying, Jesus vouched for the disciples' love by praying, *"For I have given them the words which You have given Me, and they have received them"* (17:8).

God is verbal and multi-personal. He wants to be intimate with everyone who loves Him. He does this by speaking—just like He does everything. The Bible is where we learn His voice. The Bible is a love thing.

CHAPTER FOUR

BASELINES

The subtitle of this Book Two in the *Unseen* series is *How to Unlock Bible Mysteries.* But as the saying goes, we must crawl before we can walk.

Following in this chapter are foundational study steps of critical importance. Their effectiveness is long proven. Anyone desiring to mature as a living human spirit must yield to Scripture, and proper reading is step one. The purpose of chapter four is not exhaustive training for Bible study. Rather, this chapter provides a baseline habit so your study of the unseen world is truthful.

> Be diligent to present yourself approved to God, a worker who does not need to be ashamed, rightly dividing the word of truth. (2 Timothy 2:15)

Without the foundational methods in this chapter, we easily make the Bible say what we want it to. Many have gone astray for just that reason such as the scribes and Pharisees described above. Like the devil, we can read the Bible and misuse it.

We yield to the Bible, not vice versa. Inductive Bible Study protects us from manhandling God's Word.

INDUCTIVE BIBLE STUDY

Christians pioneered Inductive Bible Study long ago. It is one method among many, true, but it is the foundational one. Without inductive study, we easily read things into the Bible. Such reading makes us like Jesus' crucifiers: we only accept what we like. We make it mean what

43

we want it to mean. But Inductive Bible Study holds everyone equally accountable to the text.

Inductive study applies to any written text. We start with the text. We observe its words, phrases, patterns, outline. Inductive observation singles out the who, what, when, where, and how. Inductive interpretation confines itself to those facts; none are imported or added from elsewhere, as true as they may be. Finally, inductive application obeys what's found, whether it is command, promise, example to follow, example to avoid, or warning. Such a careful method protects us from our preconceptions. By studying the Scripture inductively, we skirt many dangers. We disarm the urge to manipulate its meaning. Instead of manhandling the text, we yield to it. What God says in it becomes plainer.

This study protocol has many champions, such as InterVarsity Christian Fellowship and Kay Arthur's *Precepts* ministry. As a bachelor, I asked God for a wife who could hear His voice in the Bible. He sent Diane Davis. Like me, she had grown through those two ministries. We married quickly, and served twelve years as InterVarsity staff. Together we trained hundreds of college students to study the Bible for themselves with this method.

EVANGELISTIC BIBLE STUDIES

Inductive study is not only good for us living spirits. This method makes every reader equal, so in fact, unbelievers can read it more genuinely. We found unbelievers would study the Bible inductively with us. Our outreach welcomed anyone to read the Bible for themselves and reach their own conclusions inductively. These study groups, we called evangelistic Bible studies.

The dangers described in Chapter 2 can inoculate well-meaning Christians against seeing anything challenging. But people outside Christian fellowship rarely have the baggage of preconceptions. Often, they shy away because they don't want to become like the Christians they know. But unbelievers know there's a God. They know that the Bible is different, and they are curious.

In 1982, a Christian student named Trudy developed an unlikely friendship with Rose, the boisterous veep of the gay student group. Trudy was tiny, black, and shy. Rose was a huge white attention hog. As unmatched as they were, they were constant companions. This brought Rose into repeated contact with Christians. We stood for things she hated and she was plain about it, even incendiary. Rose was honest and spoke her mind.

So I told Trudy, if she would invite Rose to study the Bible with her for five weeks, I would help. To her credit, Rose agreed. The three of us met for five weeks in the very public university cafeteria. We studied Jesus in Mark's gospel, using Inductive Bible Study. On the fourth week, Rose read this statement by Jesus in Mark 8:34.

> Whoever desires to come after Me, let him deny himself, and take up his cross, and follow Me.

She read it aloud a second time, and more quietly, a third. We could see the wheels turning within her. Suddenly—in the cafeteria, with the shyest friend in the world—Rose violently stood. The force knocked her metal chair a few feet back onto the tiled cafeteria floor. All eyes were on Rose and Trudy, whose eyes widened as she slunk under the table. Rose pointed at the Bible and yelled loudly for all to hear, "He's crazy! He's asking me to DIE for him! He's crAA-a-zy!"

Rose was right. Jesus plainly asks us to give up all we hold dear, life itself. Christians habitually disarm such statements in the way we read the Bible. We think we know what it must mean; that Jesus couldn't be that harsh or strange. But unbelievers can cut to the quick. So while Trudy sank beneath the table in embarrassment, I rejoiced. A few weeks later, Rose surrendered her life to that crazy Man. In subsequent years, she served as a missionary in the red-light district of Amsterdam. Jesus played to Rose's strengths as someone to love the outcasts.

Such is the explosive power of the Bible. Inductive Bible Study serves as the fuse.

INDUCTIVE DETECTIVE

For inductive study, there is a contrary method: deductive reasoning. The argument begins with its conclusion and aligns facts to support that conclusion. I believe X. Therefore Y + Z = X. Such reasoning starts with a belief and imposes that belief upon the facts. Detective fiction illustrates both methods; let's try it.

The fictional Sherlock Holmes uses inductive discovery (although his author Arthur Conan Doyle mistakenly calls it deduction). Holmes has no monopoly, however. Hercule Poirot, Miss Jane Marple, Father Brown, and all the famous detectives use inductive reasoning. And in each case, there is a foil: Scotland Yard and the police. They bungle around misinterpreting every clue by using their deductive reasoning. "I know this person is the culprit, so every fact justifies arresting him (or her)."

Each detective ends their episode with a climactic who-dun'it unveiling. What does the detective always list? The facts and their inevitable meaning if taken as a whole. Inductive reasoning starts with the observable facts and refrains from prejudgment. (Of course, for drama's sake, you don't get all the facts until that point.)

First step in Inductive Bible Study: take in the facts without pre-conceptions. This step is called Observation. Suppose you're called to the scene of a newly discovered murder. The victim has no wounds. He is a male, and his body has an unusual boot print on the shirt—bearing a dirt marking. Sampling of the residue identifies it as dirt found only in one place. The police have apprehended a man seen in the area that evening. On his boots was the same dirt. The scarred soles of his boots exactly match the prints on the corpse.

Inspector Lestrade arrests the man, charging him with the victim's murder. His theory of the crime: his suspect violently kicked the victim in the chest and killed him. Lestrade sets about identifying the facts that support the theory. He reasons deductively. All that's needed now is a motive, and even that, he can make up.

A respectable gentleman friend of the arrested man visits Sherlock, who stipulates, "I can guarantee nothing. Your friend may be guilty after all." Hired despite his objectivity, Sherlock then exclaims, "Come along, Watson!" and the theme music begins.

Second step of Inductive Bible Study: Interpretation. Let the facts speak what they mean—and no more. The observed dirty boot print on the corpse belongs to Lestrade's suspect. The only definite meaning is that the suspect's foot met the victim's clothes somehow. But does it mean that the suspect was the murderer? Sherlock refuses to reach a conclusion without more facts. Also, without visible wounds, the dead man may not have been murdered.

Inductive Bible Study is like Sherlock's case (which I have made up). He doesn't have enough information to justify any conclusion. So he refrains from making one. To identify the accurate case of the victim's death, he requires more facts. **Inductive Bible Study repeats step one a lot: Look again more deeply for more facts. Interpretation always waits on Observation.**

To seek these facts, Sherlock dispatches Watson, who learns that the dirt on the body came from a secret boxing ring. It's secret because of the illegal gambling on boxing matches. At the hidden gym, Watson is told the dead man was a frequent boxer who even bet on his own fights. After Watson reports, Sherlock confronts the respectable gentleman friend who hired him. The gentleman admits both he and the suspect took part in the illicit boxing, as well as the dead man. In fact, the night they found the dead man, he had lost a fight against the very man Lestrade had arrested, and they had parted on good terms afterwards.

Again, consider the meaning of the facts observed, with interpretation. Gambling means there's another person with a motive: the bookie for that fight. Watson returns to the furtive hideout. His inquiries reveal that the dead man made a £25 sterling bet on himself to win that night, but lost the fight and the bet. When Watson heard the bookie's name, he recognized it: London's most notoriously violent oddsmaker.

Lastly, apply the facts and the meanings developed. This third step is Application. Sherlock posts an advertisement in the Times: THE 25 POUNDS STERLING OWED BY [the dead man's name] MAY BE COLLECTED AT 221B BAKER ST AT 4 PM ON THE MOR-ROW. Lestrade is informed and begrudgingly waits in hiding. The bookie himself arrives at 4:00 PM. Sherlock and Watson refuse to pay the violent man and he threatens, "I'll kill you the same way I killed [naming the dead man]!" Protesting disbelief, Sherlock challenges the bookie: "The police have already arrested the man whose boot print marked the victim." The bookie retorts, "I killed [name] right after the two of them fought. I knew those ignorant coppers would fall for it." And of course, Lestrade hearing this, makes the arrest, and releases the falsely accused boxer.

COURTROOM

A criminal trial courtroom also exhibits both deductive and inductive reasoning. I have served on five criminal trial juries, an unusually high number, but we all know the courtroom rules from shows like *Law & Order* or *20/20*.

In the courtroom are two sides, the prosecution and the defense. Each presents a theory to the jury in their opening speech. The prosecutor says, "The defendant is guilty and I will prove it with facts." The defense attorney then says, "My client is innocent and I will prove it with facts." Both claim to have facts, but their facts are subservient to their intended conclusions. The trial proceeds as each side calls witnesses and presents evidence to support its theory: "I believe X. Therefore Y + Z = X." This is deductive reasoning.

Other parties are in the court: the judge and the jury. Neither may use deductive reasoning, nor may they start with any theory at all. The judge may not take bribes to favor either side or prejudge the case. As our courthouse statues signify, blindfolded Lady Justice is impartial, weighing facts objectively without prejudice.

As for the jurors, the attorneys screen them pre-trial in the *voir dire* process. "Have you formed a conclusion about this case? Do you have a personal involvement in this case? What do you believe about [some influential viewpoint]?" Only jurors with full objectivity survive the screening. Once the judge swears in the jury, he restricts what they can hear.

The jury will render the final verdict, but first they hear both sides. That's when they retire to the jury room, apart from all outside influences. During their conversation, they will review all the facts observed and presented. They limit themselves only to the facts presented in the courtroom, and import none from elsewhere. This is the interpretation process when the facts are evaluated as to their meaning. It concludes with the application of their conclusion: a verdict in the case. The jury emerges and hands their written, unanimous decision to the judge. The jury exemplifies inductive reasoning, withholding all prejudgment until all the facts are presented and interpreted. They provide a verdict limited entirely to those facts and their interpretation.

INDUCTIVE JURY

One jury on which I served as foreman had a "he said, she said" case. An older manufacturing supervisor had accused a young teenage employee of theft from the company. The older man was white and the younger was black, which increased the tension. The theft itself was indisputable, but the supervisor was the only witness and accuser of the young defendant. After hearing both sides, we retired to the jury room.

Unlike the other four juries I served, unanimity was not immediate. Six favored conviction and six, acquittal. An accused is innocent until proven guilty. The standard of conviction is beyond a reasonable doubt. In order to convict, we had to rule out all reasonable doubts. Even one reasonable doubt required acquittal.

After they elected me foreman, I led an inductive review of all the facts presented. The process was laborious. Some jurors shared the supervisor's racism, therefore they preferred deductive reasoning. They believed a young black man probably was a thief and an old white guy probably told the truth. All the facts they heard in trial had to fit those beliefs.

First, we wrote all the facts we heard on a big marker board. This is the Observation step. When we did that, we saw something not evident in the courtroom: all the facts were statements of the accuser.

Second, we interpreted the meaning of each fact, in this case, the supervisor's accusations. "If he was truthful in that statement, what else would have to be true? If we believed what he said, what else would we have to believe?" The trial's map of the scene showed us that the accuser required unusually high agility in order to see what he said he saw. But we had observed in court that the accuser had a shuffling walk. This gave reasonable doubt that he really saw what he claimed to see.

Our facts included the supervisor's repeated reference to his thirty-five years of service. More than once, he strongly expressed feelings of entitlement in court. We had to discuss if he could steal from the company and justify it? The answer was a unanimous yes. This possibility alone created reasonable doubt: that the supervisor himself was the thief, only scapegoating the young defendant.

Third, we applied the conclusion required by the facts. Such reasonable doubts kept mounting—both that the accused couldn't have done the crime, and that the accuser was untrustworthy, at best. We applied our interpretation of the observed facts and wrote down our verdict: not guilty. The outcome was rewarding. When I read our verdict, the defendant's family erupted with joyous shouts. Then we all realized one more fact. The accuser never had a single supporter or guest in the courtroom—not a family member, not a coworker, and not a boss.

OBSERVATION

You can find many resources about Inductive Bible Study today. For the *Unseen* series, we list the three primary steps of the inductive method. **The first, most valuable step is to observe the facts.** When first learning inductive study, it sounds like this: "Whoa, hold your horses!" During observation, we patiently delve into the details of a Bible passage.

The Scripture requires our submission and we must still our hearts. If we do not, we can reach half-baked conclusions, satisfy ourselves with baby food, and forsake our Father's invitation to intimacy.

I wait for the LORD, my soul waits,
And in His word I do hope. (Psalm 130:5)

Surely I have calmed and quieted my soul,
Like a weaned child with his mother;
Like a weaned child is my soul within me. (Psalm 131:2)

Our personal character plays a leading role in the observation stage. Patience means we do not demand any detail to produce a meaning. They may mean nothing or everything. Like the jury, we withhold assessment of each fact we find. Meekness recognizes how easily we read into the Bible what we want it to say. Humility with God's Word does not rush through it. We humbly yield our thinking to the facts it actually says.

First identify the genre and type of literature. Earlier we did this with Revelation 19. We must study each genre on its own terms. Is it wrong to read a biology textbook as a romance novel? Yes, of course. Likewise, each Bible genre has its own rules of reading. By identifying the type of literature, we protect ourselves from misusing it. For example, Bible narratives can be historical, didactic, or prophetic. Its poetry can comprise both worship and laments. The Psalms alone include everything from antiphonal readings for congregational worship, to private devotions for the deeply depressed.

Next, the interrogatives jump-start our observation: Who? What? When? Where? An earlier example observed facts about the sword in Jesus' mouth. We also used the interrogatives to learn about Philip and Simon. Our five senses and our imagination are also resources for observation. Put yourself into a scene and imagine the smells, sounds, feelings, and tensions.

Count the repeated ideas, words, and phrases because every author uses repetition for emphasis. Diagram a complex Bible sentence to drill down to the core message. Doing so also reveals why the subordinate statements support that core message.

Learn from the techniques of observation we use in the Unseen series. With slow, deliberate practice, observation will become your habitual pattern of thought.

Outside the Bible we can also find unexpected inductive training, such as Mark Twain. Despite his antagonism to religion, Twain's mental habit of observation was exemplary—the true source of his humor. Twain wrote a hilarious essay about a deceased author's writing, which he titled "Fenimore Cooper's Literary Offenses."

> Search the title and you can read the short essay at
> gutenberg.org. Many additional classic works of literature
> are digitally available there, at no cost).

In the early 19th century, Cooper wrote the fantastically popular *Deer-slayer* fiction. His protagonist was Natty Bumppo, a frontier woodsman of the 1700s. This woodman is known to us in movies such as *Last of the Mohicans*. Bumppo silently tracks enemies and animals through the woods of frontier New York state, using expert "woodcraft." Twain observes Cooper's books carefully, as carefully as we want to observe what the Bible says. When he does, he finds problems with Cooper's favorite woodcraft techniques. They are not based on reality, because Cooper was a poor observer.

> If Cooper had been an observer, his inventive faculty would have worked
> better; not more interestingly, but more rationally, more plausibly.
> Cooper's proudest creations in the way of "situations" suffer noticeably
> from the absence of the observer's protecting gift. Cooper's eye was
> splendidly inaccurate. Cooper seldom saw anything correctly. He saw
> nearly all things as through a glass eye, darkly. Of course a man who
> cannot see the commonest little every-day matters accurately is working
> at a disadvantage when he is constructing a "situation."

Twain's humorous analysis of Cooper's literary offenses shows the value of observation. We are poor in spirit and need protection from ourselves. With poor skills of observation, we can misuse the Bible. Like Cooper, poor observers invent unrealistic and harmful interpretations of the Bible.

In contrast to Cooper, we observe a Bible passage very carefully and thoroughly when we study it. We trust the Author of the Bible. The Holy Spirit is skillful at writing. He inspired the Bible's authors. By knowing Him, we know the Bible is reliable. No fear is needed that He poorly observed reality, as was Cooper's "woodcraft" failing. We spare no detail when observing the contents of a Bible text. Every single detail we can observe will hold up. As Paul said in Romans 3:4, *"Let every man be a liar, and God be true."*

A second famous training essay for vigorous observation skills is *The Student, The Fish and Agassiz.* Professor Agassiz made a student look at one dead fish for weeks; the result was a lifelong habit of observation. Also readable online, it shows—with far less humor—the value of persistently, repetitively looking at an object of study.

The Bible deserves rigorous observation much more than a dead fish. The basic facts can be easy to see. If we hurry on, we betray a self-confidence akin to preconceptions: "I know enough." But after you get the observation habit, you realize that the greatest joy rises up as you plumb the same passage repetitively.

The appendix contains images of my own Bible study notes in Esther, to depict the results of such patient, repetitive reading.

INTERPRETATION

If observation requires patience, interpretation requires meditation. For five decades I have studied the Scripture inductively. Meditating on one passage easily requires a week.

To interpret your observations requires reflection. There is no hurry to milk God's meaning from a passage, other than our impatience and immaturity. He will not judge us as thickheaded unless "we get something out of it," as we often say. When studying a passage is our plan, being under pressure to go fast is a red flag. Find out why you feel that, and ask the Holy Spirit to calm you before His Word.

Interpretation requires a dictionary—not only an English language dictionary, but also a Bible dictionary. We are 2,000 years removed from the Bible's last contributor and 3,400 years from its first. A Bible atlas is also useful since we are over 5,500 miles away from where its events occurred. Books about daily life in Bible times are available. The crowd-funded series *The Chosen* provides cultural background. Such resources help us understand and interpret the terms, locations, distances, physical exertions, movements, and cultural norms in any passage.

The Bible's original languages are Hebrew, Aramaic, and Greek. Knowing them is beneficial but unnecessary in our times. Whose idea was it to reveal Himself in a Bible authored by multiple people over thousands of years and miles? Did He know that not every reader would speak those languages? Of course He knew we wouldn't. So when God chose a Book-centered plan, He also committed Himself to the translation of its languages. Knowing the Greek language of the New Testament helps my understanding. But the important message is available plainly in any translated language.

We use all the interrogatives in the interpretation step: *Who? What? When? Where?* And also *How?* and *Why?* The last two are especially helpful here. I led my jury in asking *Why?* questions, which can reveal the motives of the people we read about—such as the entitled racist supervisor. Many unstated facts light up also when we apply *How?* questions to a passage. For instance, *How did they get to Caesarea Philippi?* yields the realization that Jesus took a journey to the remote locales requiring a week's walk— which gives rise to *Why?*

The Bible's clearly stated facts presume many unstated truths. We find them with a simple question: what else must we believe to be true if this stated fact is true? The jury identified what the accuser was asking us to believe, if he was correct. Inductive interpretation asks the same thing of the Bible. What else has to be true if the Bible says fact XYZ is true?

The Bible says, Jesus died for our sin—so what else has to be true? The penalty for my offense must be transferable to a substitute. That substitute must be qualified to bear it. The substitute must be willing. Jesus' death must also satisfy God the Father for our sin. And the Trinity itself must love me enough to endure such a tear.

[pause]

Interpreting a passage requires correlation. What is near it (the context)? What says the same thing (cross references)? An example is the disciples' agreement that Jesus was the long-awaited Messiah, which Peter expressed in Matthew 16:16. We observed that this conversation occurred in a Roman city named Caesarea Philippi. Interpretation asks, *Why there?* The passage doesn't say why Jesus picked it. The city is far out of Jewish lands. Interpretation looks at the context. We then learn that Caesarea Philippi is actually the third remote location where Jesus has removed the disciples.

Interpreting observations is not a rigid process. Questions multiply the closer we get to understanding. Why did Jesus try three times to remove the disciples from Jewish lands? What benefit did He see? Was He try-ing to accomplish something He couldn't in Jewish territory? Caesarea Philippi was the last such trip—what made that stop satisfactory to Him?

Answering our interpretive interrogatives usually sends us back into observation. Like Sherlock earlier, we need more facts. We suspend judg-ment about a passage's meaning until we have the facts about it. Inductive study is a patient process requiring deliberation and contemplation.

PREVALENCE

Question: Is a truth less true if found in the Bible only once? Answer: no. As we discussed, proper meekness doesn't hurry into rushed con-clusions—but neither does meekness discount any truth for appearing infrequently. We wait on the Holy Spirit, but not because one Scripture isn't enough.

If we seek more Scriptures to confirm a truth present in one or two, that can be a symptom of our insecurity before God. We want confirmations. It can increase when obeying His Word feels like walking a gangplank. How many swords do we need to poke us in the back before we walk it? One verse? Ten verses?

The authority of a single verse or passage does not permit proof-texting. Meek readers don't wield their favorite verse as a sword against others. Instead, we treasure the intimacy of receiving from our Father something private—like Mother Mary.

His mother kept all these things in her heart. (Luke 2:51)

An example is speaking in tongues. On Pentecost, the flames fell, the wind blew, and right away, the 120 are speaking in tongues. Did they know what it was? Did Jesus prepare them those forty days before Jesus ascended? Acts 1:1–8 suggests He was tight-lipped about what would happen. In the intervening ten days, they studied the Scripture intensely. Their recorded focus was on explaining Judas' betrayal. Were they ready for speaking in tongues? The book of Acts doesn't tell us. We only know Peter recognized the entire event as the Spirit's pouring out, which Joel prophesied.

The gospel had spread for decades before the first explanation of tongues recorded in Scripture. The Corinthian church required correction for abusing the practice. Apostle Paul explained it in 1 Corinthians 14—the only place the Bible explains speaking in tongues. Paul, a genuine scholar of the Old Testament, had only one verse about speaking in tongues: Isaiah 28:11.

Is frequent mention necessary to be true? If so, some important doctrines miss the mark badly, such as the Trinity. Speaking in tongues is just one example. And yet it happened then and continues today. The Church is waking up because tongues enable us to pray what God wants prayed. Power is being released among Christians globally.

APPLICATION

James warned us in his letter not to be hearers of the Word only. Jesus said listening without applying is like building a house on sand.

Application is required for benefit. We have a choice. The preferred choice is submission to the Word of God, willingly. Otherwise, our accountability to it will pierce us, inevitably.

> Be doers of the word, and not hearers only, deceiving yourselves. (James 1:22)

> Whoever hears these sayings of Mine, and does them, I will liken him to a wise man who built his house on the rock... everyone who hears these sayings of Mine, and does not do them, will be like a foolish man who built his house on the sand. (Matthew 7:24, 26)

> For the word of God is living and powerful, and sharper than any two-edged sword, piercing even to the division of soul and spirit, and of joints and marrow, and is a discerner of the thoughts and intents of the heart. (Hebrews 4:12)

Observation and Interpretation have standard procedures that apply to any literature. Application questions are the least rigid category. Applying what God has shown you in the Bible is like putting on a fine, supple glove—customized to your hand. We sometimes delay meeting our Father in the Scripture for this reason. He is up close and personal. After all, His Spirit lives in us.

Christians can take the Bible like an additive in our gas tank. I've found an even greater power there: Scripture unveils what is in me. There really is a distinction between my soul and my spirit—and God's Word pierces right into it (Hebrews 4:12). The Bible doesn't look like a mirror, but it sure functions like one.

When I yield to God, His Word shines a spotlight on my *want-to*. Whatever the Scripture might ask of me, if I *don't* want to, I am convicted. If I *do* want to, I am supported.

Application isn't merely doing. Our habits of thought also require application. The Bible corrects your ideas like a scalpel in the Physician's hand. God wants worshippers in spirit, and equally in truth (John 4:24). Doctrine is not the only truth Jesus meant. Your personal truthfulness with Him is the target of His statement, as it was with the Samaritan woman at the well He said it to. When your mind excuses the choices of your heart, He wants to expose that to you. God's Holy Spirit within you knows your mind. He also knows Jesus' mind. He wants to bring the two into sync.

Now we have received, not the spirit of the world, but the Spirit who is from God, that we might know the things that have been freely given to us by God. (1 Corinthians 2:12)

The God who inspired the Bible is holy. Therefore, conviction of our sins is a frequent application. We have slowness to mature also—not "a sin" yet born of sin. Conviction is the kindness of God, stimulating us to synchronize with Him. Every rebuke we accept from His Bible gives us momentum away from our own way and toward His way.

God's kindness is intended to lead you to repentance. (Romans 2:4)

Momentum is a sign to watch. It shows whether we are applying the Bible. The opposite is stagnation. Not even God can steer a parked car. How many of us have friends repeating the same problem over and over? They are like a washing machine that tumbles and tumbles without ever changing the load. The Bible has a solution. They may see it repeatedly in their Bible studies. Yet they refuse to apply the solution. You can repent and ask for help. When problems are repetitive, deliverance ministry is a very effective way out.

Praise and worship also reveal the effectiveness of our Bible study. The Bible is a love thing, the boudoir of my intimate relationship with God. He loves the world and He gave us His Word to express that love. Simultaneously, we see depravity in ourselves, and magnanimous, unjustified love in Him. How could we read such a written revelation without worship?

I have barely described the three foundation steps of the Inductive Bible Study Method. The Resources appendix contains many in-depth resources and sample images from my own study Bible. Sharpening our skills of Inductive Bible Study is life-long, not once-and-done. Time, expense, and effort are rarely rewarded so richly as when we study the Bible inductively.

INTERPRETIVE METHODS

How do we know whether to read a Scripture literally or figuratively? Our interpretive methods heavily influence how we read a passage. Two such methods are historical and typological.

For years I favored only the historical method, also known as the historico-grammatical method. In studying Church history, one finds many abuses of typology.

By it, medieval priests justified the Church's control of life. I once read a medieval homily justifying chivalry. Using Genesis 2, the priest told his parish, "women were more pure than men." He noted that God made Eve from Adam's rib, but Adam from dust. Women are pure because water poured over a rib eventually runs clean—but not water poured over dirt.

Such misuse of the Bible was not uncommon. Typological interpreters ran wild. They ignored the plain meaning of Bible passages and indulged flights of allegorical fancy. After Jesus' resurrection, John records the miraculous catch of 153 fish. For centuries the early church leaders debated what 153 typified. Their proposals were outlandish and contrived. Now, some modern interpreters use typology likewise. Followers clamor for their hidden plums in the Bible.

My liberal religion professors trained me to believe the scientific method was the foundation of all legitimate Bible study. Historical interpretation focused on the original intent of the original author for the original recipients. This was ascertainable, and once determined, could be beyond debate—or so they told us.

But the differences between conservative and liberal Bible interpretation became unavoidable for me. I learned that no interpretation was beyond debate. In the following decades, my conviction grew that the Scripture would become whatever a person's heart wanted it to be. God has put His Word upon the earth. All of us are accountable to it. Whatever our heart chooses our mind excuses. The Bible confirms our choice—a scary thought for someone so poor in spirit.

Fifteen years ago, I experienced a surge of visions, dreams, and prophetic activation. The heavenly realms became inescapable for me. Using typology, I compared these experiences with Scripture; they matched. The explanatory power of typological interpretation was undeniable. I relented from my close-minded, one-sided viewpoint and yielded.

The historical method is not problematic. It's the same way we read any text, Bible or otherwise. What is the grammatical context of the statement? We also identify the historical context of the statement. After learning who wrote it, and who first read it, we ask, what would it mean to them? Finally, we apply it. If that's what it meant to them, how does that affect me today? The Bible itself uses this method of interpretation in the Bible. Hebrews 4 is one example, where the author does such a study of Psalm 95.

This interpretive grid seeks a one-to-one correspondence between a Scripture and objective facts. Its focus is on correlating a Bible passage to what happened in this visible world. Expository preaching expounds the meaning of the passage to its original recipients. Historico-grammatical interpretation usually favors one primary understanding of any passage: the original meaning to the initial hearers or readers. None of this is bad. Historico-grammatical interpretation is very important.

The problem arises when leaders limit interpretation to the historical method. Such limits are unsupportable unless we find fault with Jesus; He Himself used typological interpretation. Sure, typology has been misused, but so has the historico-grammatical. The scientific materialist viewpoint has seduced our Western education. This is a choice of the heart. The academic mind justifies limiting all interpretation to that worldview.

As happens with people in power, they use the historico-grammatical to cement their control of others. Full circle: medieval priests limited everyone to typological method and used it for control. Now academic "priests" limit us to the historical method, to strengthen their control. Against such controls, regular Christians are arising.

People are encountering the unseen realm more directly; we crave explanations for what we are witnessing. The historical correlation of a Scripture to its original recipients is good, but unsatisfying in our day of miracles. When someone is verified to be brain dead and a month later shakes your hand, the historical correlations are not top of mind—that, I can tell you.

In the Bible, God reveals the unseen realm. It is a world outside of our timeline. The Scripture presents itself using both interpretive methods. The historical method is limited to our timeline, and cannot handle the eternal NOW of the unseen realm. Typology accommodates the Bible's independence from time. Because God is outside our linear timeline, typological interpretation recognizes He is free to intersect human history at multiple points, without restriction. Because of this, typological interpretation is significant in the modern prophetic movement begun in 1988.

Jesus and the apostles used typological interpretation frequently in the New Testament. Anyone who limits interpretation to the more scientific method must explain this away. Typology rightly identifies repetitive biblical patterns in God's dealing with us. The assumption is that these biblical patterns characterize His ongoing behavior because He does not change. After we identify such patterns, we find they explain other Bible passages. Chapter Six is *Coder and Code, Decoder and Key.* God's pattern of coded activity is one such type, instrumental in unlocking Bible mysteries.

INTERPRETIVE EXAMPLES

Our Old Testament was the entire Bible for the apostles. In its types and patterns, they found Jesus. Without typology, they would not have recognized many Scriptures that explained Jesus. Their antagonists, the Pharisees, were Bible students *exemplar*, yet they missed Jesus because they disdained the typological patterns in the Old Testament. Likewise, those limited to the original intent miss God's patterns in our day.

The New Testament writers studied the Old Testament and declared many prophecies fulfilled. They used a typological frame of reference. One example is Jesus' virgin birth. Isaiah prophesied that *"the virgin shall conceive and bear a Son, and shall call His name Immanuel"* (7:14). Matthew, Luke, Mary, and Paul all regarded Jesus as the fulfillment—but not because they used the historical method of interpretation. Isaiah gave the prophecy to a king inspecting water supplies. What it meant to him is not what it means to us! Nor did Mary name her child Immanuel. They interpreted Isaiah's prophecy typologically.

Typology complements the historical method. To the one-to-one correspondence of Scripture and event, typology adds a fulfillment of Scripture's patterns. Consider the Passover given in Exodus 12. With only the historico-grammatical method, the law for the Passover could never have referred to Jesus, 1,400 years later. Nothing given in the Passover was for atonement. Apostle Paul could not have written 1 Corinthians 5:7, *"For indeed Christ, our Passover, was sacrificed for us."* John the Baptist could not have said, *"Behold the Lamb of God!"* (John 1:36) And we would not be celebrating communion, when Jesus said, *"Unless you eat the flesh of the Son of Man and drink His blood, you have no life in you"* (John 6:53). All these interpretations of the Passover in Egypt are typological.

Typology is even more reasonable now. God is revealing to us the unseen world found in the Scripture. Unseen time is not bound to our linear timeline. The always-NOW reality of the unseen manifests itself repeatedly in human history. That's one reason we have the saying, "history repeats itself." God captures such patterns in Scripture so we can recognize the pattern when it repeats.

Isaiah chapters 13–14 give our final example and are pertinent to the *Unseen* series. These two chapters demonstrate both historical fulfillment and typological patterns. You've heard the name Lucifer. It's one way to translate one word that appears in only one place—here in Isaiah 14:12. Whatever the translation, this rebellious archangel casts a long shadow throughout the *Unseen* series. Chapter 13 provides the context for chapter 14; its historical interpretation gives us indispensable information.

Isaiah lived in the southernmost of the two Jewish kingdoms, named Judah. He prophesied both before and after the northernmost kingdom, called Israel, was conquered and its survivors deported. That disaster occurred in 721 BC. The terrorizing empire that vanquished the northern kingdom (and many others besides) was Assyria with the capital in Nineveh.

But Isaiah records a vision in 13:1 naming the empire of Babylon—a mere province of the Assyrian Empire in Isaiah's lifetime. Isaiah sees the destruction of the Babylonian Empire before it even begins one hundred years later. In verse 17, God says, *"Behold, I will stir up the Medes against them."* That Median empire under Cyrus the Great was even further out, 180 years afterward. That is exactly what happened: Cyrus led the Medes and the Persians in the conquest of the Babylon Empire. Everything that Isaiah prophesied about Babylon in Isaiah 13:17–22 has happened.

But not everything in Isaiah 13 has occurred. Isaiah saw things that occur in the book of Revelation, which is God's prophecy of judgment in the unseen and seen alike. The correspondence with Revelation tells us Isaiah is describing events in the unseen world. Revelation 6:13–14, 20:11 and 21:23 allude to Isaiah 13:10, where the sun and moon no longer shine. In Isaiah 13:13, the earth moves out of her orbit, revealed again in Revelation 16.

With typology we identify more in Isaiah 13; take verses 2–5 for example which begin with God speaking, followed by Isaiah's visionary confirmation report.

"Lift up a banner on the high mountain,
Raise your voice to them;
Wave your hand, that they may enter the gates of the nobles.
I have commanded My sanctified ones;
I have also called My mighty ones for My anger—
Those who rejoice in My exaltation."

The noise of a multitude in the mountains,
Like that of many people!
A tumultuous noise of the kingdoms of nations gathered together!

The LORD of hosts musters
The army for battle.
They come from a far country,
From the end of heaven—
The LORD and His weapons of indignation,
To destroy the whole land.

History records that Cyrus and the Medo-Persian empire conquered the Babylonian Empire. But God's statement tells who brings about the fall of Babylon: *My sanctified ones* and *My mighty ones...* Isaiah's confirmation enlarges the description: *from a far country,... His weapons of indignation.*

Would God actually identify the Persian army under Cyrus with those terms? Yes, as a first fulfilment—but the Medes don't fit two details. They are not sanctified unto God, and they do not come *from the end of heaven.* These details are satisfied by only one group in the entire Bible: His multinational Church of Christians, sanctified by the blood of Jesus. Thus Cyrus is a type of Jesus, and his army is a type of us.

The battles of the Old Testament focused on earthly nations and their violent changes. Are we the Church called to a violent physical overthrow of governments? Interpretation finds no such command or calling for the Church in other Scriptures. Even though civil government would kill Jesus, He organized no overthrow—much to the chagrin of Judas. Nor did the apostles turn their spiritual power against the very authorities who had plotted Jesus' crucifixion. Instead, Apostle Paul affirmed: *"Be subject to the governing authorities"* (Romans 13:1).

In Revelation chapter 16–17, Babylon reappears as a type. It represents the world and darkness in a twofold alliance. In Isaiah 13, Babylon stands for *the kingdoms of nations,* the *nobles,* and everyone who defies the exaltation of the LORD.

Typologically, we conclude that the overthrowing army in Isaiah 13 is the Church, and the enemy to be destroyed is the unseen kingdom of darkness. Judging by Matthew 16:18–19, Jesus read the prophecy in the same way. The disciples, led by Peter, had just affirmed that Jesus was the Messiah.

On this rock I will build My church, and the gates of Hades shall not prevail against it. And I will give you the keys of the kingdom of heaven, and whatever you bind on earth will be bound in heaven, and whatever you loose on earth will be loosed in heaven.

The Church will invade the enemy gates just as Isaiah wrote above. We, His Church, will be His sanctified ones, truly mighty, an army from the ends of heaven, bearing His indignation and destroying all the territory of hell.

UNLOCKING MYSTERIES

These baseline habits of thought have positioned us. We can advance to unlocking the secrets that God has hidden in Scripture. We know God is a revealer and loves our friendship. He can open His Bible mysteries to reward our faithfulness.

We can elect to be satisfied with our existing Bible reading habits and study skills. Many do. Their intimacy with God is satisfactory enough. In the unity of Christ, we accept one another because we all need mercy. Unity and mercy recognize many different interests, talents, and habits of thought among Christians. Yet an accountability exists because the Word of God imposes it upon us, as the author of Hebrews wrote in 5:12–14.

> For though by this time you ought to be teachers, you need someone to teach you again the first principles of the oracles of God; and you have come to need milk and not solid food. For everyone who partakes only of milk is unskilled in the word of righteousness, for he is a babe.

Together with this high accountability are the rewards of maturity as Bible students.

> Then you will understand righteousness and justice,
> Equity and every good path,
>
> When wisdom enters your heart,
> And knowledge is pleasant to your soul,
> Discretion will preserve you;
> Understanding will keep you. (Proverbs 2: 9–11)
>
> It is the glory of God to conceal a matter,
> But the glory of kings is to search out a matter. (Proverbs 25:2)
>
> If you abide in Me, and My words abide in you, you will ask what you desire, and it shall be done for you. (John 15:7)

Your word I have hidden in my heart,
That I might not sin against You. (Psalm 119:11)

Your testimonies also are my delight
And my counselors. (Psalm 119:24)

I will walk at liberty,
For I seek Your precepts. (Psalm 119:45)

I will never forget Your precepts,
For by them You have given me life. (Psalm 119:93)

Your word is a lamp to my feet
And a light to my path. (Psalm 119:105)

CHAPTER FIVE

ADVANCED BIBLE LOGIC

Chapter Four listed some rewards of maturity. Desiring them makes our Bible reading more productive. The Bible's mysteries yield to our maturing spirits. He is in the Bible to be found. His Holy Spirit is calling us into the Word of God.

Obstacles can arise when we come to the Bible. We can read it but not understand. Other times we understand a little, yet feel that we are missing out on something. Even in the boring times when we've seen everything in a Bible passage, this Book of power is pulsating with His mysteries. Persisting past the obstacles to understanding can feel very uncomfortable. What can we do?

LISTEN TO THE BOSS

We read Scripture for knowledge, but not only that. We love the Bible because we love Him. Our goal is fellowship with God Almighty and the intimacy He intends and invites. With the human pressure to be religious, we may have used the Bible. We see it as a means to an end, as warned earlier. To study God's Word in our own way is still our own way.

Sometimes part of the Scripture doesn't speak to us. We can't put our brains in His hands. Maybe if we could put our eyeballs in His hands, He could aim them at specific words or verses. After patiently reading a passage that yields nothing to us, what do we do?

Ask the Lord for permission to move on. Don't leave until you have it.

Asking is so simple. By recognizing God as our Bible schoolmaster, we patiently await His voice. This habit protects us from persistent, shallow reading. Listening to Him penetrates every area of life, as we know. Wouldn't it be nonsense if we didn't listen to His Spirit about our Bible study?

HIS WORD, HIS PREROGATIVES

Our Father has the prerogative to dictate our relationship with His Word. To begin with, He can set our *depth* of study. It may be only a brief revisit to a familiar passage, or skimming a verse. *Frequency* can vary. Occasionally, one reading satisfies the Holy Spirit. Other times, He asks us to read the same passage repeatedly. Daily verse devotionals have benefit as well.

But the Lord also calls us to deep study. A limited spiritual diet of daily devotional verses and sermons does not meet His standard for us. Several motives cause us to choose such a limit. We can fear misunderstanding the Bible or embarrassing ourselves. Sometimes the Bible threatens us with conviction we don't want. In some churches, ostracism is a risk if you study the Bible too much. To prevent exposing our poverty of spirit, we can fall into popular habits of shallow reading. We can assuage ourselves that we are reading and hearing the Bible. Whatever the motive, studying His Word in our own way is still our own way.

Relying only on inspiration and instruction is a pitfall of many Christians. The Holy Spirit has individualized ministry for each of us. Following Him deeper into His Word is serious business. If I back off fearfully from His invitation to go deeper, what am I saying about Jesus? about my love for Him? *Holy Spirit, please help me study Your Word because I love the Lord Jesus.*

God's Spirit also has the prerogative to select the passage. He may direct us to a book study or a topical study. Often, God interests me in a specific event, person, or place. When we ask Him what to study, we have a high confidence we will hit paydirt.

The puzzles I see in the Bible are a major tool He uses to lead me. People may not recognize the Spirit's leadership in their questions about the Bible. Religion trains us to have answers, not questions. With insecurity, we can be "answer people," to avoid looking like "question people." But did God make us? Does He live in us? Yes, so our curiosity and interests are something He knows. He even gives them to us. God's Holy Spirit lives in us and can tickle our fancy in His preferred direction. Tickling up an interest within us for His Word is one of His prerogatives.

After the negative influence of religion, we can feel ungodly if something in the Bible seems weird to us. Instead, since God wrote this enigmatic Book, it's godly to pursue what intrigues us. If I trust Him within me, then appealing puzzles are His road signs; they point me where to study His Word. He uses Bible things interesting to you to motivate you deeper into it.

The Holy Spirit also has the prerogative to lock you onto one study or passage. He may keep you in a passage for a strangely uncomfortable duration. You try to leave and read something different, thinking you have seen everything in it. But if He wants you locked down in that study, His conviction quickly sends you back into it. I believe this happens to many Christians who do not recognize it as His doing. We want the rewards of obeying His leadership with His Word. The alternative? to argue with His selection. Then we really miss out.

A lockdown in one passage can feel like wasting time or treading water. But consider how well your Father knows your needs. For example, do you know what temptation will assail you in ten days? Even if you did, how could you get ready? But your Father knows. He might put you in one Bible passage all ten days. His motive is to prepare you. You don't know that's what He's doing. Whatever you need on day ten, He installs through your study days one through nine.

If we can trust Him for our salvation, we can certainly trust Him if the Holy Spirit locks us in one passage of Scripture. His leadership becomes my source of confidence. The passage is important to Him. For reasons I don't know yet, and don't need to know, He wants me to dwell on it. If He keeps me in one Scripture, it can't be fruitless. When I'm frustrated that obedience keeps me in one passage, it's an opportunity to yield to Him. I even accept the boredom because I trust Him. Wherever He may keep us in the Bible, we trust Him.

I completed a study in the summer of 2017 and asked the Holy Spirit what to study next. This is my habit. He led me strangely to the middle chapters of Ezekiel. Who starts in the middle? This mystified me, but He's the Boss and I obeyed, with His help. You hold the result in your hands. The entire nine-book *Unseen* series was born from that single study.

INTERROGATE THE BIBLE

Shortly, we will review God's use of vocabulary, language, and translation. For the moment, let's admit there are some really weird things in the Bible. The unseen world bursts like a bomb into everyday lives of

Bible people. In Scripture, people do asinine stuff; God at times gives bizarre instructions.

Our religious impulse can discount the weirdness of it all. Our pious excuses are myriad: "I shouldn't question it. Things were different back then. That's what everyone else says. I'm not qualified to assess this. My pastor knows about that; I don't need to bother with it. It's not God's will for me to understand."

Such religious deference is beneath the high heavenly status of our living spirits. God said He seated us in the heavenly realms. He revealed we are the army behind Jesus. Jesus delegates authority to us for His limitless supply. He desires intimate fellowship with you and with me. He implants mysteries in His Word to entice us. Deeper understanding of His mysteries strengthens our intimacy with Him. He wants us further up and further in.

We owe Him our obedience. When He lays a trail of breadcrumbs in His Word, God wants our curiosity to follow the trail. When He invites, our curiosity is an honor to His invitation. Shall we cower instead, afraid to investigate God's Word? Shall anything in the Bible be too delicate to stand scrutiny, or too false to survive our questions? In Romans 3:4, Apostle Paul quotes Psalm 51:4 to assure us, God's Word can withstand any interrogation. No question people can ever ask the Bible will wither it.

Indeed, let God be true but every man a liar. As it is written:

"That You may be justified in Your words,
And may overcome when You are judged."

WHY IS THAT THERE?

The more passive our Bible reading, the quicker we skip things that deserve interrogation. But we want our engagement with Scripture to mature. We freely stop at unexpected content to ask, why is that there? When Bible contents seem unusual, that's normal. There are many candidate Scriptures for this pause: why is that there?

How can we develop the mental habit of pausing for things that don't make sense? The previous chapter cited Mark Twain's essay about Fenimore Cooper. A river that Cooper described in *Deerslayer* is too small for the boat or scow that Cooper places on it. Twain's criticism exemplifies our expectation of the Bible.

When a stream acts like that, it ought to be required to explain itself. Fourteen pages later the width of the brook's outlet from the lake has suddenly shrunk thirty feet, and become "the narrowest part of the stream." This shrinkage is not accounted for.

When we read something unexpected, we ask why it is there. Whether it is Cooper's woodcraft, Agassiz's fish, or the Bible, we need not fear asking. Quite the opposite: such misfits are God wooing us to Himself. When we ask, "Why is that there?" we respond to our Father.

We can ask with two emphases. "Why is that THERE?" Something can seem out of place. The writer had a logical reason for it—but why THERE? In Mark 11:20–26, it amazed the disciples that a tree withered at Jesus' verbal command. Jesus then teaches them about faith. To illustrate its power, He escalates from withering trees to moving mountains. But suddenly Jesus segues to forgiveness. How does that fit? Why is He teaching forgiveness THERE, right after the faith teaching? Are the two subjects related? Or was it a random idea? Is it like those times I forget to tell my wife something and have to blurt out now before I forget again?

When I explore this, the answers bring me closer to the Lord. He shows me that unforgiveness stems from a lack of faith. When I don't forgive someone, it's a symptom I don't trust God. I trust myself more than Him. No wonder He thought it applied to mountain-moving, tree-withering faith.

A second emphasis asks, "Why is THAT there?" Moses exemplifies this. Bushes were no oddity after forty years of tending sheep in that mountain range. But one bush burned without burning up. Why is THAT there? Moses did what the event deserved. He turned from his path to look at it more closely. A voice speaking his name from the bush would be shocking, but Moses stayed there with the curiosity that God deserved.

IN DEBT FOR CURIOSITY

One mental discipline is interrogating written material. This habit benefits our entire lives: news reports, political communications, family life, and neighborhood interactions. When we have this mental habit, hidden motives become visible. The same benefit occurs for our Bible reading: mysteries are revealed.

Job complained as if God were in debt to his questions. But the indebtedness is the other way around. We owe God our curiosity. He inspired the

Bible. He installed in it the natural questions which arise within us. We are following these questions like His trail of breadcrumbs to discoveries He has for us. We ask the Holy Spirit the questions that His Bible passage demands from us. Our questions are the payment on our debt to Him: curiosity, receptivity, and hunger for intimacy with Him.

We can investigate the Bible with careful thought, but we do not demand answers. Instead, we yield to what He reveals in our study. It may not answer our inquiry directly. Meekness accepts Scripture's output, regardless of the outcome. Job thought God owed him answers; we do not think that. Job demanded that God justify His actions; we do not demand that. We are active in inquiring, but not demanding like babies.

We trust our Father to reveal what He wants us to know in the Bible. That was Jesus' trust. He had long waited for the disciples to recognize Him, and Jesus' trust was honored in Matthew 16:17.

> Blessed are you, Simon Bar-Jonah, for flesh and blood has not revealed this to you, but My Father who is in heaven.

INTERROGATION EXAMPLE

An example pertinent to the remaining books of the *Unseen* series is Ezekiel 28. Our first step is simply observing. The initial reading shows focus on a city-state named Tyre. With our map, we find Tyre on the Mediterranean coast, now within Lebanon. The context shows both chapters 26 and 27 pertain to Tyre as well. Skimming those two, we find repeated reference to laments over this city-state. We know from 26:1 that Ezekiel wrote these three chapters in 593 BC. The slightest level of background inquiry tells us that Tyre was leveled in 322 BC by Alexander the Great—271 years later.

Our observations produce natural questions for interpretation, such as these three. Why is Tyre the focus here? It's not a Jewish nation. Tyre's not prominent in the Bible. Next, we ask why chapter 28 repeats lamentation. Laments follow the death of someone or something dear, but why was Tyre dear? In Ezekiel's day, Tyre's global power was at its zenith, famed for commercial trading. God even lists its trading contracts in chapter 27. Why is this a lament, as if Tyre died? The third question: what does this have to do with me today, and with the Church? What continuing benefit did God have in mind for placing this in His Bible? Our questions follow one simple pattern: why is that there?

Interpretation asks why God describes this prince with such lofty language. The human prince of Tyre cannot walk on the mountain of God. The lament says he was created in perfection, plainly contradictory to other Scriptures about humans. Only one explanation is plausible, only one alternative. The prince of Tyre is a symbolic type of satan's origin. Conclusion: God uses typological symbols in chapter 28.

During interpretation, we think of other Scriptures that relate. Here, we remember that Isaiah 14 and Revelation 12 also reveal satan's origin. These three chapters are the Bible's total revelation about it.

The origin of satan may not be appealing. How could it be relevant? Why is it in there? It doesn't make us feel close to God. For such reasons, we can easily skip chapter 28. Such mysteries may seem over our heads. But we honor God's Bible puzzles with the inquiries they deserve. We believe God included chapter 28 to reveal something to us. We owe Him our curiosity at least. With a desire to unlock His inviting mysteries, we instead interrogate the passage. "Why is that there?"

> You defiled your sanctuaries
> By the multitude of your iniquities,
> By the iniquity of your trading. (28:18)

God is speaking to satan who is the *you* and *your*. For the moment, let's confine our curiosity to the trading (thoroughly considered in other books of the *Unseen* series). God put trading in His own comments there. He wants us to ask, "Why is that there?" If this verse were a trial witness, we would have many questions.

What are the sanctuaries? Aren't sanctuaries reserved for God? Didn't God know Lucifer had them? How did trading defile them? How did Lucifer trade? Who was he trading with? Trading is an exchange of value. What value did he have to trade? What value could others give him? How did trading promote iniquity in him?

Paul says that the love of money is a root of all evil (1 Timothy 6:10). Is that the reason Lucifer's trading sparked his iniquity? Trading is a simple exchange of value; is that bad? Is buying and selling sin? What about bartering? Should we avoid all trading?

Or is God singling out only the trades of Lucifer? Was there something Lucifer did that made his exchanges iniquitous? God says it was a *multitude*. The word *trading* matches *multitude*; together, they imply a repetitive practice rather than a single action. A long window of time is implied by repetition. How did so many iniquities accumulate?

There are many puzzles in this one verse. We can't put the verse in any witness stand, but we ask God who inspired it. We apply our mental stamina to learn. What is in the verse for us? With meekness, we wait for His leadership. When we study this way, something will definitely happen.

These mysteries occupy the remaining seven books of the *Unseen* series. Ezekiel 28 is a primary source for the next volume, *Nobody Sees This Creation: The Origin of the Devil and His Replacements*. In this Book Two, our purpose is to hone our skills for His Word. Those skills will yield the solutions for the above puzzles, which are answered throughout the Bible. Suffice it here to say, Lucifer's trading was the symptom of one total package: disdain for God. This cherub guarded the throne of God and trod the fiery stones around God's very throne. No angel was closer to the Triune God than Lucifer. By his trading, he undervalued his high privilege in heaven. He had the multiple sanctuaries, which we might call protected trading outposts. His privilege was proximity to God, but Lucifer focused elsewhere, as if something else were more important.

NO EXCUSE FOR PRIDE

The Bible requires our meekness. If we refuse, the Bible then helps us become obnoxious. Our habit of critical thinking is like every other talent God gave us. We use it for Him, and at His direction. If we misuse this talent, we are arguing with God. If we criticize, judge, or gossip, we are agreeing with satan. Meekness presumes no personal superiority over anyone. The poor in spirit avoid such comparisons. Otherwise, logical thinking only renders us know-it-alls. We become unwelcome among people, never at home with family or friends, always nomadic in relationships, and perpetually dissatisfied—like satan.

COMMON KNOWLEDGE NO LONGER

When a Bible passage has not yet satisfied your questions, ask if there's some common knowledge that is missing from your reading. This takes two forms. The first is identifying what you are taking for granted. So often we think we know something and give it no thought. With a book as deep as the Bible, that's unwise. We don't have to explore every question immediately, compulsively, or anxiously. We can simply register that there is a question to revisit as the Holy Spirit leads. When He feels you are ready, He will bring it to your attention again. Or you may not have time right now, among your responsibilities.

A simple example is using the bathroom. Human beings all have to expel the results of digestion and drinking; Jesus was no exception. But if you take it for granted, you might underestimate 1 Samuel 24. King Saul had a right to privacy when he used the bathroom; his guards did not follow him into the cave he chose, and no one knew David and his army were in the same cave. Other examples are Elijah's taunt for the pagans in 1 Kings 18:27, and God's strange instruction to Ezekiel in 4:12 of his prophetic journal.

The second form of missing common knowledge is past habits of society. The society in which they wrote the New Testament is two thousand years and several cultures distant from us. Every culture has an unstated body of knowledge. People outside the culture don't see it. Some Bible statements may seem out of place without that common knowledge. It signals to look for some knowledge common then but unknown now. An example is the response to Jesus' teaching in Matthew 7:28–29.

> And so it was, when Jesus had ended these sayings, that the people were astonished at His teaching, for He taught them as one having authority, and not as the scribes.

This follows the Sermon on the Mount, which begins with Jesus' Beatitudes. We appreciate it, but our reaction is rarely like the one described above. What are we failing to see? We lack the common knowledge summed up in one phrase, *not as the scribes.* Scribes were the scholars of the Law. Their name as a group comes from their role in the transmission of the Law by hand-copying. These scholars, like ours today, stated nothing categorically. All their statements appealed to a higher authority, like a celebrity endorsement. Jesus stood in strict contrast to their deferential desire for the endorsement of others. He needed no authority but the Holy Spirit's leading within Him. The verse tells us how dramatic the contrast was.

Sometimes our interrogation of a Bible passage doesn't explain what we find there. We can then interrogate our assumptions. Maybe we lack appreciation for some common knowledge that solves the puzzle.

REVERSE ENGINEERING THE PIECES

Today the connotation of reverse engineering is thievery. But for Bible study, the process is valuable.

Competitors buy a newly innovated product and disassemble the product to each component piece. They assume the original innovator had good reasons for each part and its placement. From those pieces, they identify manufacturing requirements.

With this reverse-engineered information, they create a copycat manufacturing process to make the identical product. With no cost for research and development, and less costly regulation, they can sell the pirated item at far lower prices than the original innovator.

Reverse engineering has beneficial uses as well. The first phone call by Alexander Bell resulted from an accident: "Mr. Watson, come here! I want to see you." Neither of them knew why the device finally worked after many unsuccessful tries. They had to reverse engineer to the reason, working backwards step by step to identify the components of successful sound transmission. All our phones have their origin in Bell reverse engineering his lab accident.

We ask a verse, "why is that there?" Reverse engineering can reveal why. Our beginning premise: the writer had a rational reason for putting this verse where he did. If the reason isn't clear to us, the weak link lies with us, not the writer and not the Holy Spirit who inspired the verse.

In the Bible, the individual pieces are words, sentences, and paragraphs. (The upcoming chapter seven, *God's Words*, reviews His word selection in greater depth.) Reverse engineering a passage, we disassemble to these individual pieces and evaluate them.

Every word's dictionary definition is the *denotation* of the word. Words often have *connotations* as well. The context and usage determine the connotation, which is unique to each language, culture, and time. Unlike the denotation, the word doesn't have the same connotation in every use. Connotation influences the translation of Scripture. We identify each word's denotations and connotations in the version being used.

We next review the grammatical relationships among the pieces. For instance, the relationship of pronouns to the individual persons and places named may not be clear. By isolating the proper nouns and pronouns in a passage, we can match them together. Often, this single step fills an entire study period with exciting discoveries.

We also see the grammar relationships by identifying each sentence's individual pieces. Read a sentence using only the verbs, subjects, and objects. By reducing each sentence this way, we find the writer's reasons for the adverbs, adjectives, and other modifiers. Thus, we reverse engineer to the writer's intent.

This is a fluid process and is not rule-bound. Our efforts may or may not lead to any discoveries. The thieves who steal innovations are not like us. We are hungry to know God and walk in His ways. We love the Bible as a book for that relationship—not for earning points in a religious IOU system.

REVERSE ENGINEERING TO THE UNSTATED FACTS

For each clearly stated Bible truth, a simple question is possible. What else must be true? Every truth stated leads to a crowd of truths unstated. After all, the Bible doesn't state everything that is true, as reviewed earlier.

For an example, let's sample a tantalizing Bible phrase: *in the midst.* It is a modifying phrase which Ezekiel uses far more often than other biblical authors. Is that accidental? Maybe, and maybe not. We love the Bible, so we explore, whatever we might conclude.

Reverse engineering inspects the surrounding pieces that this mysterious phrase affects. Water is one piece that is affected whenever the Holy Spirit caused Ezekiel to write, *"in the midst."* Ezekiel repeatedly uses *"in the midst of the seas"* and *"in the midst of his rivers."*

Judgment is another piece that often appears with the waters of the phrase, *in the midst.* God names each nation's judgment in Ezekiel, and each pronouncement refers to waterways. He clearly states that for their pride, He judges their waters. The middle chapters of Ezekiel are about God's judgment on Israel and her neighbors. Now we know the basis of the prophet's disproportionate use of this phrase. The nations' waterways are *in their midst,* and a key factor in their offensive pride.

But judging water makes no sense, by any modern reading of the Bible. Have we hit upon something that God is revealing—or is it a meaningless correlation? We do not dismiss it readily. The Author of the Bible lives in us and we owe Him our curiosity. We meditate on the possible meanings of what He inspired.

An inspection of Ezekiel's middle chapters started this process. We reverse engineered from its explicit statements to this possible truth: God judges nations' pride by drying up their waters, rivers, and aquifers.

TESTING OUR REVERSE ENGINEERING

We must also test the Bible truths produced by our reverse engineering. One test uses the questions of our society, culture, and peers. Multiplying modern questions appears to defy the validity of our output, and we do not dismiss them offhandedly. God's Word can stand any scrutiny. Questions shoehorn us deeper into the Scripture.

Climate change and desertification are dominating theories as of this writing. How is a nation's pride with its waters? Why penalize earth's waters for its inhabitants' sin? Why would God be environmentally destructive? The questions pertain to individuals as well. Our nation is turning its back on high fructose corn syrup and sugary drinks. We are drinking much more water than recent decades. But does God's judgment on the waters mean that water is evil? Is Scripture telling us not to drink the water? Our nation has many rivers—is that a bad sign for us?

A second test is the actual condition of the nations named in Ezekiel. If the Holy Spirit inspired Ezekiel to communicate this reality, we would expect the nations to be deserts now. After all, God judged their waters for the sin of those nations. In fact, they are deserts, as a terrain map shows.

A third test uses other truths and facts plainly stated elsewhere in the Bible. Our reverse-engineered theory is that God's judgment on nations' pride affects their waters. What other passages correlate to that? One involves yet another mystery: Leviathan, with only five references in Scripture. In each one, Leviathan is evil, and in each, God's judgment involves its waters. We can test our reverse engineering from Ezekiel's overused phrase. Our test should show that pride and Leviathan are associated. In fact, Job 41:34 specifically verifies it: *"He is king over all the children of pride."* Our strange conclusion may in fact be accurate.

IT CAN'T MEAN THAT

The preconceptions discussed earlier have their deadliest effect when we tell a Bible passage what it can't mean. We can fear the Bible might mean something threatening to us or our beliefs.

How do *we* know? To adapt the childhood rebuttal, who died and made *us* king of the Bible? Who are *we* to say what it can and can't mean? The Bible is not a normal book, but a book of the unseen God in which He reveals the unseen realm. It does not kowtow to expectations formed in the seen world.

If you want to know its mysteries, you have to identity the urge: it can't mean that! When you relinquish that urge, you may be close to paydirt, like Gamaliel in Acts 5. He was a Jewish leader on the Sanhedrin. The apostles were on trial and refused to stop preaching Jesus. They even told the high priest, *"you murdered* [Jesus] *by hanging him on a tree."* Predictably, these murderous leaders planned to kill the apostles as well.

Peter did not accidentally choose *hanging on a tree* to describe crucifixion. This was inspired verbal argumentation. The Scripture explicitly states in Deuteronomy 21:23 that someone hung on a tree was accursed. Peter knew their belief: "the Messiah cannot be a cursed person."

In fact, the apostles knew that Jesus hanging on the tree was the basis of our salvation. In the Law was only one command that could make Jesus become sin for us—hanging on a tree. That's why they used the phrase versus the Sanhedrin's version. Apostle Paul spells it out in Galatians 3:13.

Christ has redeemed us from the curse of the law, having become a curse for us (for it is written, "Cursed is everyone who hangs on a tree").

The Jews believed Deuteronomy 21:23 can't mean that! But one leader on the Sanhedrin maintained an open mind: Gamaliel. He was old and respected. He also heard Peter's verbal taunt from the Law. But Gamaliel accepted the possibility: the curse of someone hanged on a tree might actually include the Messiah Himself. His open mind prevented the Sanhedrin from executing the twelve apostles.

The Word of God must offend us if we are to understand it. Sometimes our theory about a passage feels just impossible. That signifies the Spirit's invitation. He is inviting us to rest in that passage. The interpretive process of slow meditation will yield understanding and possibly confirmation.

Above we considered *in the midst*, Ezekiel's outsized phrase. Our reverse engineering revealed the effect of God's judgment on nations' waterways. It's so foreign to modern thinking. Surely it can't mean that God will turn fertile earth into a desert! While suspending our conclusion, we do not reject it. If that's the correct understanding, we can expect it to be confirmed in other ways.

An easy example is the Canaanite woman seeking healing for her daughter, in Matthew 15:21–28. Three times He repudiates her in no uncertain terms. Jesus actually ignored her repeated plea, told her no, and even compared her to the beggar dogs under a family's dinner table. Our preconceptions object strenuously: it can't mean that! Why is He so mean?

But persistent meditation yields its fruit. Our Jesus was capable of sarcasm, such as Mark 7:9: *You have a fine way of setting aside the commands of God in order to observe your own traditions!* (NIV). Tongue-in-cheek speech is a related verbal technique, but in written speech, it is indiscernible. The Cambridge online dictionary defines the idiom: "If you say something tongue in cheek, you intend it to be understood as a joke, although you might appear to be serious."

If Jesus was speaking tongue in cheek, we read in fact that He was inviting the Canaanite woman to keep asking, and she did. Certainly, He rewarded her for it. We confirm this reading by His other statements on the necessity of persistent asking, such as Luke 11:5–10 and 18:1–6–. *"He spoke a parable to them, that men always ought to pray and not lose heart."*

When your study of this unique Book provokes a feeling, "it can't mean that," it is the Spirit's invitation to meditative interpretation. Ask the Boss what it means, and wait for His answer. Maybe that's what Gamaliel did after the apostles' trial.

UNIFYING THEME

Earlier, we surveyed the army in Revelation 19. We questioned the sword from Jesus' mouth. What is the point? We don't know—but we assume that God chooses His words carefully; He showed John this vision purposely. These tiny details help unlock the unifying theme of a passage.

Consider the way we ourselves talk. We don't utter random sentences in a string. When we express ourselves, every word and phrase contribute to our meaning. There's no cause for someone to say, "Ignore every fourth word Mary says; it's not meaningful." How much less cause is there for God's words to be ignored, disdained, or taken lightly? Each paragraph, each word and phrase, each punctuation—they all contribute to one unifying theme.

Not every encounter with the Bible is a thorough study. The habit is necessary, however. We want to practice thorough thinking, so it becomes habitual. Habits train us so we are ready when He speaks. When He has a mystery to reveal to us through a unifying theme, we won't be twiddling our thumbs unable to see it.

The unifying theme is almost never visible when we first read a passage. We read every passage the way we always have. Christians start out as baby spirits and rely on the teaching of our elders. Deferring to authority is an essential skill, but not if we defer to what others say it means. Because of our past deference to religious authorities, only effort can transcend this pre-installed interpretation. By digging into the Scripture as this book advises, we give ourselves the opportunity to rise above those deferential limits.

Earlier we observed Jesus' three trips out of Jewish lands. There is a unifying theme, but what? Meditation enables interpretation of the apparently unrelated details. Evaluating possible explanations, we arrive at only one unifying theme which makes sense of these travel details. Jesus is seeking a place of anonymity and privacy for a serious talk with His disciples.

He first takes the disciples to the towns of Tyre and Sidon on the coast of Lebanon. But He was recognized there, where He healed the daughter of the Canaanite woman. Jesus then returned to the Decapolis area east of Galilee, but thousands accumulated; He multiplied fish and bread a second time. He left there and went to a region called Magdala, but the adversarial religious leaders pursued Him with tests. Jesus warned the disciples about the falsity of the leaders' teaching, and took them to the Roman city of Caesarea Philippi. There anonymity was finally available. Jesus' much-desired privacy with the disciples comprises the next fifteen verses.

Yet questions remain. This private conversation was so important to Jesus, but why? What could He only achieve by such time-consuming effort?

After all, the thirteen men didn't get on a train or bus. They walked those distances for days and days. We have no conception of walking such distances. Capernaum in Galilee was Jesus' local base. Tyre was 32 miles from there, an eleven hour walk for men in their thirties, not counting breaks. Caesarea Philippi is also 32 miles away. Our passage records four such journeys in this period, a walk of 126 miles, forty-four hours' worth. This was a major effort, but why? If you had been a disciple, wouldn't you have wondered about it? "Why is Jesus making us walk so far?"

The unifying theme emerges when we reverse engineer from the conclusion of the travel: a mountain climb in Matthew 17:1–8 (emphasis added.).

> Now after six days Jesus took Peter, James, and John his brother, led them up on a high mountain by themselves; and He was transfigured before them. His face shone like the sun, and His clothes became as white as the light. And behold, Moses and Elijah appeared to them, talking with Him. Then Peter answered and said to Jesus, "Lord, it is good for us to be here; if You wish, let us make here three tabernacles: one for You, one for Moses, and one for Elijah."
>
> While he was still speaking, behold, a bright cloud overshadowed them; and suddenly a voice came out of the cloud, saying, "*This* is *My* beloved *Son*, in whom I am *well* pleased. Hear *Him!*" And when the disciples heard it, they fell on their faces and were greatly afraid. But Jesus

came and touched them and said, "Arise, and do not be afraid." When they had lifted up their eyes, they saw no one but Jesus only.

The days so full of walking culminate in God's voice from heaven. The Father endorses Jesus. Peter had just affirmed that Jesus was the Messiah and the Son of God—but then he argued with Jesus that the religious leaders would not reject Him. Jesus rebuked Peter. Now here they are on this mountaintop, and the top two Jewish icons are with Jesus.

With our preconceived notions, this looks like Moses and Elijah endorsing Jesus. Far from it—endorsers are superior to the endorsed. Only Jesus' face is like the sun; only His clothes become like the whitest linen. The other two are not transfigured. Father God is showing the disciples, Jesus is superior to Moses and Elijah. The Father's statement affirms Jesus' rebuke of Peter. Jesus is the superior of this trio, and He needs no endorsement from respected leaders.

My italics above show the proper emphasis for understanding the Father's voice on that mountain. He singles Jesus out. Jesus has the inside track—not religious leaders. He wants us to listen to Jesus directly and accept what Jesus says as the sole authority. Don't reject what Jesus says when it differs from your expectations. Don't defer to religious leaders. Hear Him, not them.

UPROOT DEFERENCE

Our deferential response to religious authorities greatly hinders our Bible understanding.

Jesus was patient with the limits of His twelve followers. They faced the biggest paradigm shift in history, and He gently stretched their capacities. But Jesus' reaction to Peter was His most explosive, most abrupt, and verbally violent in the gospels. By today's superficial sensitivity, Jesus deserves harsh judgment. Twitter and Facebook would "deplatform" Him and ostracize Him for this outburst. Plus, Jesus was always spreading misinformation and making hurtful statements. He even seemed to imply that the persistent Canaanite woman in Tyre was a dog (Matthew 15:26).

The unifying theme of the four trips outside Jewish lands is for Peter and also for us: any deference to anyone which supplants our deference to Jesus. Who is the Lord: them, or Him? The Bible tells us to respect our elders but does not prevent exceeding their discoveries. However, like the disciples, we habitually defer to superiors, unwilling to risk their displeasure or advance past them.

Peter exemplified this; he was the disciples' vocal leader. The Jewish leaders wouldn't reject Jesus, he said. The disciples all had a preconception: the religious leaders must endorse Jesus. Peter may have felt he was only the first of many to recognize Jesus' identity. Like all the disciples, he believed the entire nation soon would affirm Jesus as the Messiah of Israel. Judging from the continual crowd responses, we would have thought the same.

But Peter rightly identified the crowds' deference to the religious leaders. The Jerusalem priests and Pharisees could sway the crowd toward or away from the Messiah. The disciples' plan for the Messiah was His public endorsement by the religious leaders and the subsequent crowning by the Jewish nation. Isn't that what we would expect, in Peter's shoes?

That's why Peter objected to Jesus' teaching about His rejection.

Peter didn't want the other disciples discouraged, so he asked Jesus to step aside privately. Jesus complied with Peter's request and listened to Peter's rebuke—up to a point. He suddenly burst forth with His own rebuke. But this one was not private; Jesus spun away from Peter toward the other disciples. Jesus saw the devil in Peter's deference to religious authorities. Think about it: here in front of Peter was the Messiah Himself, and Peter tells Him that He is wrong. Peter tells the Messiah that He needs the endorsement of the Jewish leaders—as if they are superior to Him.

God likewise pinpoints our unquestioning deference to religious leaders. He dislikes it when we let them interpose themselves between us and Him. He is superior to all. When we defer to others, we demote Him. The Father was having none of that; the Transfiguration was His doing. "*This* [not the others,] is *My* beloved *Son*. In *Him*, I am well pleased. Hear *HIM!*"

Our deference to anyone above our deference to Jesus deafens us to what He says. Peter and the disciples show this. The disciples never responded to Jesus' promise of His resurrection. They could not hear it; no record shows they ever asked about resurrection. In Mark 9:32, they were afraid to ask about any of what he was saying about rejection. All they could hear was the conflict with their preconceived notion: religious leaders must endorse Him, not reject Him.

The Father's voice on the mountain prohibits ranking Jesus lower than other leaders. We are not meek when we refuse faith in this, when we tolerate our demeaning deference to leaders. We can value the response of others and of Christian leaders. We respect our teachers. Meekness does not presume our reading of Scripture is always correct. But the same faith that sprouts meekness also makes us trust 1 John 2:20. *"But you have an anointing from the Holy One, and you know all things."*

One sign that we doubt this: we palliate our desire by asking authorities. Over forty years, many have asked me what a passage means. My first response is always, "What do *you* think it means?" Their guess is in sync with the passage nine times out of ten. The obstacle is not the Bible passage, but their lack of trust that the Holy Spirit will teach them.

People defer to religious authorities to tell them what the Bible means. These are the authorities who never taught them to trust God's leadership. Lacking the belief that He actually lives inside them, they doubt that He can lead them into truth.

I did not become secure with the Bible overnight. But neither did I doubt my ability to read for myself. Instead, I trusted in His ability to instruct me. As a new Christian, I was a religion major. My professors all disdained the integrity of Scripture and ridiculed faith in Christ. Perplexity was frequent as I weighed their arguments against trusting the Bible. But my anxiety had to wait on Him.

Anxiety signals our susceptibility to using God and His Word. We love something else more, so we turn Him into a means of protecting it. Holy Spirit exposed my anxiety whenever I used the Bible that way. He taught me that waiting on Him is not only waiting. It is enjoying Him. What's the hurry? Being with Him is the whole point of everything.

With this attitude, questions and perplexity were no threat. I could study the passage patiently without rushing. After developing a theory of the meaning, I would consult others, both the living (in person or in writing) and the historical (such as Bible commentaries).

Passively deferring to what authorities say about the Bible retards our Christian growth. Hebrews 5:12–14 rebukes Christians for such deference. The Emmaus walkers exemplify slowness with the Bible, in Luke 24:19–20. Like Peter, they were perplexed that the religious leaders did not endorse Jesus. Their deference to these visible authorities was greater than their deference to Jesus' teaching. Therefore, the walkers were blinded to the prophetic imperatives for these events. These imperatives are well known to Christians, such as Psalm 118:22–23:

> The stone which the builders rejected
> Has become the chief cornerstone.
> This was the Lord's doing;
> It is marvelous in our eyes.

We wonder, how could the disciples miss that and the other Old Testament prophecies fulfilled in Jesus? The answer is, they deferred to authorities. They esteemed the religious authorities as being more authoritative than Jesus. The disciples suspended belief in what Jesus said, because it conflicted with the teaching they had from religious authorities. Jesus rebuked the timid deference of the Emmaus walkers: *"foolish ones and slow of heart to believe"* (Luke 24:25).

The irony is that deference to religious authorities is not meekness to God, but its opposite: rebellion.

If God truly lives in me, John's letter is right: I have an anointing to know the truth. Same with you. A true spiritual authority refuses to interject themselves between us and Lord Jesus. Instead, they nurture our faith that we have a direct relationship with Him. The genuine spiritual leader does not reinforce self-doubt but builds our trust in God's Spirit. Sadly, many preachers and teachers have the preconception that we need them. It's understandable because so many Christians defer to them. The marketplace of spiritual influencers is close to an argument with the Holy Spirit: *"He will guide you into all truth"* (John 16:13).

What can we do to avoid that argument? Let us nourish our direct love affair with Him. Sit before His Word; soak in it like a bubble bath. What's the hurry? We can trust Him to lead us. When we have questions about our accurate perception, we can ask leaders of spiritual authority. Asking leaders what it means is beneficial. But passivity to explore the Word of God for ourselves is substandard. We must not subject our Bible exploration to the approved regimen of interloping religious authorities. That makes us like Peter, who argued with the Son of God right in front of him.

If you are a Christian, God lives right in you. Be filled with the Holy Spirit, as the Bible commands. Do not subject His direct leadership to the evaluation and endorsement of others. In love, He will correct you, as He did Peter, and it could be explosive. Exposing the devil and destroying his works is a prime objective.

RECOGNIZING COUNTERFEITERS

Paul instructs us in Ephesians 5:11, *"Have no fellowship with the unfruitful works of darkness, but rather expose them."* To obey this requires us to recognize the devil's counterfeits.

Scripture indicates that God creates from nothing, *ex nihilo* in Latin.

The kingdom of darkness cannot create like that. Another difference is that God imagines from nothing. Look in the mirror; who made you up? Who thought of making you? He did. But the kingdom of darkness can only copy what He imagines. The Bible enables us to tell who's who.

Second Thessalonians 2 and Revelation 13 reveal that the kingdom of darkness can do miracles. For example, Pharaoh's sorcerers duplicated Moses' cane-snake and blood-water miracles in Exodus 7–8. Jesus condemned the miracle-working, demon-casting prophesiers in Matthew 7:22, but not for lying. They really did those things and He didn't argue the point. The apostles traveling the then-known world also faced counterfeiters, as Apostle Paul described in 2 Corinthians 11:13–15.

> For such are false apostles, deceitful workers, transforming themselves into apostles of Christ. And no wonder! For Satan himself transforms himself into an angel of light. Therefore it is no great thing if his ministers also transform themselves into ministers of righteousness, whose end will be according to their works.

Bible study is our protectant against deception by the counterfeits. Failure to know the Word of God makes us sign-chasers, driving from conference to conference, from miracle to miracle. What we want is in us already: intimacy with the Holy Spirit of God.

> Ho! Everyone who thirsts,
> Come to the waters;
> And you who have no money,
> Come, buy and eat.
> Yes, come, buy wine and milk
> Without money and without price.
> Why do you spend money for what is not bread,
> And your wages for what does not satisfy?
> Listen carefully to Me, and eat what is good,
> And let your soul delight itself in abundance.
> Incline your ear, and come to Me.
> Hear, and your soul shall live. (Isaiah 55:1–3)

Reverse engineering is a very simple habit for exposing the works of darkness. In Scripture are three ways to reverse engineer from counterfeit to counterfeiters.

The first test for identifying counterfeits: the identity of Jesus. The kingdom of darkness has spawned competing "sacred" writings. They all lower Jesus' unique identity. The kingdom of darkness promotes religion with an IOU system for putting God in our debt—only necessary because by lowering Jesus, His death for sin becomes inadequate and incomplete. These counterfeits have billions of followers. Apostle John in 1 John 4:2–3 tells us to test the spirits of everyone by their honor for Jesus as the Son of God. Apostle Paul also identified counterfeiters that way in 2 Corinthians 11:4.

> By this you know the Spirit of God: Every spirit that confesses that Jesus Christ has come in the flesh is of God, and every spirit that does not confess that Jesus Christ has come in the flesh is not of God.

> For if he who comes preaches another Jesus whom we have not preached, or if you receive a different spirit which you have not received, or a different gospel which you have not accepted—you may well put up with it!

The behavioral or results test is in the Bible also. After all, the Christians in Corinth weren't falling for snake oil salesmen. The counterfeits of darkness make positive impressions. They were doing miracles also, not for love but for self-promotion. Paul described the after-effects in 2 Corinthians 11:20. Jesus summarized this test also, in Matthew 7:20.

> For you put up with it if one brings you into bondage, if one devours you, if one takes from you, if one exalts himself, if one strikes you on the face.

> Therefore by their fruits you will know them.

Counterfeiters are also revealed by a third test, which exposes interloping authorities as well. Do they insert themselves between the Christian and Jesus? Being intimate with God is a privilege offered only to human beings. Darkness can't have it and jealously obstructs it. Abusers want to have people but disguise it as love. They do not love people, but use them. Their impressive counterfeiters oppress and subjugate people.

God Himself warned Cain about it in Genesis 4:7. *"Sin lies at the door. And its desire is for you."* The Galatians certainly suffered that way from the deceivers who impressed them. In Galatians 4:17, Paul put it this way.

They zealously court you, but for no good; yes, they want to exclude you, that you may be zealous for them.

These tests reveal a tremendous contrast. To the shallow and easily misled, the appearance may be identical, or even favor the servants of darkness. By applying the above tests, we preserve ourselves for the kingdom of God.

REWARDED

Are these habits of thought only for getting details without purpose? I feel that way often when I study the Scripture. I've discovered: the prize includes the habit.

Why should God reveal much from the Bible to us if we lightly regard it? We honor Him by honoring His Word with every curious bone in our bodies. And to such, He reveals His mysteries.

It is the glory of God to conceal a matter,
But the glory of kings is to search out a matter. (Proverbs 25:2)

We don't need to squeeze blood from a turnip, as the saying goes. We simply want to be good stewards. God wanted you to have a Bible in your hands or device. He went to great lengths. He marshaled effort from millions of people—not to mention those who paid with their lives. Honoring His Word has many benefits for you, which are tangential to Bible study.

We are smarter and enhance our ability to absorb from any source. We enjoy others' respect for our thoughtful responses. Slow meditation on His Word makes us better listeners to others—both their spoken and unspoken words. The habit of waiting on Him teaches us how to enjoy people more than knowing stuff. His exposure of our anxieties about the Bible's meaning helps heal anxieties in all areas. This is a brief list.

He often directs our attention to something in the Bible. If we are obedient and give Him that attention, He enjoys honoring us in other areas of life.

FRAME OF REFERENCE

We often incorporate deceptions of darkness into our frame of reference without knowing it. Our hidden grid for interpreting life is usually unquestioned. Dark counterfeiters use our frame of reference for their footholds.

Thus, we give unwitting agreement to the kingdom of darkness. They eagerly drive through the doors we open to them. Our preconceived notions and our deference to religious authorities support our frame of reference. The maturing process for our spirits includes identifying our frame of reference, as discussed at length in Book One of the *Unseen* series, *Nobody Sees This You: How to Live as a Spirit in the Unseen Realm.*

An important pilgrimage is from our fragmented and mixed grid to the integrated grid Jesus imparts. This happens several times in a growing Christian's life. It's a major reason my wife and I named our ministry *Paradigm Lighthouse*, with the logo of the lightbulb.

Blessed is the man whose strength is in You,
Whose heart is set on pilgrimage. (Psalm 84:5)

Studying the Bible occurs within our frame or grid. The word *template* comes from the computer world. We impose this template on everything we do and read, without knowing it. One purpose of God in our Bible study is to replace our old template. We can adopt His—the only authentic way to interpret everything. But how if we don't know our own template?

The habits of thought and study contribute to this process. No one way exists. No one can say, "Today I will change my grid for interpreting everything." Change in our frame of reference results from a cumulative process. It is a pilgrimage.

Recurring throughout this book, we have an example. We keep revisiting the unwelcome consequences of deferring to religious authorities. By this point, you may have a new frame of reference about the Holy Spirit teaching you from within. I didn't plan on doing that. I realize it only as I write this paragraph.

The seeds for changing our grid are the Beatitude qualities to which we now turn.

CHAPTER SIX

CODER AND CODE, DECODER AND KEY

Spiritual mysteries pertain to the unseen. Mystery about the unseen realm beckons us further up and further in. Although mysterious to us, the unseen world is the home sweet home of its age-old, unseen inhabitants.

But God keeps mysteries—from the unseen inhabitants and from people alike. During conflict, communication requires care. Chapter One was titled, *War Engaged*. By understanding wartime communication, we can unlock Bible mysteries. The first step is resignation to a simple fact: the unseen realm is at war with God, and we are God's fighting force.

Books Three through Five of the *Unseen* series review the Bible's mysteries about people, the devil and fallen angels, and the war against humankind. Four sentences could summarize these mysteries: They thought they beat God. He outsmarted them. They fell into God's trap. We replace them.

His full plan for people was a secret. It's in the Bible, yet a secret—how?

THE AMBUSHER

Book Six of the *Unseen* series is, *Nobody Sees This Warrior: God's Secret Ambush*. Ambushing is His well-proven habit in the Bible, first revealed during Israel's conquest of Canaan. Jesus said His Church would invade the territory of hell and push back its gates (Matthew 16:18). The book of Joshua records events occurring around 1500 BC, with many types for the Church.

If God were applying for divinity with us today, we would not hire Him if He listed "ambusher" on His resumé. A fair guess says no reader has heard a sermon, "God the Ambusher." Why not, if it's important in the Bible? As we have seen, the Bible responds to our willingness; God honors our choices. Scripture is not an ordinary book. It is the power of God for salvation (Romans 1:16) but also for delusion (2 Thessalonians 2:10–11).

Joshua 6 tells the familiar event of impregnable Jericho's defeat after Israel marched around it seven days; archaeologists have unearthed the ruins of its famous walls. But Joshua 7 brings bad news: one soldier violated the command of the LORD, and plundered goods from the defeated Jericho (6:18–19). He did it secretly. It became very costly.

The next city to conquer was a small town named Ai (Aye-EE or A-eye). Its size warranted only a small attacking contingent. To the shock of Joshua and Israel, the men of Ai defeated their forces (7:5). In verses 6–9, Joshua and the leaders fall to pieces. They weep and grovel over this defeat—not because thirty-six of their 1,000,000-man army died, a small number. Their courage failed because it called God's support into question. Twelve of the fourteen spies had convinced the wandering Hebrews forty years earlier that their migration and conquest of Canaan was against all odds. Now Israel had arrived, and their survival was still against all odds. Without God's support, the Canaanites could extinguish the Hebrews. That forty-year-old fear roared back to life with this defeat and reduced Israel's leaders to weeping.

In 7:10–14, the LORD rebukes Joshua for groveling. He reveals that a spiritual compromise caused their defeat: the costly, secret disobedience of one soldier. By casting lots and faith in God's guidance, they weeded out tribes and clans one by one until Achan stood before Joshua. Evidently, he was hoping someone else would suffer for his crime; the death of thirty-six Hebrew soldiers didn't sorrow him. He had hoped for the accusation to land on someone else—falsely. But once the lot singled out Achan, he confessed and relinquished the evidence of his theft. At God's instruction in 7:15, the nation stoned Achan and his family to death, then burned their bodies. They erected a monument at the burial site to remind everyone: the entire nation suffers when one person disobeys the Lord God.

The stoning of Achan ends Joshua 7, but Ai still looms in Israel's fears. God next solves the fear.

In Joshua 8, the LORD instructs Joshua to lay an ambush. The men of Ai were confident after their previous victory over Israel. God used it against them; He combined a feint and an ambush.

An ambush hides a portion of an army where the enemy cannot see them. The other portion is left visible to the enemy; a feint is its pretense of retreat. That visible weakness entices the enemy to give chase. The enemy overextends themselves while giving chase, exposing their rear to an attack. Then, the visible army stops all pretense of retreat, and turns to attack the pursuing enemy. The unseen units, hidden for the ambush, spring out in the enemy's rear. The enemy is caught in a pincer movement—trapped between the two portions of the army.

This warfare tactic, portrayed in Joshua 8, is a pattern in God's dealings with darkness.

At God's instruction, Joshua hid five thousand soldiers out of Ai's sight. Joshua and his visible forces staged a halfhearted attack. Ai's soldiers all poured out of the city to vanquish Israel and remove the threat.

> For they will come out after us till we have drawn them from the city, for they will say, "They are fleeing before us as at the first." (Joshua 8:6)

The visible portion with Joshua executed a feint; they ran away as if beaten by the men of Ai (8:15). As predicted, the king of Ai spared no manpower (8:17) in pursuing Israel. Soon the battle line was distant from the city and the men of Ai were too far away to defend it. That's when Joshua released the hidden, ambushing force, who invaded and burned the defenseless city. Joshua ended the feint of the visible army and turned to face the men of Ai. Seeing their city afire, the fighters of Ai were now caught in a vise between the two contingents of Israel. The victory of total annihilation was secured, as the Lord originally commanded—and the crippling fear would never return to Israel.

Modern sensitivity recoils at God's total war declaration, but it is a type of unseen war. Never after the conquest of Canaan did God command such total destruction. In the New Testament, God never directs Christians to exhibit such violence against people. Instead, He deploys His Church as spiritual warriors against the unseen puppet-masters who mercilessly lead people in evil. His is a total war against the kingdom of darkness.

Later prophets and today's archaeological discoveries have shown the evil in Canaan. The unseen abusers of humanity deeply insinuated themselves throughout Canaan. That is what is at stake. Do modern people really want to give quarter to unseen evil? Will modern people tolerate the devil's work to destroy human beings? Sadly, yes. How about us Christians? Jesus promised us expanding territory in Matthew 16:18. Will we countenance the unseen enemy's presence in it?

The subtitle of Book One of the *Unseen* series is *How to Live as a Spirit in the Unseen Realm.* Our enemies there are manifesting in the seen world in new ways. We, the Church, are His sanctified, mighty ones who come from the end of heaven as His weapons of indignation (as seen in Isaiah 13). By our hands, behind the King of kings, the kingdom of darkness will fall, as Revelation 19 taught us earlier.

God's habit of ambushing makes sense, considering that Christians are His appointed army. We are a perfect feint. One look at our qualifications would fully vaccinate any unseen spirit against fearfulness. The fallen angels, seeing the Church's poverty of spirit and meekness, would need no booster vaccination.

Joshua used the feint of retreat to draw his enemies into full exposure. God's feint is human meekness and frailty. We and our spiritual condition are God's feint. His unseen opponents see His favor for mankind as weak. Mortal humans are the weakest creatures He made. The fallen Lucifer and his allies consider themselves so close to victory, they launch every weapon. They fall for the feint, and our God springs the ambush.

FEINT AT THE CROSS

God outsmarted the kingdom of darkness with a feint and an ambush. The pattern was just like His ambush of Ai's army. The plan centered on Jesus' crucifixion.

Paul explained the plan in his first letter to the Corinthian Christians. The genre is epistle, a letter written to solve church problems. Paul wrote most New Testament epistles, and the church at Corinth got the longest two letters because of all their problems. It's not a compliment to them, but definitely a blessing for us. Their problems included vulnerability to the sensational.

When the Holy Spirit was poured out, a new power came onto the earth. It was very new and subject to misuse. The economy of magic arts was empire-wide, with many sorcerers. Some became traveling "apostles" who amazed people as Simon of Samaria had done, and they preyed on new churches. They borrowed the credible title "apostle" and used their powers to control and use people—as the kingdom of darkness always does.

Some such "apostles" arrived in Corinth. The Christians there quickly disdained Paul and glommed onto these sensational miracle workers. Like the Samaritans who followed Simon in Acts 8, the Christians of Corinth were fascinated. Sorcery was common throughout the ancient world. Sorcerers wowed people and won influence. Counterfeit miracle power was not unusual, and the Corinthians fell for it.

Paul's meekness was a deep contrast to those methods. To the Corinthian Christians, meekness discredited Paul. It was a weakness. The sensationalists used it like a wedge to supplant his influence among them. In 1 Corinthians 2:7-8, Paul gives the reason that meekness is not weakness: God's ambushing habit.

> But we speak the wisdom of God in a mystery, the hidden wisdom which God ordained before the ages for our glory, which none of the rulers of this age knew; for had they known, they would not have crucified the Lord of glory.

He flatly states that if *"the rulers of this age"* had known what God had hidden from them, *"they would not have crucified the Lord of glory,"* Jesus. Now Jesus was crucified by Romans at the instigation of the Jews. Are they *the rulers of this age* to whom Paul refers? Interpretation tells us no, because *the rulers* mean the unseen principalities (Ephesians 6:12). A very large time span is signified by *this age*. Look how we name long historical periods, such as the Bronze Age. The context confirms this: God ordained a hidden wisdom *before the ages*, plural. His plan was conceived before not merely one but several very long periods.

This hidden wisdom, none of the unseen powers knew. Paul tells its subject and purpose: *our glory.* That word appears twice. *The Lord of glory* is the One they crucified. The purpose is glory for human beings.

Paul reveals what God did not want the kingdom of darkness to know: through the crucifixion of Jesus, God would glorify living human spirits. *Our glory* was dreadful for those invisible rulers and principalities because we are their death knell. We mortals replace the devil and the evil angels who once inhabited God's courts. A human being is King of kings and Lord of lords. (Book One of the *Unseen* series lists all eight aspects of *our glory*, titled *Nobody Sees This You.*)

The fallen angels could not imagine God's plan for pouring out His Holy Spirit into you and me. The kingdom of darkness did not know what killing Jesus would produce: God Himself would fill human beings.

Had they known, they would have kept Jesus alive at all costs, rather than enable the outpouring of God's Spirit. Jesus, being without sin, fathered by God Almighty, would not have died. Darkness would be happier for Him to have a long career of teaching—two thousand years' worth so far. Isaiah prophesied a global teaching center in Isaiah 2. The devil would have preferred that over what actually happened: our glory.

93

They would have tried to keep Jesus on earth physically, rather than kill Him. It was killing Jesus that led to our glory.

In Paul's statement, God is revealing the priorities and fears of our unseen enemies. They fear our glory because we are their replacements. Other books of the *Unseen* series unveil our glory; here our subject is God's mysteries in the Bible. So we ask: how did God keep it from the unseen *rulers of this age*?

CODED COMMUNICATION

A feint only works if unknown to the enemy. Otherwise it backfires and the planned ambush can't occur.

In both war and peace, the nations of earth use cryptography to encode internal communications. Adversaries must not know the assets, the weaknesses, and the plans of a nation. If enemies could decipher the code, they could disable the self-defense. They could disrupt internal planning. In wartime, the nation would be potentially defenseless if its code were deciphered. Plans could be anticipated, and attacks repulsed.

Code is generated with keys for decoding. Cryptography uses different alphabets, numbers, and puzzles. Anyone with the keys can decode the encrypted message. The WWII Nazis used a decoding typewriter. The movie *Enigma* portrayed Turing's success at deciphering it.

A good code performs two functions. First, it hides your plans from enemies. Second, it allows misinterpretation by adversaries. Your code lets them think they know your plans. They may deceptively smile at you as if friendly but in secret are working to defeat you. This deception becomes impossible when they misinterpret the code. They thus confirm their enemy status. After that, the enemy cannot pretend to be friends. Their antagonistic stance is confirmed; they cannot regain trust.

Coded communication is a fact of life. American military used the Navajo language for coded communication in WWII, as seen in the movie *Windtalkers*. I have friends who serve America as cryptographers.

GOD'S CODE

God also uses code. That's how He prevented the devil from knowing His plans. The Bible doesn't use the word *code*. Paul described it above as *"hidden wisdom"* and *"mystery,"* a frequent New Testament word. Secrecy is necessary—but how did He keep secrets hidden from unseen spirits in the kingdom of darkness?

We saw above that the spiritual enemies did not recognize the trap of Jesus' crucifixion. How could they be so blind? Since its founding, the Church has known that the cross was God's plan all along. The Old Testament reveals that Jesus' death was long-planned and prefigures His crucifixion in many types. Apostle John wrote in Revelation 13:8 that Jesus, the Lamb, was *"slain before the foundation of the world."* Within the first ten days after Jesus ascended, the new apostles identified in the Scripture that Jesus' betrayal by Judas was long prophesied (Acts 1:16). Rapidly in her infancy, the Church identified Isaiah 53 as a prophetic declaration that Jesus would die for our sin, such as verses 4–6.

Surely He has borne our griefs
And carried our sorrows;
Yet we esteemed Him stricken,
Smitten by God, and afflicted.
But He was wounded for our transgressions,
He was bruised for our iniquities;
The chastisement for our peace was upon Him,
And by His stripes we are healed.
All we like sheep have gone astray;
We have turned, every one, to his own way;
And the Lord has laid on Him the iniquity of us all.

How did God keep this *hidden wisdom* encoded from the kingdom of darkness? What code could elude detection by the fallen Lucifer? The solution is one of the most elegant that God has revealed. It explains why Jesus had to die, and how He Himself knew it. God's code used symbols predominantly, communicated in human language. To decode His cryptographic communication, you need a decoder and a code key.

OUR DECODER

A message is encoded at its origin, then sent to the intended recipient. Decoding is required. After describing God's hidden wisdom, Paul next talks about our decoder in 1 Corinthians 2:11–14.

For what man knows the things of a man except the spirit of the man which is in him? Even so no one knows the things of God except the Spirit of God.

Paul says the Holy Spirit of God is privy to all God's mysteries. He is the third person of the Trinity. It may not seem very mysterious to say that God's Spirit knows all God's thoughts. But it doesn't stop there.

> Now we have received, not the spirit of the world, but the Spirit who is from God, that we might know the things that have been freely given to us by God.

Paul's statement means that Holy Spirit lives in us, the only living human spirits on earth. He who knows all God's mysteries inhabits each of us individually, as well as the Church corporately. Jesus promised this in John 14:17, 23.

> You know Him, for He dwells with you and will be in you.... If anyone loves Me, he will keep My word; and My Father will love him, and We will come to him and make Our home with him.

Apostle John described it as a birthright Christian experience. I don't need to know everything. The One who knows everything lives in me and talks with me.

> But the anointing which you have received from Him abides in you, and you do not need that anyone teach you; but as the same anointing teaches you concerning all things, and is true, and is not a lie, and just as it has taught you, you will abide in Him. (1 John 2:27)

Paul wanted to protect the Corinthian Christians from the deceptions of sensational traveling "apostles." Like those Christians, we may not even suspect their origin. Good things can originate in unseen evil influence. We too can be wowed by impressive words and deeds. Endorsements and track record go a long way with us. But none of these are necessary. Like the Corinthians, we have all we need—right inside our born-again spirits.

> These things we also speak, not in words which man's wisdom teaches but which the Holy Spirit teaches, comparing spiritual things with spiritual. But the natural man does not receive the things of the Spirit of God, for they are foolishness to him; nor can he know them, because they are spiritually discerned. (1 Corinthians 2:13)

Since the Holy Spirit was poured out, humanity has fallen into two groups: the ones alive in spirit, and the ones alive only in the natural. This *us-them* was considered in Book One, *Nobody Sees This You.* The communication barrier between God and man remains, but not for the saved. The barrier remains only for the dead in spirit. By contrast, we are living spirits by faith in Jesus. The Holy Spirit of God lives within us, and decodes the thoughts of God. Our Decoder lives in us. And we can understand Him.

THE CODE WITHOUT THE KEY

The key to God's code is in a different language altogether—one the devil and his fallen angels could never learn to speak. This code key, darkness could never wield.

Jesus knew He was the Messiah. He didn't learn it from the people around Him. The crowds were fickle, and the disciples were slow to believe. The best Bible students of His day were rigid—in fact, murderously rigid. Instead, He knew His identity from the Scripture. He said so on the Emmaus walk.

> "O foolish ones, and slow of heart to believe in all that the prophets have spoken! Ought not the Christ to have suffered these things and to enter into His glory?" And beginning at Moses and all the Prophets, He expounded to them in all the Scriptures the things concerning Himself. (Luke 24:25–27)

First Corinthians 2:8 said the wisdom was hidden, as we know now, in the Old Testament. How could Jesus see it when no one else could? He had the key.

Everyone around Him loved their Bible. If ever a nation was constructed based on the Bible, it was first-century Israel. Why didn't they see who He was? How could they miss the plain Scriptures about Jesus, knowing the Bible so well? They did not have the key.

The "wise men" of Matthew 2 needed directions. They stopped to ask the local king Herod, who asked the religious leaders. The answer from Micah 5:2 was unequivocal: Bethlehem, where the worshipping astrologers then found Him. In Luke 2:47, the twelve-year-old Jesus amazed those same temple leaders with His Bible wisdom. The testimony of His strong spirit was widespread even as a boy (Luke 2:40).

Fast forward eighteen years to age thirty. When Jesus began preaching, the leadership corps found fault. The leaders knew the Bible and treasured certain Messianic prophecies focused on Bethlehem. He grew up in

Nazareth, not in Bethlehem (John 7:41–42). Presuming themselves in full possession of the facts, they deductively formed a theory for all facts to fit.

They could easily have changed their theory. Maybe their elders recalled the astrologers' inquiry thirty years before. The leaders plugged their ears to that. They also conveniently forgot Herod's bloodbath in Bethlehem (Matthew 2:16). Even Scriptures that didn't support their theory were even disdained, like the one Matthew recorded in 2:23.

> And he came and dwelt in a city called Nazareth, that it might be fulfilled which was spoken by the prophets, "He shall be called a Nazarene."

The Jewish leaders esteemed their grasp of Scripture complete. They policed their nation by it. Influences that didn't match their explanation of the Bible had to be taken out—like Jesus.

These religious leaders read the words but misinterpreted the code. Like their unseen puppet-masters in the kingdom of darkness, they lacked the code key. And when they acted on their misinterpretation of God's code, they confirmed their enemy status.

> And all the people answered and said, "His blood be on us and on our children." (Matthew 27:25)

THE KEY

God's code uses words and symbols portrayed in words. The Word of God contains the entire code. His code key is in a completely different "alphabet" than the code. The kingdom of darkness can read. Not only can they read the Bible; they use it to tempt us. Yet without the code key, they are outsiders, confirmed as enemies. God elegantly devised a code key they could never, ever fabricate—meekness.

Jesus Himself was meek. The evidence includes His self-management:

> Take My yoke upon you and learn from Me, for I am gentle and lowly in heart. (Matthew 11:29)

> The Son can do nothing of Himself. (John 5:19)

> My doctrine is not Mine, but His who sent Me. (John 7:16)

> I have not spoken on My own authority. (John 12:49)

Like Jesus, we have the Decoder, living within us, and meekness is our code key. The purpose of God's mysteries is greater intimacy with us. That relationship grows in proportion to our code key.

Moses wrote more of God's revelation than any other person in the Bible. Meekness was his key as well. He craved to see the glory of the LORD in Exodus 33:18. Even then, his meekness was clear, in Exodus 34:8–9.

> "Please, show me Your glory."... Moses made haste and bowed his head toward the earth, and worshiped. Then he said, "If now I have found grace in Your sight, O Lord."

Meekness is not sinlessness. Moses didn't get to enter the Promised Land because he sinned, even after all his revelations. Jesus said, *"You must be perfect even as your heavenly Father is perfect"* (Matthew 5:48). But in the same place, He said, *"blessed are the poor in spirit"* (5:3). How could it be both ways?

Jesus designed the Sermon on the Mount to produce a recognition: we cannot put God in our debt, no how, no way. By putting perfection out of reach with such high standards, Jesus was instigating our mournful poverty of spirit. Being Beatitude people doesn't perfect us in holiness; it perfects us in selfless humility.

Moses saw God's glory. Instead of inflating his ego, his meekness grew. His protégé Joshua saw this. He was closer to Moses than anyone, for over forty years, and saw Moses leading military actions against both Israelites (Exodus 32:27) and Amalekites (Exodus 17). After Moses' death, Joshua added a summary of Moses' attitude in Numbers 12:3.

> Now the man Moses was very humble, more than all men who were on the face of the earth.

Moses met the Beatitude conditions. Did he enjoy the Beatitude consequences? The LORD Himself defended Moses in Numbers 12:6–8.

> Hear now My words:
> If there is a prophet among you,
> I, the LORD, make Myself known to him in a vision;
> I speak to him in a dream.
> Not so with My servant Moses;
> He is faithful in all My house.
> I speak with him face to face,

Even plainly, and not in dark sayings;
And he sees the form of the LORD.

This is effectiveness in the spirit world. For us, as for Moses, it only comes through this humility. Such a code key of meekness is beyond the dead in spirit, and such we were. Such character is an alphabet that only God can supply into our hearts. Jesus affirmed this in Matthew 11:25–26 and 16:17.

"I thank You, Father, Lord of heaven and earth, that You have hidden these things from the wise and prudent and have revealed them to babes. Even so, Father, for so it seemed good in Your sight."

Jesus answered and said to him, "Blessed are you, Simon Bar-Jonah, for flesh and blood has not revealed this to you, but My Father who is in heaven."

God invites our search (Proverbs 25:2). Unlocking what God has hidden motivates us. Many seek the one symbol that unlocks all the others—especially those focused on the end times. Others love the acrostics in the original manuscripts. But the code and key are different alphabets.

The code key is in plain sight: Jesus' very first recorded teaching. God's code uses words, types, and symbols. But the key to God's code uses a different alphabet. Instead of words or symbols, the alphabet of the key is attitudes—namely, the Beatitudes.

BEATITUDES

The Beatitude code key in Matthew 5 was not new. Quite the contrary, these attitudes are prominent in the Old Testament. We just reviewed the meekness of Moses. Isaiah 57:15 is another instance.

For thus says the High and Lofty One
Who inhabits eternity, whose name is Holy:
"I dwell in the high and holy place,
With him who has a contrite and humble spirit,
To revive the spirit of the humble,
And to revive the heart of the contrite ones."

Jesus perceived this code key also in His Bible and crafted an elegant summary: the Beatitudes of Matthew 5. Jesus' nine Beatitudes are in

Matthew 5:3–11. Each has two clauses: the blessed condition, and why it is blessed. To call these conditions blessed is surprising. What the world values is a stark contrast.

The Beatitude Attitude	Its Contrast
poor in spirit	rich in spirit
mourning	happy
meek	proud, confident and deserving
hunger and thirst for righteousness	satisfied with own morals and righteousness
merciful	exacting and demanding
pure in heart	secretive, guileful, and plotting
peacemaker	agitator
persecuted for righteousness' sake	goes along to get along
revile and persecute and say all kinds of evil against you for Jesus' sake	congratulated, defended, respected; always receiving the benefit of every doubt

The second clause begins, *for.* In it Jesus tells why we are blessed to be such people. No one wants to be poor in spirit, to mourn, and to be persecuted—at least, not without a good reason. When the conditions are in us, what do we get?

The Beatitude Attitude	Its Consequence
poor in spirit	"theirs is the kingdom of heaven:" they are royalty
mourning	comfort
meek	inherit the earth
hunger and thirst for righteousness	satisfied, filled
merciful	obtain mercy
pure in heart	see God
peacemaker	called sons of God
persecuted for righteousness' sake	"theirs is the kingdom of heaven:" they are royalty
revile and persecute and say all kinds of evil against you for Jesus' sake	rejoice and be exceedingly glad, for great is your reward in heaven

101

Few of the consequences match with their Beatitude in any human sense at all. What Jesus paired is nonsensical in this life. He didn't survey people. "Whose is the kingdom of heaven?" If He had, we might reply, "Well, the rich in spirit. I try to be a better Christian. I know I'm not perfect. But my preacher, my role model, my mom, my grandma, my dad ..." We think of the Christian we wish we were—someone rich in spirit.

Jesus' pairs are not only surprising. These Beatitudes are comprehensive. We cannot pick and choose. "Well, I like being merciful, but I don't want to be meek. Someone I know will walk all over me." Instead, the Beatitudes are a package deal. One attitude builds upon the previous. I may not have the first attitude if I don't have all the attitudes.

BECOMING MEEK

Vigilance to mature spiritually is one way we honor God's great love. This diligence makes us meek. Meekness is the surest preventive against arrogance. A meek person lives in submissive obedience to the Holy Spirit. Such a Christian can yield to God's plan for His Church. They know it is the temple in which He lives on earth (1 Corinthians 3:16, Ephesians 2:22).

Meekness does not mean everyone else is always right and you are always wrong. Jesus was meek even as He was clearing the temple. His motive was zeal for God, and bravery enabled Him to defy the status quo. Zeal, courage, and meekness are not exclusive of each other.

Instead, as meek people, we do not lock horns with the disagreeable or hurtful. We leave them to their Lord. Paul clarified this in Romans 14:4. It's the antidote to the backbiting and critical attitudes within the Galatian church (5:15).

> Who are you to judge another's servant? To his own master he stands or falls.

> If you bite and devour one another, beware lest you be consumed by one another!

To find when the Decoder gave you His code key, look when the Holy Spirit filled you. The Beatitudes are opposite to our sinful nature, but the Holy Spirit is submissive and under Father's authority. Jesus made this plain about Him in John 16:11–12.

He will not speak on His own authority, but whatever He hears He will speak.

His *presence* in us produces His *qualities* in us. We don't become meek by a decision or action. The third person of the Trinity within us *produces* what He *promotes*. The filling of the Holy Spirit is the security deposit: God has implanted the Decoder and His code key in me. As Paul wrote in his first letter to the Corinthians:

But God has revealed them to us through His Spirit.... Now we have received, not the spirit of the world, but the Spirit who is from God, that we might know the things that have been freely given to us by God. (2:10, 12)

CONTRARY EVIDENCE

The Beatitude code key resists inspection and measurement. It brings its own satisfaction. We don't measure whether we have this key.

Assessing ourselves calls our meekness into question. A poor in spirit person never says, "I am sufficiently poor in spirit." When we have the code key, we do not say, "I am meek enough." Someone claiming to be meek unwisely usurps the assessment reserved for our Lord alone. Such claims invite others to argue about our meekness. This is to their harm and ours.

Nor does a Beatitude person call attention to their meekness. Self-promotion is as contradictory as self-assessment. Sadly, hypocrites are a fact of life in our churches as they were in Jesus' time (Matthew 6). Without meekness, hypocrisy is right at hand.

A meek Christian does not boss God like a butler or use Him. It's inconceivable to the humble that we should instruct Him. The Beatitude person wouldn't presume to tell God what to do. For example, Jesus didn't make the Father reveal things to people. He actually got exasperated waiting on it (Matthew 17:17). He responded only when the Father's revealing was evident (Matthew 11:25, 16:17).

Job attempted using God. The book by his name is the oldest book in the Bible. Job lived during the childhood of humanity. God responded based on Job's childishness, with rebuke and challenge. Job then became *child-like* instead of *childish*. The Beatitudes are child-like. In contrast, childishness is demanding and cannot coexist with meekness.

Nor does a meek person merely parrot Christian words. The Pharaoh of Egypt did. He repeatedly confessed his sin to Moses, and repeatedly expressed prayer requests to Moses. Yet his heart hardened each time. We might take courage if a wicked oppressor humbled himself to ask for prayer. But without meekness, Pharaoh's prayer requests were like Job's—just using God. But we are not like Pharaoh, nor are we like Job in his immaturity. Instead, our genuine confession and repentance make us meek.

REVEALING ENEMY INFLUENCE

The Beatitude code key is very effective for confirming the enemies of God. By definition, people who have the contrasting attitudes are prideful. Considering themselves rich in spirit, they are confident. As so-called elites, they justify their exacting and demanding oppression of others. That fits the kingdom of darkness. None of them are guilty of having Beatitude attitudes. That's why meekness is such an effective code key. By it, God hid His mysteries from the kingdom of darkness.

God's symbols draw the proud into a misinterpretation. They think of God's plan as being like theirs. That is why the kingdom of darkness could only see a king like Caesar. A king riding on a lowly donkey was beyond their conception. That's why Zechariah 9:9 was a good code, which Matthew cited in 21:5.

Shout, O daughter of Jerusalem!
Behold, your King is coming to you;
He is just and having salvation,
Lowly and riding on a donkey,
A colt, the foal of a donkey.

The kingdom of darkness can see nothing but pride. Its archetypal symbol in Scripture is Leviathan, whom God describes in Job 41:34 as *"king over all the children of pride."* Isaiah 14:13–14 reveals the iniquitous attitude found in Lucifer with five *I will* statements of pride.

For you have said in your heart:
'I will ascend into heaven,
I will exalt my throne above the stars of God;
I will also sit on the mount of the congregation
On the farthest sides of the north;

I will ascend above the heights of the clouds,
I will be like the Most High.'

Not only are the unseen enemies exposed by lacking God's code key. People in the seen world confirm their animosity to Him as well. Church history shows Christians and leaders can be bereft of all meekness. They may know and use the Bible expertly, without God's code key. Far from meek, they are controlling, judgmental, fault-finding, divisive, manipulative, and falsely modest. Such wounding Christians still love the *"works of the flesh,"* as Paul described them to the back-biting Galatian Christians (5:19).

But if you bite and devour one another, beware lest you be consumed by one another!... Let us not become conceited, provoking one another, envying one another. (Galatians 5:15, 26)

Many are hurt by such Christians, leaders, and Bible students. If you've been hurt by such people, call it what it is, and forgive them.

The Bible tacitly recognizes that visible church is mixed. Paul lists seventeen specific *"works of the flesh."* He lists these to warn a *church*, not individuals. Jesus dictated letters to seven regional churches in Revelation chapters 2–3. All seven letters promise rewards, but only to individuals. The promised rewards are not for the church, because it is mixed. Only some are vigilant to overcome. He warns everyone in church that we must grow and overcome. The alternative is being cast out.

In every church are people who know the Bible and claim to be Christians, yet lack meekness. Paul warns that such *works of the flesh* exclude a person from the kingdom of God (Galatians 5:21).

Of which I tell you beforehand, just as I also told you in time past, that those who practice such things will not inherit the kingdom of God.

This meekness code key is not words or symbols. It is divine character in our fallen flesh. If we choose it, we are blessed. If we refuse it, we become like Achan in Joshua 7—excluded. Even worse: we fall victim to the unseen beings who see us as their plunder.

When an unclean spirit goes out of a man, he goes through dry places, seeking rest; and finding none, he says, 'I will return to my house from which I came.' And when he comes, he finds it swept and put in order. Then he goes and takes with him seven other spirits more wicked than himself, and they enter and dwell there; and the last state of that man is worse than the first. (Luke 11:24–26)

CODE SYMBOLS

God's code is very symbolic. This makes typology indispensable for interpretation. A good example is the stone of Isaiah 8:14 and 28:16. The apostles cited these 750-year-old prophecies as fulfilled in Jesus. In context, Isaiah's prophecy is God describing His own actions.

"He will be as a sanctuary,
But a stone of stumbling and a rock of offense
To both the houses of Israel,
As a trap and a snare to the inhabitants of Jerusalem.
And many among them shall stumble;
They shall fall and be broken,
Be snared and taken." (8:14–15)

Behold, I lay in Zion a stone for a foundation,
A tried stone, a precious cornerstone, a sure foundation;
Whoever believes will not act hastily. (28:16)

Jesus knew the stone symbol was about Himself. He used the stone of Psalm 118:22 to rebuke the self-satisfied scribes who were the scholars of the Law in Jewish leadership.

Then He looked at them and said, "What then is this that is written:
'The stone which the builders rejected
Has become the chief cornerstone'?
Whoever falls on that stone will be broken; but on whomever it falls,
it will grind him to powder." (Luke 20:17–18)

The code symbol of the stone is two-sided. For some the stone causes stumbling. For others it serves as the chief cornerstone. This hidden symbol helped Jesus identify who was friend and who was foe. Because it is a well-designed code, its second purpose was next achieved. The adversaries revealed their true nature and confirmed their animosity in Luke 20:19–20.

And the chief priests and the scribes that very hour sought to lay hands on Him, but they feared the people—for they knew He had spoken this parable against them. So they watched Him, and sent spies who pretended to be righteous, that they might seize on His words, in order to deliver Him to the power and the authority of the governor.

The Bible is not only symbols but also words. Any literate person can read them. Chapter 1 was *War Engaged*. If the Bible is encoded for war, what's the effect on its words?

CHAPTER SEVEN
GOD'S WORDS

Simple words on a page: anyone can read or hear the Bible. We can read it as we read textbooks, newspapers, and histories. With the historico-grammatical method, we can easily identify what event or person a passage describes. It's not even necessary to be a Christian. Many people read the Bible as opponents of its revelation.

God has made His Word available to friend and foe alike. Through early human history He created a book to introduce people to Him and the unseen realm of spirits. But people are dead in spirit. So God's book could not be an ordinary book; the Bible must have the power to midwife your birth as a spirit.

> I am not ashamed of the gospel of Christ, for it is the power of God to salvation for everyone who believes. (Romans 1:16)

> Christ also loved the church and gave Himself for her, that He might sanctify and cleanse her with the washing of water by the word. (Ephesians 5:25–26)

THE VOCABULARY OF JESUS

The idea of Jesus having a vocabulary may be new to you. In fact, He had several; Jesus was actually multilingual. When young, His parents fled to Egypt for safety; He may have learned Egyptian. Jewish boys learned Hebrew in synagogue using the Old Testament. Latin-speaking Romans governed his people; most Jews knew a smattering. Growing up in Nazareth, He spoke the everyday Jewish language, Aramaic.

Only five miles from Nazareth, the Roman rulers commissioned the construction of a comprehensive Hellenic city. Its name was Sepphoris, built during Jesus' lifetime and now excavated. The Greek word for Jesus' profession was more contractor than carpenter. If Jesus and Joseph helped build Sepphoris, speaking both Latin and Greek would have been required.

Jesus had functional fluency in Aramaic, Greek, Hebrew, Latin, and possibly Egyptian. He could take the disciples to Tyre, Sidon, and Caesarea Philippi. In each place, He could talk with non-Jewish people. In His society, it was useful to be a polyglot (speak multiple languages). Notice that Pilate's placard over Jesus was in Hebrew, Greek, and Latin (John 19:20).

HOLY SPIRIT MADE THE BIBLE WITH PEOPLE

After Jesus was resurrected, He was here only forty days, then He ascended to heaven. This departure was not in sync with the disciples' expectations, judging from their question in Acts 1:6. *"Lord, will You at this time restore the kingdom to Israel?"* Nor would we have conceived of such a departure.

God liked the plan, though. At the Last Supper, Jesus said, *"It is to your advantage that I go away"* (John 16:7). He explained why. His presence would no longer require a bodily proximity. Instead, He would be present with us permanently as spirit.

> If I do not go away, the Helper will not come to you; but if I depart, I will send Him to you. (John 16:7)

> And I will pray the Father, and He will give you another Helper, that He may abide with you forever— the Spirit of truth, whom the world cannot receive, because it neither sees Him nor knows Him; but you know Him, for He dwells with you and will be in you. (John 14:16–17)

> I am going away and coming back to you. (John 14:28)

When Jesus ascended, He poured out His Spirit as promised. Immediately, the disciples experienced His presence and power. Healings and miracles had required His physical action before this. But now people were healed *en masse* through the new believers. He was in them as a Spirit. Even their shadow and handkerchief could be activated (Acts 5:15, 19:12).

The power of the Holy Spirit included a far more lasting effect, with less obvious drama: the composition of the gospel documents. We call them the New Testament. Two millennia of history had authenticated the Scriptures used by Jesus and the apostles—our Old Testament. But God's book was incomplete.

Within a few decades, the Spirit of God began the final stages of compilation. He completed the canon (the authoritative list of books) of our Bible in the fourth century AD, when the New Testament contents were authenticated by a council of the entire Church. Until 1456 AD and the printing press, the Scripture's components were hand-copied by devotees.

We have a Bible because God used people to write it, compile it, copy it, and translate it. Jesus said this was better than having Him in person. We might be nervous about this plan. Putting the Bible in the hands of fallen people? Wouldn't angels be better stewards of it?

But this plan matches His habit of ambush and feint. The Bible is how He unlocks the unseen realm for us. A book He made with people stores His mysteries. People are His means for producing it. The kingdom of darkness would never create such a weak plan.

Darkness makes up competing literature, like the sorcery textbooks discussed elsewhere. But the Bible is not for magic. God authorized no one to use the Bible like a talisman or a rabbit's foot. The Bible is a historical record of people, places, and situations. Each of them reveals the unseen world. The Bible releases the mysteries of God to us when we mature. The Holy Spirit tends the words, phrases, organization, transmission, and translation.

If we trust God, we can trust the Bible He produced. If we love our Father, we rely on Him for our daily bread: His Word.

The words that I speak to you are spirit, and they are life. (John 6:63)

When He, the Spirit of truth, has come, He will guide you into all truth. (John 16:13)

If you then, being evil, know how to give good gifts to your children, how much more will your heavenly Father give the Holy Spirit to those who ask Him! (Luke 11:13)

GOD'S VOCABULARY

Were you stretched thinking about Jesus' vocabulary? Consider the Father's lexicon. We think of vocabulary for elementary school lessons, or foreign language learning. But God didn't have to memorize vocabulary words in third grade. He is the Master of vocabulary, the Definer of words. *"The Word was God"* (John 1:2). We understand the Bible better when we recognize God has a vocabulary. He always deploys the right words.

When He confused the people at Babel, He didn't merely obscure their understanding of the original language. He instantly supplied each person with the new language He designated for their ethnic group. Imagine if He had to apply for the job, "Divinity." His resumé would include "Master of vocabulary" and "Knows every word in every language."

God created us as spirit, soul, and body. Our new birth as spirits through Christ restored our dead spirits. We now live in the unseen. Our Father wants us to live in the world of spirit. He limited Himself to human language for revealing it.

Our Father is the one who first multiplied the languages. Thus, He subjected His revelation to the necessity of human transmission and the frailty of translation. Reading the Bible in translation is no accident, nor is translation a handicap. It was God's idea.

God likes words; He also likes the translation process. The Old Testament is predominantly Hebrew with some ancient Aramaic. The New Testament uses the everyday Greek spoken throughout the Roman Empire. You can learn those languages; they are well known.

Far easier: buy a translation. No book in history has magnetized as much love from the academic professions: teachers, translators, lexicographers, archaeologists, printers, and many more. Their education to gain such skills required decades of time, tuition, and long nights. These dedicated people have translated the Bible from its original three languages into thousands of others.

God has given so much prominence to His written Word. Yet the human process of compiling, preserving, and translating the Bible has frailties. Everywhere we turn, God uses human weakness for His kingdom. For more on the amazing miracle of the Bible, see my wife's upcoming book, *The Bible: the Life of a Book*, by D.D. Renfroe.

HOW GOD CHOOSES HIS WORDS

Vocabulary is a significant element of Bible study. What words does God choose in the Bible?

The *Unseen* series uses the New King James Version. There are many widely used English translations. Bible websites such as Biblegateway.com and Bible.org/netbible are free. Translations as a broad category includes several methods.

Two of the methods are paraphrases and dynamic equivalence. They may be more easily understood; they translate on a thought for thought basis. However, for a study of word choices, those translation methods are inadequate. They do not translate every word from the original languages.

A third method of translating the Bible is a word-by-word basis. Such translators usually work in committees, considering alternative words. Their goal is the right English word to equal the original word's meaning to the original Greeks or Hebrews. Through debate and correspondence, they select words that convey the equivalent concept to our culture.

We can compare word choice among these word-by-word translations. Word choice has three layers to consider, beginning with the word choice of the *translator*. My first-grade grandson is exploding in vocabulary. Sometimes he doesn't always choose the right words. Other times, his words are accurate, but assembled within nonsensical statements. Recently he explained why a story was fictional: "Because chickens don't bake." In contrast, I often pause while looking for the right word. Most of this book has been rewritten three times, in a calculus to find just the right word.

The second and far more important layer of word choice is *God's*. God has no such limitations with His words. When He inspired the Scripture, He also committed Himself to oversee the translation process. In any translation we consult, His word selection is accurate and telling. He often uses His expressions to arouse our curiosity, to snag our attention. The nature of reading provides Him opportunity galore.

Word choice has a third layer, based on the nature of reading. Our brains do not wait to finish before predicting the meaning of what we read. We perceive the meaning before we finish, in a "pre-reading" process. Each word adds more meaning, and we "pre-read" the coming words. It's like a spouse or good friend finishing your sentence for you. They pre-read your sentence because they are confident, "I know what he means."

Doing this with the Bible relies upon what we think we know already. But most of us know: the sentence-finisher is not always right. Our pre-read word choice may be wrong.

We must meekly yield our predetermined pre-reading to God's actual word choice. In the Bible, He laid out hooks to catch our interest. He loaded them with bait. If we are after Him, we don't swim past those hooks; instead they look like food. We welcome those "curiosity invitations." We want to be caught by Him.

Why do you spend money for what is not bread,
And your wages for what does not satisfy?
Listen carefully to Me, and eat what is good,
And let your soul delight itself in abundance.
Incline your ear, and come to Me.
Hear, and your soul shall live. (Isaiah 55:2–3)

NOTIFICATION SYSTEMS

Good habits of Bible reading include a notification system, like your car's seat belt alert. One such notification is agitation. Mark Twain famously quipped, "It ain't those parts of the Bible that I can't understand that bother me. It is the parts that I do understand." When we notice that a Scripture bothers us, we are that much closer to its mysteries.

When you feel agitated over a Bible passage, your spirit sees more in the passage. Because we pre-read sentences, we easily skip over an out-of-place word or disregard a phrase that doesn't fit. Even though God and the translators purposely chose the words in your Bible, they don't fit your predictive reading expectation. But there is a value when a passage misfits your expectation. It is a fishhook to catch us. I want the bait; so do you.

For example, consider Psalm 139:18: *"When I awake, I am still with You."* In my thirties, I memorized all of that psalm and recited it multiple times daily. That verse agitated me every time. After a few weeks, I realized why; the verse seemed backwards. My memory wanted to say it backwards: "When I awake, *You* are still with *me*." The agitating misfit was the Lord's hook for me. I patiently meditated on it. There was no hurry; I just kept returning to it throughout the day, for months.

Somehow during that period I was thinking about lab experimentation. My high school biology teacher had drilled us repeatedly to have only one variable at a time. The Spirit of God within me dug up 139:18 during that reflection. "What's the variable—you, Paul, or Me?" Suddenly I understood why David phrased it, *"I am still with You."* The variable was himself, coming and going. It was not the presence of God that came and went. This invaluable understanding built my faith in His love so much, thanks to my notification system which caught the unexpected word and agitated me.

In any passage of the Bible, we can pre-read the word X, but find He uses the word Z. We can skip the discord between His chosen words and our expected words. We miss out if we do, possibly to our harm. A good notification system keeps us out of stagnancy. In my case agitation notifies me. Such Bible reading alert systems protect us. In place of boring, mechanical Bible reading that puts us to sleep, our love for Father drives us to reflect on His choice. "I would have used the word X. I wonder why God said Z?" We know He has a reason because he is a verbal God. His resumé says Master of Vocabulary.

A TIME TO READ AND A TIME TO STUDY

He drops these hooks into the Bible, like a fisherman, to snag our interest. You and I are the fish He seeks. God doesn't need to hear Himself talk. His vocabulary is not limited or inflexible. What you see are the words and ideas He purposely chose for the Bible. Every word, thought, and phrase contributes a meaning—His Word to you.

Simply spending time with the Bible is not identical to good study habits. By skimming the surface habitually, we sometimes avoid God's hooks. But the baseline habits of Inductive Bible Study (Chapter 4) lower us into the water, where His delicious bait dangles for us. Observation, interpretation, and application are a response system—a way of thinking. We are not under pressure, but we are each accountable to honor His speech. Such habits show our honor for His Word.

Not every Bible reading can be a study; we might put it off otherwise. Each of us must honor His will for our time usage. God's Word is so deep that we could abandon every activity except reading it. For good and ill, many have lived that way. We easily run out of time to pursue a new mystery in the Bible. Developing more understanding often requires multiple returns to a passage or a theme.

We could feel guilty for not putting aside the affairs of daily life. God knows that people's availability, interest, training, and skill can all vary. These delays protect us from manhandling the Bible our way or jumping to preferred conclusions.

Waiting also permits us to consider the passage from several real-life angles as we go through the day. One day I was reciting Psalm 139 from memory while driving. A stoplight put me behind another car whose license letter combination I verbalized: WAY 893. Suddenly I understood David's statement, *"You are familiar with all my ways."* I thought, "even my way #893!" My patient meditation on the Scripture came to fruit at the right time.

We wait on Him and hold His puzzles in our minds. This way, even the timing of a red light and the positioning of license plates become His tools. By listening to my notification system about a slightly unexpected grammar, I became open and His Spirit unlocked an unexpected meaning. I could never have pre-read that meaning.

Our God is amazing. The fruit of this license plate reflection was life-changing. It has persisted in my life and benefited many through my ministry.

Much Bible fruit is low-hanging, right in reach, easy and quick. Many readings are simple communion with our Lord. But He wants us to seek the hidden fruit as well, requiring time. Like fruit hidden high and close to the trunk of the fertile tree, extra effort is required if we want it. He designed the Bible to honor us when we patiently seek what He hid there. Interpreting a Bible passage benefits from ruminating, and interpretation benefits from such meditation over days and weeks.

When we have good response habits, we come out far richer for the effort. Listen for the habitual intensity described in Proverbs 2:1–4.

> My son, if you receive my words,
> And treasure my commands within you,
> So that you incline your ear to wisdom,
> And apply your heart to understanding;
> Yes, if you cry out for discernment,
> And lift up your voice for understanding,
> If you seek her as silver,
> And search for her as for hidden treasures.

What if humanity searched the Scripture like Powerball jackpots? Solomon describes our jackpot in the continuing verses of Proverbs 2:5–12—but this jackpot is sought by few.

> Then you will understand the fear of the LORD,
> And find the knowledge of God.
> For the LORD gives wisdom;
> From His mouth come knowledge and understanding;
> He stores up sound wisdom for the upright;
> He is a shield to those who walk uprightly;
> He guards the paths of justice,
> And preserves the way of His saints.
> Then you will understand righteousness and justice,
> Equity and every good path.

When wisdom enters your heart,
And knowledge is pleasant to your soul,
Discretion will preserve you;
Understanding will keep you,
To deliver you from the way of evil.

DISMISSING GOD'S WORDS

Passing over the Scripture's little hooks is not a desirable habit. We don't want to practice saying no to the Holy Spirit! Simple questions avoid that: "Why is that there? Why did God choose word Z instead of word X?" Sadly, we have many ways to dismiss God's word selection.

Pride is so sneaky. Since we would have used word X, we figure God meant to, but mistakenly chose the word Y. We just assume He meant X. We actually finish God's sentences for Him. This calls for a humble apology, like with a spouse. "Oh, I did it again—I'm sorry. Please forgive me."

Our instinct does not easily admit, "I don't know why God used that word." To avoid it, we will make up an answer. Like children, "I don't know" is hard to say. Adding the word *yet* is a good habit. This three-letter word subordinates my limited understanding to the momentum in my life. I am growing; my understanding of the Bible is growing. Meekness has hope, and freely says, "I don't know yet." Pride resists such an admission, and insists the present interpretation is good enough—no growth needed—which is the opposite of meekness.

Another dismissive excuse: "That is how they talked back then." Yes, we are culturally distant from the people of the Bible. We can bridge the gap; that's why we study the Bible. We also slough off God's hooks as quick as a thought: "That's not important." We can also defer to Christian leaders. "I don't need to think about that. If it's important, my pastor will explain it."

I've even heard people excuse their accountability to Scripture by saying, "All we have is a translation; we're missing so much." We wait for preachers and teachers to tell us the meaning of Greek or Hebrew words. The habit came honestly; preachers often do say, "What the word really means..." Every church needs someone who knows an original Bible language; I'm glad I do because it assists fuller understanding of God's Word. But often the resulting assumption is that others can't really understand it. That's when knowing a Bible language deters people from reading the Bible for themselves. The net result: readers then dismiss God's purposeful attention-getters.

The Holy Spirit has skillfully managed the translation process for thousands of years. True preaching breeds a specific confidence in Christians: "God manages His Word perfectly, I can understand it, and I can hear Him in it." With simple openness and honor for God's Word, preachers can instill faith in Scripture. Teaching from the original languages must impart faith in God, just like any Bible preaching should.

WHAT IT HAS TO MEAN

Being open may be simple—but it isn't easy, as the saying goes. We have to repent for squeezing God's Word into our molds. We habitually make the Bible mean what we want it to say.

A gate-keeping motive may exist; leaders may want more control. The Jewish leaders had that pride when they heard Jesus use the Scripture. "He can't be right! We already know what it means." Like them, Christians can make the Bible support our favorite doctrines. Book Seven of the *Unseen* series is *Nobody Sees This Church: Resisting Darkness.* It outlines the strategies used by the kingdom of darkness against us. We cover such misuse of the Bible in depth there.

For example, Christ loves the Church and gave Himself up for her (Ephesians 5:25). We love the Church because it is His. But an extremist position arose in the fourth century AD, still taught today: there is no salvation apart from Mother Church. Book Seven reviews its origin. The Bible has been used to support this misinterpretation.

We have to explain away or ignore verses that contradict what we want it to mean. As for the Mother Church doctrine, Jesus dictated letters to seven churches in Revelation and rebukes them. Even the churches threatened with lampstand removal had individuals in them who could overcome. Clearly membership in Mother Church was not the secret. When the proponents of a position avoid contrary Scriptures, it reveals their true motives.

Christians of every stripe have squeezed the Bible into our doctrines, but the Holy Spirit inspires righteous indignation among us. As numbers and agreement grow, reform comes. The Protestant Reformation of 1517 was not the first; many reformers preceded that time. Many have arisen since.

Reformers can have their extreme positions as well. The zeal required to bring reform can also motivate wrong ideas just as passionately. For example, a persistent Protestant extreme arose: a person can do nothing to be saved. Some Scriptures reveal God has chosen who to save and who to damn. But other verses are contrary to that, presuming we have a free will. What about those? The mark of an extreme position is avoiding contrary Scriptures, which must either be subordinated to the favorite position, explained away, or ignored.

HYPOCRITES

A common complaint about churches is hypocrisy. We must admit hypocrisy can only exist because of the Bible. It creates a standard and we feel it acutely. Three responses are available to us. Either we meet that standard, or we confess and repent—or we pretend to meet it. Hypocrisy thinks it sees the Bible standards, and dumbs them down into pills we can swallow. "Looking good on Sunday" is our culture's phrase for this habit.

But the Bible standard begins with meekness. Only meekness can inoculate us against hypocrisy in ourselves. Meek people recognize poverty of spirit in themselves and feel no need to point at others' poverty. Looking good spiritually is of no value to us, but rather a dangerous condition. Such a Beatitude person has the code key that the Holy Spirit Decoder requires. As a Church, we are growing in meekness. The Bible rewards our humble contemplation. Our understanding of Scripture benefits as our Beatitude character grows.

IN THE MIDST

The prophet Ezekiel saw the origin of God's war in the spirit world. One phrase God used frequently with Ezekiel: *"in the midst."* It hooked my attention, and I ruminated on it for weeks. The Holy Spirit lifted the curtain on the unseen world after my persistence. *In the midst* was the spark for this nine-book *Unseen* series. We considered it earlier regarding reverse engineering.

Comparing Bible books helps identify the revelation unique to each one. *In the midst* occurs 72 times in Ezekiel's prophecy. The next most frequent use is Deuteronomy, with 24 times. What God revealed to Ezekiel required prominence for this concept.

We can compare any word or phrase under consideration with alternative phrases. The unique meaning of the phrase comes to light. God compiled His Word through human authors. Authors differed in their unique time, place, culture, and idioms. God's selection of them was on purpose, to package His revelation in ways they could record for us.

Alternative terms for *in the midst,* with similar meaning, appear in other Bible books. "Between" (209 times), "among" (902 times), and "middle" (40 times) are three. What alternative phrase would we select today, instead of *in the midst?* Our top choice today might be "in the center of," but something is missing. Consider a crowd. I could be in the center, but only observing. By contrast, *in the midst* of a crowd, I'm a participant. God is precise in His word selection, and the words we read are the packages of His revelation.

The phrase is definitely there. Whether it is purposeful is a different question. It may only be an idiosyncrasy. But *in the midst* may have a significance in Ezekiel's revelation. It's something we can test further. We shall return to this intrigue in Book Three, *Nobody Sees This Creation: The Origin of the Devil and His Replacements.*

BOOKS IN THE UNSEEN REALM

Chapter five was *Coder and Code, Decoder and Key,* about God's ambushes and feints. To hide them from the kingdom of darkness, He uses encrypted communication with us, His army. That encryption is the Bible.

In the unseen realm, they write. Several prophets before Jesus saw the unseen; God commanded them to write it down. The new Jerusalem has writing, the apostles' names on its foundation. Jesus' thigh has writing on it, like a tattoo. Both Ezekiel and Apostle John received writing implements to write what they experienced in the unseen realm.

The Bible not only describes the unseen realm. The Bible itself also appears in the unseen realm, and forty-three additional, distinct books. This library is revealed in the Bible with three words. "Book" is used 180 times in the New King James Version. "Scroll" appears 26 times, and "tablets," 32 times. Bible authors mention history books and chronicles of government actions. Three times, they refer their readers to an assortment of books or scrolls.

Four types of books are only in the spirit realm. God does not reveal how these books get written. Angels are capable of many physical things, so it's plausible that God's large angel corps includes transcriptionists. However, His speaking alone could produce writing, as even our text-to-speech software does.

One book is only in Apostle John's vision: the scroll that contains the end of this Creation. It first appears in Revelation 5:1. The unsealing of this scroll starts everything John sees afterward.

And I saw in the right hand of Him who sat on the throne a scroll written inside and on the back, sealed with seven seals.

A second book is the Lamb's Book of Life. God reveals it eleven times from Moses to Revelation. Only in John's vision of Judgment Day is it named *"the Lamb's Book of Life."* It appears to consist only of names. Everyone welcomed into God's favor for eternity is listed. No one whose name is missing may enter heaven; quite the opposite, that person is cast into eternal damnation.

But there shall by no means enter it anything that defiles, or causes an abomination or a lie, but only those who are written in the Lamb's Book of Life. (Revelation 21:27)

This book has an owner: The Lamb, which is Jesus' symbolic name as our Savior in John's Revelation. But the book's existence was revealed much earlier, before its owner Jesus was born. Neither Moses nor David had our revelation about the salvation and damnation of people. However, both men knew that God kept a book of names—the people He favored. They also spoke as if God could blot out someone's name. On Sinai, Moses conversed with God about this book and the blotting out.

Moses returned to the LORD and said, "Oh, these people have committed a great sin, and have made for themselves a god of gold! Yet now, if You will forgive their sin—but if not, I pray, blot me out of Your book which You have written."

And the LORD said to Moses, "Whoever has sinned against Me, I will blot him out of My book." (Exodus 32:31–33)

The next two books in the unseen realm are custom-written for each individual. One is the book of days. Job may have referred to it, but David was the prophet who most clearly received this revelation. David's Psalms 56 and 139 refer to such a book. Though its contents aren't spelled out, the Scripture reveals clearly: each living soul has a book of their days. The book of your days both records and determines everything that will happen throughout your life. God personally writes this book for each and every human soul ever born, and it is completely individualized. Our great number does not exhaust His individual attention. He records what He wants our individual lives to include, even our wanderings and our tears—one by one. How many days we live, and the contents of each: all written before we were born.

When I still tried to play golf well, I wondered if God wrote the flight of my golf ball in His book of my days. My frustration at golf certainly seemed predetermined. Maybe God wrote I would be good at other sports instead. Frustrations aside, God has not revealed what level of detail is in them except the number of our days to live, our wanderings, and our tears.

The last individualized book type contains our words and deeds, and is also the most revealed. Job, David, Daniel, and John all spoke about this type of unseen book, as did Jesus. Job wished *"that my words were written,... that they were inscribed in a book,"* and *"that my Prosecutor had written a book"* (Job 19:23, 31:35). He didn't know what he was asking for. If heaven is like earth, we might humorously blame brother Job—as if God got the idea of these books from his complaint.

Daniel and Apostle John wrote their books over 600 years apart, in about 535 BC and 90 AD. In their visions, each prophet actually saw these books opened. Apostle John saw each soul judged by God, using the content of the books of our words and deeds.

> I watched till thrones were put in place,
> And the Ancient of Days was seated;
> His garment was white as snow,
> And the hair of His head was like pure wool.
> His throne was a fiery flame,
> Its wheels a burning fire;
> A fiery stream issued
> And came forth from before Him.
> A thousand thousands ministered to Him;
> Ten thousand times ten thousand stood before Him.
> The court was seated,
> And the books were opened. (Daniel 7:9–10)

> And I saw the dead, small and great, standing before God, and books were opened. And another book was opened, which is the Book of Life. And the dead were judged according to their works, by the things which were written in the books. (Revelation 20:12)

Culturally, we limit Jesus to being loving. This limitation conflicts with His own statements. He emphasized He is also the Judge of our eternal destiny, such as Matthew 25:31–46 and John 5:22–30. Jesus also warned us that all our deeds and words would receive publicity, in Luke 12:2–3.

> For there is nothing covered that will not be revealed, nor hidden that will not be known. Therefore whatever you have spoken in the dark will be heard in the light, and what you have spoken in the ear in inner rooms will be proclaimed on the housetops.

This publicity is not only for our misdeeds and sins. Sixteen times, Jesus said that our good deeds and words are recorded in our individual books, so God can reward us. Mark 9:41 rewards a small behavior; Matthew 16:27 gives the big picture.

> For whoever gives you a cup of water to drink in My name, because you belong to Christ, assuredly, I say to you, he will by no means lose his reward.

> For the Son of Man will come in the glory of His Father with His angels, and then He will reward each according to his works.

All will hear the contents of these books of our words and deeds. This will occur whether our name is in the Lamb's book or not. I am saved by the grace of God. By faith and obedience, I'm confident that my book of deeds will include some rewards, like yours probably will. Nevertheless, publicity for my sins and embarrassments on Judgment Day is not appealing. I don't really want to hear yours either.

But God did not ask our opinion. That is what will happen. It provides a powerful motive for holy obedience to God and His words. By listening to the Lord attentively, and obeying Him carefully, I hope to stop adding embarrassing contents in my book of deeds and words.

These books will provide the basis of our eternal judgment. They will be inspected and read in His presence. Each of us has at least one such book of words and deeds. This creates a very serious problem for every person: we sin, and we will be blotted out. *"Whoever has sinned against Me, I will blot him out of My book"* (Exodus 32:31–33). Embarrassment is the least of our concerns.

Only one book can override the sins recorded in your book and mine: the Lamb's Book of Life. This override process is the last step on Judgment Day, in Revelation 20:12–15.

And I saw the dead, small and great, standing before God, and books were opened. And another book was opened, which is the Book of Life. And the dead were judged according to their works, by the things which were written in the books. The sea gave up the dead who were in it, and Death and Hades delivered up the dead who were in them. And they were judged, each one according to his works. Then Death and Hades were cast into the lake of fire. This is the second death. And anyone not found written in the Book of Life was cast into the lake of fire.

READING BY GOD'S ENEMIES

Can the unseen enemies of God read? Yes, the kingdom of darkness definitely reads. The tempter quoted Psalm 91:11–12 to Jesus, to tempt His disobedience.

If You are the Son of God, throw Yourself down. For it is written:
'He shall give His angels charge over you,' and,
'In their hands they shall bear you up,
Lest you dash your foot against a stone.' (Matthew 4:6)

Can the kingdom of darkness read these books in the unseen world? The phraseology of Scripture suggests that the books in the unseen realm are off-limits until Judgment Day. This appears to be true for everyone, seen or unseen, holy or evil. Our books of deeds and words are closed until that Day as well. Each vision that reveals them also reveals their opening and presumes they were closed previously.

SCHOOLS FOR THE KINGDOM OF DARKNESS

Apostle Paul describes the kingdom of darkness as a counterfeiting operation in 2 Corinthians 11:13–15. They disguise themselves as righteous, explaining the false religions of the world. The Bible reveals much about this counterfeiting.

For such are false apostles, deceitful workers, transforming themselves into apostles of Christ. And no wonder! For Satan himself transforms himself into an angel of light. Therefore it is no great thing if his ministers also transform themselves into ministers of righteousness, whose end will be according to their works.

Sorcerers, soothsayers, astrologers, and fortune-tellers advised kings. Israel's kings even used them. Trusted advisers do not spring up out of nowhere. They were the graduates of schools and had to qualify rigorously. These emissaries of darkness could not be walk-ons, to use a college football term. They also had to prove their accuracy. Like alumni groups in our own times, these advisers invested in their schools. Professional associations enabled them to network, confer, and execute concerted action. And they sold their courses to others (Acts 19:15).

We see these sorcerers several times in Daniel's accounts. Daniel and his three friends were forced into such a school in Babylon. Joseph, Moses, Samuel, and Ezekiel all refer to sorcery schools as well. We saw that Simon of Samaria had schooling. Apostle Paul's first journey included a head-to-head conflict with a proconsul's magician advisor. And the book of Acts relates several such occasions.

The Bible reveals that darkness always has representatives. No one is born with the knowledge or power; they have to desire it and learn it. Whether in secret or public, they have schools and textbooks just like any college.

The schools and associations for darkness kept secret for centuries. Today, our entertainment industry uses sensationalism to make evil things appear harmless. Take the fictional drama out of Hogwarts, and you find the real thing of magic assumed. The kingdom of darkness is creating public acceptance and enabling the evil unseen to unveil themselves. Their bold display is visible throughout our American society.

WRITING BY THE KINGDOM OF DARKNESS

Book One mentioned angels' physical capabilities (fully discussed in Book Eight of the *Unseen* series, *Nobody Sees These Friends: Partners in the Unseen*). In the Bible, angels light fires, walk, and grab people. They furnish writing implements to prophets. Angelic abilities certainly include physical writing.

When satan and his partners were cast out of heaven, they kept their angelic nature. This plausibly includes the ability to write.

We know darkness to be counterfeiters. However, Jesus' commands prohibit us from witch-hunting other Christians. We can disagree with other Christians; it doesn't mean their writing is the fruit of darkness. Such accusations are unnecessary because darkness has provided us several "inspired" books.

The Koran and the Book of Mormon are two examples. Islam teaches that God dictated the Koran to Mohammad. Mormonism believes that the angel Moroni directed Joseph Smith to the location of long-hidden buried silver plates, inscribed with revelation from God.

The literature "inspired" by darkness contains some truth that agrees with the Bible. Muslims manifest a tight discipline to what the Koran reveals, and have since their beginning. Thus, Islam swept Christianity out of North Africa because of the laxity tolerated among Christians. Muslim discipline won the hearts of everyone affected by Christian double-dealing and fractiousness.

Mormons exhibit a similar fidelity to the tenets and practices of their beliefs. Everyone has seen predictably clothed Mormon youth on bicycles. They are serving two years of missionary service. The family values advertised by Mormonism are appealing. And they serve our society desirably, from genealogical libraries to their work ethic. Whatever the reality, Mormonism portrays clean-cut Americana—aggressively so.

The desirable truths embedded in the falsity are part of the counterfeiting operation that Paul described. Jesus' closest twelve friends included a counterfeiter, Judas Iscariot. Think of the power Judas manifested. He also had gone out two-by-two, healing people and casting out demons.

Matthew, the former tax collector, was a practiced record keeper who had demonstrably complied with accountability. He was the obvious choice for keeping the money bag, yet some quality of Judas commended him over Matthew. No discrediting behavior was visible; Judas wouldn't have been trusted as treasurer if so. Even the last night when he left to betray Jesus, none of his fellow disciples knew Judas' counterfeit identity.

How do we discern the counterfeit writing? As counterfeits of God's Word, they claim God's endorsement, inspiration, or dictation. These books always dilute the fully divine and fully human nature of Jesus Christ. Either they lower Him from His unique identity (as in the Koran) or they give us that identity (as in the Book of Mormon). The books of darkness deny the sole adequacy of His death for sins. In their books, something must be added by us. His substitution for us is unnecessary in these counterfeit scriptures because other means of salvation are available.

The lives of their followers betray their origin in darkness. The believers of these counterfeit "inspired" books live as slaves—unable to think outside the approved boundaries. Those who dare it either conform or become persecuted. From simple ostracism to death for their families, the penalties for freedom are real. No freedom is tolerated.

This slavish rigidity opposes God's plan for variety, described in Book One. His system to multiply agreement includes a force of constant change. The literature inspired by the kingdom of darkness restricts that multiplication. The counterfeit scriptures cement their victims into goose-stepping uniformity.

CHAPTER EIGHT
TIME TRAVEL

This chapter is about time and the Bible. Naming it "Time Travel" is not tongue in cheek. A single question can open our understanding. Is it truly biblical to impose upon the unseen realm the limits of the visible world?

But how can we communicate the things of spirit in natural words? Our vocabulary choices are either too narrow or they connote too much weirdness. Communication is 10 percent what I mean to say and 90 percent what you understand me to mean. How can I take natural words and describe things of the spirit realm, so that when you hear/read the natural words, you understand the unseen?

God spoke to Moses about this divide in Deuteronomy 29:29. Jesus also expressed this dilemma to Nicodemus in John 3:11–12.

> The secret things belong to the LORD our God, but those things which are revealed belong to us and to our children forever.

> We speak what We know and testify what We have seen, and you do not receive Our witness. If I have told you earthly things and you do not believe, how will you believe if I tell you heavenly things?

Paul describes God's elegant solution in 1 Corinthians 2:7, 10, 12. He lives in us and reveals to us. By imparting knowledge directly, He can bypass the limits of language.

> But we speak the wisdom of God in a mystery, the hidden wisdom which God ordained before the ages for our glory.... God has revealed them to us through His Spirit. For the Spirit searches all things, yes,

the deep things of God.... Now we have received, not the spirit of the world, but the Spirit who is from God, that we might know the things that have been freely given to us by God.

Jesus was acutely cognizant that knowledge about Himself and the unseen realm required this straight-to-knowledge interaction in Matthew 11:25 and 16:17.

I thank You, Father, Lord of heaven and earth, that You have hidden these things from the wise and prudent and have revealed them to babes.

Blessed are you, Simon Bar-Jonah, for flesh and blood has not revealed this to you, but My Father who is in heaven.

Please review the Scripture in partnership with this revealing Spirit. With Him in you to interpret, you can rely on His wisdom. Follow the questions without fear. Test these things, as John encouraged in 1 John 4:1. For me, they have unlocked Bible mysteries.

ROLLER COASTER PARADIGM SHIFTS

I've been putting off this chapter about time. Writing about God's mysteries is hard. My poverty of spirit handicaps me in perceiving truths from the unseen world of spirit. What I perceive, I can't presume to be true, and must test by Scripture. He satisfies my hunger to know Him, but it imposes paradigm shifts upon me. My brain gets juggled inside my skull—but soon settles with the ability to see anew.

Many Christians endure this process. People everywhere are exploding with His revealing within them. The unseen battle of light and dark rages. We who love Him are in His war school. Thanks to our Trainer, we are advancing. Every advance He imparts takes us farther out, far past our readiness and adequacy. But He is trustworthy.

The Holy Spirit is like a roller coaster operator who lives inside us. We have all ridden them, and know they make you feel the thrill of disaster. That's why we scream. The Holy Spirit roller coaster has its gentle moments just like ours, and its wild, out-of-control feelings as well.

Would we prefer to leave the ride? No. Can we scream? Feel free. Just hang on, no matter what. Enjoy the ride.

POV (POINT OF VIEW)

In computer gaming, one control is "POV." By using it, the player can shift his character's *point of view*. One POV motion puts the player inside the character's eyes. A different motion makes the player like a drone overhead—a third person omniscient view. Selections include the POV of an uninvolved witness to the action.

Imagine you are playing a favorite computer game. Naturally, you focus on the action. One day you accidentally hit a button or key combo that you have never used before, and suddenly you feel lost. You don't recognize what you are seeing. Explanation: you hit the POV button for the first time.

Unlike computer games, shifting the point of view is not new, but as old as story-telling and literature itself. Story creators assist their audiences to shift points of view. But consider the origin and limits of POV shifting. Did we make it up? Sure, we can shift points of view in fiction, but certainly not real life. So where did this ability originate, if not in real life?

God made us in His image. Everything we can do, being in His image, came from His own identity. When people design roller coasters and computer games, we mimic His own design abilities. This includes the ability to shift points of view. Architectural models, schematics, blueprints, and landscape designs are all depicted with differing points of view. Authors and poets relate stories both fiction and nonfiction with point of view management.

In God's image, we have flexibility in our point of view. Can we apply this flexibility to time?

OUR TIME POV

We can.

None of us were born outside of time. Fish are never born out of water, their normal environment. Likewise, time is our normal environment. But our plentiful fiction about time travel proves we do recognize our time environment.

Why does that time travel fiction persistently bubble up? Because we keep seeing something outside time, as fish look up at mysterious things on top of their water world. They can't investigate our boats on the water's surface. Think of what they see: funny shapes above them, surrounded by food and treats. Any fish who eats one is removed from the water world and taken somewhere else. They might come back and they might not.

The fish's POV of the fisherman's boat illustrates our challenge. We sense there is a fluid time world separate from our "water world" of time. Philosophers have mused about time. I enjoy reading it, but won't compete with philosophers as if my solution is more rational. The Scripture sidesteps philosophy, labeling its efforts as a cheat, empty deceit, and tradition of men (Colossians 2:8). God's Word purposely marginalizes the wise of the world, as in 1 Corinthians 1:18–21.

Unlike fish, people cannot experiment with the baited hook. The scientific method requires repeatable, verifiable experiments. But time is impervious to science. To fill their many gaps, scientists appeal to faith in the scientific consensus. Thus, we hear the phrase, "the hard and fast conclusions of science," an oxymoron that reveals a religious but blind faith in science.

The Bible claims to be God's revealing Word. It aggravates this faith in scientists. The debates about evolution and biblical Creation display the friction. Disputing or reconciling the Bible's timetables with scientifically extrapolated ones uses a lot of ink.

Time is to human beings as water is to the fish. We cannot exit it. But some of us see something funny on top of time. Someone out there drops bait into time where we can see and desire it.

Jesus was fully human and fully divine. He alone, of all people, was born with the ability to shift His time point of view. After His death and resurrection, the Father elevated Him to the throne of heaven. Now He is King of the unseen, and Father sat us next to Him—human beings, the most disobedient spirit-creatures He made. Thus, He shows throughout the heavenly friends and foes that He is love.

> But God, who is rich in mercy, because of His great love with which He loved us, even when we were dead in trespasses, made us alive together with Christ (by grace you have been saved), and raised us up together, and made us sit together in the heavenly places in Christ Jesus, that in the ages to come He might show the exceeding riches of His grace in His kindness toward us in Christ Jesus. (Ephesians 2:4–7)

HEAVENLY POINT OF VIEW

What we mean by the word *heaven* is not what the Bible means. In our culture, heaven is where we hope to go after death. But God's excellent vocabulary chose a plural word, *heavenly places*. Book One of the *Unseen* series, *Nobody Sees This You: How to Live as a Spirit in the Unseen Realm*, explored the Scripture thoroughly on this matter. Our spirits are actually there in the heavens. Heaven is not a geographical "there" but a spirit "there." It is not a future "there" but a right-now "there." It is not a place; it is the unseen realm *en toto*.

The heavens are not on top of time, like a boat on water. Our heavenly realms are not out of reach. We are not limited to looking up at them. Instead, heaven is where our spirits are. Heaven is where we relate to *Our Father, who is in heaven*, and that is right inside us, namely our spirits.

After Peter and the disciples affirmed His identity in Matthew 16:16, Jesus could have picked any topic. He could have driven a freight train of truth through that door. But He chose this one in Matthew 16:19.

> And I will give you the keys of the kingdom of heaven, and whatever you bind on earth will be bound in heaven, and whatever you loose on earth will be loosed in heaven.

For us, no curtain of separation exists between heaven and earth. We who follow Jesus Christ are in both. We are like fish who can go from water to boat and back at will. Keys represent authority, and we have authority both in our water of time and in heaven's time.

Our lifelong comfort with time makes this hard to accept. Time is our normal environment. Like any boundary, there is a freedom within it. The idea of having no time-boundaries is actually frightening. We usually leave it to fiction writers and entertainment—but what if we didn't?

VISIBLE TIME

Time in the visible world is linear. We're born, we live, we die. The sun rises, sets, and makes a day—and again tomorrow. We arrive at 2:00 PM and cannot leave at 1:00 PM; we can only leave after 2:00 PM. Baby to boy to man who sires a baby to boy to man who sires a baby, and so on for generations.

This visible world's time is also sequential. Events follow each other in a line. We cannot experience two events at one time, but only one at a time.

Time is also directional in the visible realm. The direction is one way only. People cannot go backwards. No one can undo what is done. The irreversible direction puts every happening in the past. No past event will ever be affected by human beings again. Humankind never experiences the future. People can only inhabit the present.

Linear, sequential, and directional: no liberty to reverse or move around exists on this timeline.

HISTORY

Being in God's image, we recognize influence. We assess and assign significance. Time's passing contains people, deeds, words, and events. Some, we recognize as influential. We assemble the story of them and call it history.

We cannot visit or relive history. Its people affected our happiness, but they are beyond visiting. The best we can do is retell history, generation after generation. This telling reveals the roots of our society. History explains how our life habits and thought patterns originated. Culture includes these, but culture is not a hard and fast thing. Culture is the fruit of history. Different ethnicities value each contribution differently—forging their unique culture over generations.

Above, we reviewed God's choice of words to package His revelation. By necessity, those words are the history of what has happened. No one can excuse themselves because God chose historical records as His means of revealing. "History was my weakest subject" is not acceptable. "I can't remember dates and places" is another common excuse. To know God, we must know the history He used to reveal Himself, which He compacted into our Bible.

The Bible is history. As such, it tacitly affirms our experience of time as linear, sequential, and directional. But does the Bible limit us to visible time? No, the Word of God presents an additional POV about time.

For example: How did time work before Creation? Does time affect spirits like us, like angels and demons? Faith in Jesus makes us living spirits. The Bible's mysteries include dealings outside visible time. These questions matter for our maturity as spirits and for our understanding of the Bible's mysteries.

UNSEEN TIME

Time in the unseen world is not linear. Unseen time is not sequential, nor is it directional. There is much Bible evidence of this, easily identifiable. Anyone willing to shift their point of view can understand how unseen time works.

In Genesis 3:8, our first parents heard a sound which defied visible time. In the cool of the day, they heard God walking in the garden. Like all sound, friction produced it, causing movement that squeezed air molecules against their eardrums. That friction requires a body. Does God have a body? Yes, the resurrected, ascended Second Person of the Trinity has a body. He knew Adam and Eve—before the first human birth even occurred, including His own.

For Jesus, a human being, unseen time is not sequential so He could participate in an event before His own birth. Jesus, in His body, met His parents before His body was born to their descendants. In His body, Jesus also met his patriarch Jacob and wrestled him (Genesis 32:24–25).

Something else happened in that body. The Lamb was slain before the foundation of the world (Revelation 13:8). Before Adam and Eve heard His walking sound, before Jacob wrestled Him, Jesus was already crucified. That is definitely not directional time. It is the eternal NOW of the unseen realm.

Joshua 10:12–14 tells of a time that was not linear. The defeat of the Amorites was only possible because sun and moon stopped. Isaiah 38:8 describes time that was not sequential. God gave an arbitrary sign to Hezekiah and the sun's shadow went backward on the sundial. He even specified how backward: ten degrees.

MATURING IN UNSEEN TIME

If we were discussing nations, we could study a map and see their borders. If we were reviewing history, we could look at a timeline. To know when a friend will arrive, we check our calendar or clock. Time in the heavenly realms also has a map, timeline, calendar, and clock: the Bible. Knowing how time works for unseen spirits helps us in several ways.

Changing our time point of view unlocks more Bible mysteries. Passages can be incomprehensible for visible time, but very plain when we understand time in the unseen.

This POV fluidity unlocks prophecy. Our culture incorrectly defines prophecy as telling the future like a fortune teller. Such definitions limit prophecy to this timeline. However, prophecy originates with the Holy Spirit, who is outside our visible timelines, and frees us from bondage to them. Whether the Bible's prophets or the Church's, prophecy speaks from the unseen realm into the visible realm.

We mustn't interpret Christian prophecy as if our timeline is primary.

135

Instead, we submit our linear, sequential, and directional time environment to what the Spirit says. Discipleship demands the transformation of our minds about time, as it does about everything else. Imposing our timeline on God's Word in any format obscures what He reveals. But when we yield to His eternal NOW in prophetic words, our rigidity falls away. We mature into intimacy with the Master of Time.

That is His intention. We who follow Jesus are now seated with Him. Our spirits occupy the same heavenly realms as He does. Maturing as spirits enables us to live in unseen time. Our participation in the eternal NOW becomes effective for the visible timeline. When we read the Bible, it is not merely history. We enter its relationships and relate to its people. The Bible makes history by making us, and we are history's makers.

By maturing as spirits alive in unseen time, we activate the authority Jesus intended. We can impose unseen time upon visible time. After all, Jesus said we have His authority which overrides the curtain between seen and unseen. Time travel is certainly within the boundaries of what He said to the disciples.

> And I will give you the keys of the kingdom of heaven, and whatever you bind on earth will be bound in heaven, and whatever you loose on earth will be loosed in heaven. (Matthew 16:19)

NOW

In the heavenly realms, it is always NOW. My editor won't enjoy having NOW in all caps, but how else can we communicate? The unseen NOW has no such limits as our "now."

Our "now" comes and goes. It is brief and does not linger. Our influence upon "now" is brief and vanishes instantly. Our previous "now" moment may only be one second old, but is as far away as a "now" one thousand years ago.

Spirits live in the heavenly realms. There, they witness both the NOW and visible time on an at-will basis. Spirits can experience the visible sequence of "nows" but are not bound to it. Nor are they stuck in one direction. Whether they look forwards or backwards on our timeline, they can experience it as a NOW. And we Christians are living spirits.

Past, present, and future, we can know as the present. In the unseen, everything is NOW.

For example, Jesus saw a NOW event in Luke 10:18. Upon the joyous return of the seventy-two disciples, He told them, *"I saw Satan fall like lightning from heaven."* But Isaiah 14:12 described Lucifer's fall as past tense. In fact, Lucifer's exile to earth occurred before God even created people (Ezekiel 28:17–19).

So when could Jesus have seen it? Consider the possibilities. Did He see a dethroning of satan's authority when His disciples exercised authority in the unseen? Possibly He saw it another time in His life—a vision or a prayer time. Maybe in the disciples' report, He recognized its fulfillment. If Revelation 12:11–12 is the guide, Jesus might have seen it at His birth. Maybe Jesus saw the event before His birth.

With so many conflicting possibilities, why wasn't He more specific? Was He playing cat-and-mouse with us, always hinting but never disclosing? Commentators have taken positions and Christians have debated it. Whatever their interpretation, they have the same common ground: limitation to our timeline in the seen world.

These conflicts vanish when we understand unseen time and the always NOW. Lucifer's fall and exile is a NOW. It is always visible in the world of spirit. Any person born in spirit can stand in our linear time and see that event in the NOW. As spirits, we experience the NOW, as God provides us maturity.

The question for a heavenly mystery is not its place on our timeline. Assessing unseen events with our time-based POV is unwise. We wrongly assume time for God is like ours—linear, sequential, and directional—and unavoidably so. But the opposite assumption is most plausible: spirit time must be far different from visible time.

So the far better question is, "How does this NOW relate to the other NOW events revealed in Scripture?"

Some people took the bait that God the Fisherman is dangling. They went out of our water of time and came back. These are God's prophets, our primary sources for the NOW.

PROPHETIC TYPOLOGY

We reviewed interpretive methods above, including typology. The language available to a prophet was limited to their time, place, and culture. God the Spirit inspired them to use their own language and vocabulary of concepts. With these types, He expressed His patterns in His dealings with mankind.

How do we read the prophets today? The same truths, using lasting types, applied to our time and place in our words. A musician can play a violin's tune on a flute or a tuba. The music is the same, but with a different key and instrument.

The biblical type is like that. The type reveals the lasting qualities of God and His habits of thought and behavior. It dictates the notes and provides the tempo. The instrument may change for our time, setting, or audience—but the habits of God do not.

PROPHECY

In 1988, the modern prophetic movement was born at a Christian International conference in Santa Rosa Beach, FL. As in the Old Testament, prophets disciple and train other prophets. Elijah, Elisha, and Isaiah had prophetic schools, as did others. Today, God has millions of Christians trained globally to hear His voice for others. They are marked by His love and holiness to minister what He says accordingly. My wife and I are two such trained prophets and have trained others.

But I puzzled for decades beforehand. What am I seeing? Why doesn't everyone else see it? What is God doing to me? Why me? To resolve this inner conflict, I turned to the writing prophets of the Old Testament.

More questions met me there. I relay this to convey the value of coming to God and asking Him your questions. There is no fear in questions. The Bible wants to answer them, so let it. Why are certain NOW events of heaven revealed to one prophet, but not others? Why did God reveal that NOW event to the prophet in that place? That situation? That point in history? After all, we know God is not random.

After several decades of puzzling, I completed prophetic ministry training. But I still had questions. (Really, we always should if we want to know God. There's always more of Him to know.) How and why do prophets see past events as if they are happening right before them? And future events? This question had much personal force for me because of my own visions and dreams, proven accurate.

God gives prophets what He wants to say, both in the Bible and today. But prophets can only choose from the words available in our language. To be effective, our communication must take people from the known to the new. Somehow, we have to squeeze the unseen realm into concepts that people can handle.

The trombone is one such concept.

HOW A TROMBONE WORKS

A trombone has two brass parts that slide against each other. Each hand of the musician holds a part. The stationary part has the mouthpiece, which is small. You blow into it. With your other hand, you form the notes by sliding the moving portion. It has the big opening where the music comes out.

Trombones were popular in the era of big band swing and jazz. Marching bands use them today. The trombone marcher has a little music stand attached on top. Question: which portion of the trombone holds the music stand: the stationary part or the sliding part?

Our marching musician has the music where he or she can read it, on the stationary part. The music is always the same distance from the eyes, no matter what note is played or how extended the slide may be.

The music could be on the sliding part, but that would be difficult. Every time the slide changed a note, your eyes would have to refocus, requiring mental energy and effort. But music is much faster, so the resulting tune might sound out of sync, even with the correct notes.

The music might not even be legible when the slide was farthest out or nearest in.

God reveals the eternal NOW like music on the trombone's slide. Reading a Bible prophet, we often find failures of logic and giant *non sequitur* transitions that make no sense. It's like the prophet's sheet music was on the sliding part: in and out, in and out.

TIME TROMBONE

The prophets reveal events both near and far from them—sometimes in the same sentence. It's like music on the sliding part. This sliding music unveils multiple times to them. Bible prophecies are fulfilled in both close times and far times. Multiple time fulfillment explains most Bible prophecies.

Prophecy tells the NOW of the heavenly realms. The sheet music on the little stand symbolizes that. The prophet sees it, responds to it, and plays it as a participant. But the prophetic time trombone has its music on the slide.

Some notes are tomorrow time when the slide is in closest. Far time prophecies are when the slide is farthest out—the end of the world, for example. The tempo of revelation is fast like real music. The prophet's sliding music stand goes out, in, and out real far. It might be still, followed by three times fast in and out, and then in real close.

Above, we reviewed Isaiah's prophecy of Jesus' virgin birth. He was talking with King Ahaz on an aqueduct inspection and warning the king not to ally with Assyria. Then suddenly, out of nowhere, is a prophecy about a virgin birth for Immanuel. This does not fit. What would you do?

We know what Isaiah did. He trusted God and wrote it down as God gave it to him. Isaiah said practical things to Ahaz. He also revealed prophetically the results of the alliance. But Isaiah refused to strain out what made little sense. He didn't know the music was on the sliding part—735 years out.

Apostle Peter revealed the prophets' own assessments of this strange experience.

> Of this salvation the prophets have inquired and searched carefully, who prophesied of the grace that would come to you, searching what, or what manner of time, the Spirit of Christ who was in them was indicating when He testified beforehand the sufferings of Christ and the glories that would follow. To them it was revealed that, not to themselves, but to us they were ministering the things which now have been reported to you through those who have preached the gospel to you by the Holy Spirit sent from heaven—things which angels desire to look into. (1 Peter 1:10–12)

PROPHETIC PRACTICE

People rely on what we know for safety. We are comfortable with linear, sequential, and directional time. When God welcomes us beyond it, we witness and participate in the eternal NOW. This is disorienting. Training by more experienced prophets is very helpful. Practicing in a safe training center, your faith grows and overrides your apprehension. Christian International of Santa Rosa Beach pioneered such training centers.

When we begin to sense the unseen, it's normal to feel insecure. In our trombone example, you or I might question if we are getting the notes right and playing in time. We might complain that the band director put our music on the sliding part. With embarrassment, we could feel that we had not played our best. But our band director is God. He is the one who attached the music to the slide. He is revealing the unseen heavenly realms where our spirits live.

So you trust He did it for a reason, which you may not understand. It may be completely illogical to you, but you trust Him. If you are seeing them, He is revealing. However weird the unseen realm may seem, you do the best you can.

On the other hand, you could refuse to play the trombone, but that would be mutiny and musical suicide.

PERSON TROMBONE

The typological trombone applies to people as well. Isaiah wrote the prophecy about the virgin's giving birth. He then had intercourse with his wife and had a baby which they named Maher-Shalal-Hash-Baz. The name was meaningful, with an hourglass function. God promised Ahaz that the attacking kings he feared would be desolate before the child knew right from wrong. That baby was the near-time fulfillment of the prophecy, but an incomplete one because Isaiah had sired the child.

Because of the person trombone, an individual in the Old Testament can represent someone in the new. That's how Jesus could say John the Baptist was Elijah returned (Matthew 17:10–13). Judas is another example. It apparently puzzled the apostles how their friend Judas could betray Jesus. They studied Psalms after Jesus' ascension (Acts 1:16–22). With the person trombone, they saw Judas in David's laments about his betraying adviser Ahithophel from Psalm 41 and 69.

EVENT TROMBONE

Our above review of Isaiah 13 included an event trombone. In 730 BC, Isaiah described the Babylonian Empire 100 years before it existed. Then his prophetic sliding music went even farther out; he prophesied the conquest of Babylon by the Medes and Persians 180 years in the future.

Apostle Peter identified Moses' record of the Flood as a type. Moses wrote it in Genesis, but didn't know he was writing a type of baptism. Peter recognized this type in the eight passengers on Noah's ark (1 Peter 3:20–21). The rescue on the ark was near music on the event trombone; our baptism was the far music.

Apostle Paul didn't use the words event trombone or typology. He might have if trombones existed. In 1 Corinthians 10:1–4– he says that biblical events 1,400 years earlier now represented Christians, baptism, and communion.

Moreover, brethren, I do not want you to be unaware that all our fathers were under the cloud, all passed through the sea, all were baptized into Moses in the cloud and in the sea, all ate the same spiritual food, and all drank the same spiritual drink. For they drank of that spiritual Rock that followed them, and that Rock was Christ.

Peter explained that the prophets served us the Church, and not themselves. Paul agrees, in 1 Corinthians 10:11,

Now all these things happened to them as examples, and they were written for our admonition, upon whom the ends of the ages have come.

To unlock Bible mysteries, we read it with both interpretive methods. We have to understand what it meant to its original writers and recipients—the historico-grammatical method. But Scripture's types must also be correlated to our own day and setting—the typological method.

Paul specifically says that the end of the ages is on us. Our period of time holds the end of the ages. Everything written beforehand has a purpose. But it is only fulfilled when we apply its types and examples to our time.

LIVING AS IF IT IS ALL NOW

Above I related my past exclusivity to the historico-grammatical method for the Bible. Memory reveals the exact day and event that God first pressured my stubbornness. In 1985, I habitually swam a mile three times weekly. On one such swim, a sudden headache forced me to stop and drive home. This I did only with difficulty. The headache pain left with pain reliever—but something remained.

I became confused in time. The curtain separating past from present had fallen. My memories became as real as the experience right in the moment. Another curtain vanished also, the one separating my plans from actual circumstance. Into my present experience flooded everything I wanted, imagined, and planned. Then another barrier dissolved: my night dreams became as real as right now. They were all NOW. For three days, all these were indistinguishable.

These strange headaches persisted. I quickly learned to take pain reliever at the first symptoms. But the headache pain did not even appear always. I could be suddenly in this strange EVERYTHING NOW outlook. A neurologist years later took his best shot at explaining it, with a catch-all diagnosis still used today: "a complex migraine."

As usual for Christians, I presumed this trial was for good. It wasn't painful; it was just weird. By the Lord's guidance, I realized this was like the prophets experienced. Time near and far got all mixed up for me. The prophets received all that from God, but without knowing the timeline.

TIME TRAVEL

Our entertainment fiction is full of time travel. It's an enduring ambition of modern man. Examples include H. G. Wells' *The Time Machine*, Bellisario's 1990s series *Quantum Leap*, and the *Terminator* series. Time fascinates people. Transporting physically between two times repeatedly emerges in our fiction.

Jesus put His followers in authority. One sign is how we experience time in the unseen world. When He gave us authority to bind and loose, He placed no limit on it. Instead, He used the word *whatever,* very open-ended. His authorization can include binding to our timeline, and loosing from it.

Fleshly man imagines the physical transport of our bodies through time. After all, being made in God's *image* includes God's *imagination*. Anything man can imagine, God can as well. It happened in the Bible to Isaiah, Ezekiel, and plausibly Moses.

We are more authoritative than even fiction depicts. The expectations of the spiritually dead do not determine our relationship with time. Our bodies need not be relocated through physical time travel. Instead, we can make time travel around us.

Our time travel is from a position of authority, not limitation or submission. Our bodies do not need transport. When we transcend time's passage, we do so as spirits. When we are in agreement with our Father, the visible timeline serves us—not vice versa.

> The wind blows where it wishes, and you hear the sound of it, but cannot tell where it comes from and where it goes. So is everyone who is born of the spirit. (John 3:8)

Consider an example from daily life: having a deadline and being in a hurry. Running behind evokes terrific anxiety about air flights, work, meetings, classes, worship services, and other time-sensitive activities. But if we can impose our spirit upon our flesh, we can get a new viewpoint.

After all, doesn't God Almighty live in us? We can impose His unseen time upon the time of the visible world.

When I run late, my fleshly tendency arises. My training as a whitewater canoeist resurfaces, and like navigating a river, I try to manhandle traffic. But who has authority over time? Is it the person expecting me, or the maker of the deadline? No, it is my Lord God and me, His servant. As He gave Joshua more time to defeat the Amorites, our Father can make deadlines slow down. He can alter our intended schedules for the better.

TIME AND OUR DAILY LIFE

This heavenly point of view completely transforms time pressures, as well as our understanding of the Bible.

Running late gains an entirely new meaning. Our part cannot be neglected. Did I leave too late to arrive on time? Did I forget what traffic would be like? There is no shame in asking Him to bail us out for leaving too late. What disqualifies us is not a mistake, but dishonesty and failure to repent.

Second, God will position us where He wants us when He wants us. Do we trust His placement, or do we have a better idea? An important element of our time authority is submission to His Lordship.

Third, if being on time is that important, He will reply to our request: *please slow down everything else.* He may dispatch angelic helpers. How do you know? All the lights turn green, and our meeting is running late without us knowing it—for two examples.

Fourth, when we live this way, our powerful Book interweaves with our lives. Submitting our natural experience of time to our Lord, He integrates His Word more and more with our lives. Our maturity as living spirits accelerates. And His Word yields even more powerful explanations of reality.

Christian parenting benefits from this authority. We help our children's maturity on both the visible and the unseen timelines. God made the parenting system to point every child to the only perfect Father. The raw material He uses—imperfect parents. He places parents in authority over children. Any parent who cannot admit failings defaults on the authority God intends. We must relinquish the pressure that makes us domineer over our children. He wants to welcome them into maturity, not conformity. Our children will get where they need to be when they need to be there.

UNDERSTANDING BIBLE TIME

God designed the Bible to honor our faith. When we obey its mysteries with actual behavior, more mysteries appear. Our understanding of God's mysteries feeds off our willingness to adventure with Him. The preceding consideration of time is just one area.

The visible timeline exerts a controlling influence in modern Western civilization. Predictably, the Lordship of Jesus Christ includes the refusal to kiss the ring of the time—Caesar's.

CHAPTER NINE

EXPLANATORY POWER

A danger reviewed earlier was having preconceptions. Preconceived notions can cause us to interpret the Bible wrongly. But that's not their only danger, because they also close our minds to better explanations of the Bible.

New interpretations must explain the Scripture better. The proponents of new interpretations must observe the boundaries God has set for new ideas. Better explanations are not marked by fewer questions but more, as evaluating the improvement requires adjustments in related beliefs and practices. However, if the explanation is true, it will endure our debate and survive our scrutiny. The new framework will leave fewer puzzles unsolved, and will unlock more Bible mysteries.

This standard is Explanatory Power. Our interpretations of Scripture must continually submit to that standard: does my interpretation explain the Scripture better?

The Bible contains everything that God wants us to know, as Moses told Israel in Deuteronomy 29:29.

> The secret things belong to the Lord our God, but those things which are revealed belong to us and to our children forever.

ROAD MAP BIBLE

Consider a road map, for example. Whether digital or printed, you use it. Why? Because your journey takes you where you haven't been, using roads you've never traveled. How do you know it's a good map? The roadways you already know appear on it accurately. Therefore, you trust its accuracy about the roads you don't know. Each turn you take further confirms the explanatory accuracy of the road map.

But not everyone likes maps. They may prefer their intuitions. Possibly a local can give directions. Some drivers determine their compass direction from sun, wind, or memory.

God's Word is like that road map. In it, He has revealed true reality in its entirety. Hundreds of generations have tested its map of life. Every culture and ethnic group has confirmed its accuracy about people and God.

But humankind has explored reality in our own way, ignoring His map to use our own intuition. Instead of the Bible's map of reality, we draw our own according to our preferences. Compared to God's Word, our maps are like a child's treasure map. It's written in pirate scrawl with sketchy details and a big X, all on crumpled paper.

People in every culture embrace the Bible as the best road map of life. What it says will happen, actually happens. With the Scripture's presentation of reality, we can explain life. Its explanations form our grid for interpreting ourselves, God, and others. We discussed this grid extensively in Book One of the *Unseen* series.

Any grid or template for explaining life first becomes credible when it explains what has happened. Next, it must predict correctly what will happen under the same conditions. When this occurs, the grid's framework of explanation is further accepted. People use such interpretive templates in every endeavor of life.

But like the road map that was up to date ten years ago, our explanatory grids must be updated. In the case of road maps, new roads and neighborhoods must be added. Fresh places should appear. These all require an updating process for road maps. Outdated maps will lead people astray.

Likewise, the march of time makes our templates out of date. Our interpretive grids of life clash with reality. Better frameworks must be developed. Hard work is required to gain general acceptance for better frameworks of explanation. When the updated framework involves better explanations of Bible passages, courage is required as well. People feel threatened when confronted with a better explanation than the one they have relied upon for so long.

Road maps do not reveal everything. Exploring one day on my big cruiser motorcycle, I saw a six-mile road on the digital map. After one mile, the pavement disappeared, and the rest was sandy with puddles. It was a road—but the map didn't tell me everything. I had to go get on the road to learn all about it.

Likewise, God's map of reality contains mysteries. He designed it to yield the mysteries when we get on the road with Him. God hides things in the Bible for us to find—enigmas, confusing statements, unseen truths, and puzzles. The Bible is a simple collection of ink on paper, yet it both explains and mystifies.

BIBLE BOUNDARIES

We are free to consider every possibility in our interpretation of Scripture. Apostle John said we have an anointing to know the truth (1 John 2:20). We can dismiss the Holy Spirit's insights within us because we haven't heard them from others. That doesn't mean that we can't be right.

Legend credits the Commissioner of the U.S. Patent Office in 1899 with exemplifying resistance to the new. Think about everything invented since 1899. But a bystander heard him say, "Everything that can be invented has been invented." Gratefully, the inventors of the twentieth century weren't listening to him. The new can be right; the old can be insufficient. God's Creation holds many discoveries yet to make, but His Word has the most potential of all.

Like all freedoms, our freedom has boundaries.

1. We are told to **respect our elders** in Hebrews 13:7, 17. A common thread among the proponents of falsities is pride. You may have a better explanation. But if you dishonor your elders, or those who went before you, then your so-called better explanation shows pride's poison.

Remember those who rule over you, who have spoken the word of God to you, whose faith follow, considering the outcome of their conduct.... Obey those who rule over you, and be submissive, for they watch out for your souls, as those who must give account.

2. The Bible instructs us to be **alert to falsehood.** Jesus emphasizes vigilance in His letter to the Pergamum church (Revelation 2:12–17).

We are not to love the latest interpretation. Newness is not goodness. Paul repeated this warning to several churches, as did Apostle John in his three letters. Hebrews 13:9 also says, *"Do not be carried about with various and strange doctrines."* In Colossians 2:8–9, Paul repeats the importance of vigilance.

> Beware lest anyone cheat you through philosophy and empty deceit, according to the tradition of men, according to the basic principles of the world, and not according to Christ.

Sadly, vigilance for falsehood can also exist apart from love for Jesus Christ. In Book Seven, *Nobody Sees This Church: Resisting Darkness*, vigilance for right doctrine is often mixed with Lucifer's method. We must be equally vigilant to maintain our love for Christ. Jesus chastised the Ephesian church accordingly.

> You have tested those who say they are apostles and are not, and have found them liars... Nevertheless I have this against you, that you have left your first love. (Revelation 2:1, 4)

The kingdom of darkness consistently opposes us. Its tactics include divisive arguments. Maintaining doctrine according to the Bible is a crucial service of Church leaders. But if their vigilance for proper doctrine lacks love and meekness, Lucifer's pride already infects them.

3. **We cannot add to or take away from Scripture**, as Jesus warns in Revelation 22:18–19.

> If anyone adds to these things, God will add to him the plagues that are written in this book; and if anyone takes away from the words of the book of this prophecy, God shall take away his part from the Book of Life, from the holy city, and from the things which are written in this book.

Jesus based His life on the trustworthiness of the Scripture. His life was one big "must" which He knew from the Old Testament.

> Beginning at Moses and all the Prophets, He expounded to them in all the Scriptures the things concerning Himself. (Luke 24:27)

He submitted to the Scriptures about His life. The Bible said He must die for sin. He knew His cry in Gethsemane would not be granted. The Scripture could threaten our worst dread. We could ignore the parts we don't like—taking away from God's Word. Or we could add to it what we want it to mean. These dangers come from our own hearts, and the Bible is designed to elicit them. We submit to God's Word, period.

4. **We must not love an explanation just because it's ours.** Just because we came up with it is no merit. Church history is littered with people who amassed influence around their particular interpretation of the Bible. Their influence died with them.

   Nor may we love a new interpretation, just because our entire church does. The Galatian church did, but was condemned by Apostle Paul for defying salvation by faith. Popularity is no justification either. A new explanation of a Bible truth often draws crowds. When it is monetized or enhances influence, it can overlap Luciferian behaviors. This will become clear in the following.

5. **Meekness is a fundamental requirement.** These boundaries do not trouble a meek person. Meekness is a primary quality necessary to understand God's Word. These limits are protective. When we recognize how easily we can go astray, left to ourselves, God's boundaries around His Scripture give us safety.

   God designed the Bible with traps and ambushes, which entice His enemies to reveal themselves. One such trap reveals their self-promoting pride by falling in love with their own interpretation. This, the meek person can never do.

6. **Yield to the process.** Agreement in the diverse Body of Christ requires a process we cannot shortcut. Agreement arises eventually, but not instantly. Disputed interpretations often engage multiple generations—identifying the issue in one, debating the solutions in the next, and resolving it in the third.

   Non-negotiables undergird our freedom. Salvation is by faith in Jesus (not by works). The Holy Spirit fills believers. God's Word has authority and is entirely trustworthy. The Church is His Bride. These and other gospel truths form our long-accepted foundations. Standing upon them does not shut down further inquiry.

   Meekness freely admits our interpretations are not final. An example is the debate about predestination and free will. It raged for centuries—are only the predestined saved? or do we have a free will? Opposite explanations persist among genuine Christians because the Scripture leaves room for different interpretations. Its lack of clarity on the subject is by God's design; He is the one who oversaw its composition and inspired it. By this freedom, He tests us. Will we value the unity Jesus asked for on the night of His crucifixion?

And the glory which You gave Me I have given them, that they may be one just as We are one. (John 17:22)

Another example of the process is the act necessary to be saved. For 1,700 years, you were a Christian simply by birth into a Christian family and church. Then the Great Awakening birthed a better explanation of the Scripture: we must confess our sin, accept His death as our substitute, and acknowledge Jesus as our Lord. Three centuries later, that is now the dominant understanding worldwide.

Within these six boundaries, we may consider every explanation. Investigating better Bible interpretations is a godly process. Explaining puzzles nurtures the body of Christ. Together we search out His mysteries as living human spirits.

FROM OLD TO NEW

As the Church matures, we find more in the Bible than our predecessors did. Standing on their shoulders, we mature. The Bible is constant and its contents do not change, but each generation sees more in it. This process is not smooth because people always prefer the *status quo* and protect it. A cycle of old to new frequently repeats in history.

This cycle is common to any human endeavor. Good thing the Wright Brothers or Thomas Edison or Watson and Crick didn't listen to the U.S. Patent Office in 1899.

Christians work hard to gain general acceptance for better explanations of the Bible. The term "Protestant Reformation" is used for the century following 1517. Before that, your good standing with Mother Church saved you. Priestly affirmation and Church compliance made your salvation sure. Martin Luther survived persecution and advanced a better explanation of salvation: by faith in Jesus Christ.

Suddenly there were two grids or templates for interpreting life, the

Roman Catholic and the Protestant. For the ensuing century, monarchs allied themselves with one side for political gain. Much blood was shed in war. The dispute centered on how to be saved, and what caused damnation. The stakes were much higher, national interests were engaged, and people got very intense. One side's great passion was to gain general acceptance for the new understanding. The other side's passion was to defend the previous, long-held framework.

The reformers gained acceptance for their interpretation of salvation. But their new explanation next became the new tradition. Luther's passionate discovery, salvation by faith in Christ, is now the accepted explanation worldwide. Even Catholics who once fought it have accepted this as the best explanation of the gospel.

THE CHRISTIAN OLD TO NEW

For Christians, the cycle is initiated by the Holy Spirit. We've seen that only God can reveal. At times, He releases an alternative explanation of truth from the Bible. Some people of the time receive it with open minds. These open-minded people are not usually leaders. With testing, they discover it is a better explanation of the Bible than before. The updated understanding does not discard the old. Rather, it incorporates the best of all previous explanations.

The new explanation has to be formulated for communication. They invest great effort to explain it to other Christians. Its passionate proponents apply it to many Scriptures. In consensus, these pioneers create a new interpretive framework for the Bible, which incorporates their new explanation.

Next is promulgation. Other Christians also find it is a better understanding of the Scripture. The new framework gains wider acceptance, and leaders arise for the new movement. The updated understanding is applied to church practice, governance, and communication. Priests and pastors extract new Christian behaviors from the improved framework, and promulgate them.

The new explanation of the Bible stops being new and becomes accepted. The combined investment to achieve general acceptance is so great that a new *status quo* is born—an accepted explanation to defend.

This cycle is visible in Jesus' interaction with the Pharisees, a sect of Judaism. Their passion for their Bible interpretation (our Old Testament) was intense and strict. The Jewish rules about fasting were very important to the Pharisees.

Some Pharisees asked Jesus why his disciples did not fast. Jesus saw their close-minded loyalty to the existing framework. He told a parable to illuminate the cycle, from old to new, in Mark 2:22. Their interpretation of the Law was an old wineskin, easily burst by the alternative, improved explanation which Jesus brought.

> No one puts new wine into old wineskins; or else the new wine bursts the wineskins, the wine is spilled, and the wineskins are ruined. But new wine must be put into new wineskins.

THE BIBLE OLD TO NEW

The Holy Spirit oversaw the writing and compilation of the Bible. God's Word is complete now, yet He regularly provides the Church with new wine. He instills passion in us to explore God's written Word. That passion did not stop or go away when the Bible's books were written nor when its canon was finally compiled. The Spirit refreshes our passion through new explanations of Scripture. This is how Jesus leads His Church onward and upward.

Going from old to new happens repeatedly because passion for Him is built into His bride. God gives more insight into the Bible to the next generation—but a problem can arise. Those so heavily invested in the accepted framework often oppose the new thinking. Better explanations feel like a threat to their influence.

The first wave of reformers in 1517 gained wide acceptance for their interpretive grid of the Bible. The next wave introduced an emphasis on personal discipleship and holiness; John Wesley is an example. That second wave succeeded, and following Christ as Lord is accepted now. But it was not accepted then. The first wave of reformers became guardians of their status quo. So they persecuted the second wave of reformers.

When our understanding of the Bible goes from old to new, such conflict often ensues. Resolution occurs in different ways. The passage of time is one way. Loyalty to older explanations pass when their caretakers die. The newer insights into Scripture become the new tradition.

Another resolution is to separate. One group is satisfied with the standing interpretation of a Bible passage. The other group feels great urgency and passion for their better interpretation. When one group refuses to look at the Bible differently, separation may be best.

Differing beliefs about church governance also justify separation. America's founding resulted from the Puritans' decision to separate from the

Anglicans. Resolution through separation is the historical spark causing the many Christian denominations.

MEEKNESS FOR NEWNESS

Have you ever sensed more in a Scripture, yet unsure what? Every Christian walking in the Spirit experiences this. God gives hints and incentives to improve our understanding of His Word.

Can your paradigm of reality be inaccurate or contain gaps? Of course. Everyone acknowledges the possibility—but no one admits it easily. This is true of any human consensus: science, economic concerns, home cures, dress, commercial endeavors, to name a few.

None of those subjects is deeper than God's Word. To receive His revelation in the Bible, meekness and humility are necessary. We may think the current explanation is the best and most practical. Are we proud of it? Or will we lay our dearly held premises on His altar? We follow Jesus wherever He leads. Reading the Bible meekly is a prerequisite. Meekness is the fertile soil for receiving His revelation in the Bible—especially the alternative explanations that feel new.

PRESENT TRUTH

Jesus promised the Holy Spirit's agency in revealing truth and mysteries. Through the Holy Spirit's agency, the Bible's composition was finalized. *"When He, the Spirit of truth, has come, He will guide you into all truth"* (John 16:13). This same Spirit lives in us. He is a verbal God, and He speaks to us. Jesus told us the result as we become more intimate with God. *"Out of his heart will flow rivers of living water"* (John 7:38).

Wisdom recognizes that our understanding of the Bible is incomplete. Christians study the Bible daily, to understand it better. Some may assume the Bible's mysteries solved but only by ignoring its own claim to contain mysteries. Our assumption is different: we do not have the best explanation of God's Word. Our future holds better explanations than we presently have.

Apostle Peter personally experienced the Spirit guiding him into all the truth, just like we can. In Acts 10, God revealed to Peter that Gentiles were welcome into salvation. In the subsequent years of church debate and turmoil on the issue, Peter realized and declared in Acts 15 that Gentiles did not have to become Jews first. During this process of growing in the truth, Peter made mistakes such as Paul described in Galatians 2. Experience taught Peter that walking with God includes a growth in understanding Him and His plans. He embedded this assumption in 2 Peter 1:12, *"You know and are established in the present truth."*

Our grasp of God's revelation in Scripture grows. Peter's choice of the word *present* truth implies a process which results in *more* truth. The Bible can be explored for many lifetimes, as the Spirit reveals its mysteries to successive generations. Each generation will be established in the present truth—yet still leave undiscovered truth for the next generation to receive.

The final and complete revelation of God is the Bible. The present truth denotes our present understanding of it. The kingdom of darkness has encouraged a counterfeit idea in our culture: "my truth." The Bible roundly condemns this "suit yourself" paganism. Without submission to God's Word, "my truth" is a euphemism for rebellion, which earns the wrath of God.

Yet when we settle on our preferred understanding of the Bible, we are resisting His leadership into more truth from the Scripture. Is this not perilously close to that same "my truth" attitude? The rebellion is different, but it is still rebellion.

To mature as a Church, our understanding of Scripture must deepen. This has always been true; that is how God set things up. Book One of the *Unseen* series is *Nobody Sees This You: How to Live as a Spirit in the Unseen Realm.* Maturing as living human spirits received major emphasis. We mature through our hardships and struggles, which are God's strategy for testing His Church. He uses these trials to prove whether we will mature in the heavenly realms.

Advancing in our understanding of His Word is one such hardship and test. The standard of explanatory power tests whether our interpretation of Scripture stagnates or grows under His Spirit's leadership. Individual Christians must pass this test, and the Church must as well. Part of the test is whether we will admit that our understanding of His Word can improve.

UPDATING EXPLANATIONS

This simple admission requires only meekness. Yet each generation believes they've got the final interpretation. I don't understand how a generation of Christians can consider all puzzles solved.

Such a belief quickly puts them on the defensive against momentum into the future. After all, people are in God's image, with His built-in drive to advance. History moves onward, and societies conform to our advancements. A church that is narrow-minded resists better explanations of God's Word. Among outsiders, such stubborn Christians earn an outdated, irrelevant reputation. Society then sees the Bible as an irrelevant book for antiquity. This shift is visible in American society today.

Have you ever done this? You paint the walls of a room; suddenly the trim looks beat up. And once that's painted, then the furniture looks old. And after fixing that, the floor looks worn out. Updating can be a never-ending series of improvements. But it is improvement, and definitely is more work. A lazy homeowner can avoid the work by not updating their home. The home then becomes dilapidated; no one wants to visit. The neighbors disdain the homeowner, who gains an unwelcome reputation.

No maturing Christian wants to alienate our unsaved audience. Instead, we love our neighbors and desire their salvation, and the salvation of our nations. But like the homeowner who refuses to update, laziness makes our explanations of the Bible stagnant. Our evangelism is diminished, and our good news obscured, by a discrediting resistance to improvement.

No, we want all God's blessings and we recognize effort is necessary to find them in His Word. So we study the Bible fearlessly and vigorously. God has revealed Himself in it, and we want to know Him and His thoughts. We want to show His Kingdom on Earth.

Thy kingdom come. Thy will be done in earth as it is in heaven. (Matthew 6:10 KJV)

The searching Spirit of God constantly pulls us ever deeper into His fellowship. Our explanations of His Word automatically update when we yield to His pull. We cry out for discernment.

Yes, if you cry out for discernment,
And lift up your voice for understanding,
If you seek her as silver,
And search for her as for hidden treasures. (Proverbs 2:3–4).

But yielding is our choice. He will not force it. He permits resistance to His pull. We can settle in self-satisfaction and reject the automatic update. The Transjordan tribes exemplify this in Numbers 32:5. They were invited into the Promised Land, but chose to settle along the way.

Let this land be given to your servants as our possession. Do not take us over the Jordan.

But, beloved, we are confident of better things concerning you. (Hebrews 6:9)

THE GIFT OF PUZZLES

The *Unseen* series may give you more puzzles than answers. We delve into the Bible to see the unseen realm; what it holds makes no earthly sense. Puzzles might arise faster than you thought possible. Faith is our bridge across those puzzles.

An impassable chasm confronted Indiana Jones in the movie, *Indiana Jones: The Last Crusade.* After consulting his father's guidebook, he took the leap of faith. Indiana refers to Habakkuk 2:4, *"The just shall live by faith."* That leap revealed a bridge that was unseeable, but real. It is a parable of the Holy Spirit's reciprocal invitation to each of us: *"Come up here and I will show you things"* (Revelation 4:1).

Not everyone wants to understand the Bible better. We can avoid conviction by not reading it. Passages that discredit our present understanding are agitating. But most Christians want to grow in their faith. We care about knowing God and honoring His Word. That's why you are reading this book.

So we accept Bible puzzles as God's gift to us. When a question arises, it's an invitation we do not take lightly. God uses questions and puzzles to test our desire for Him. If we accept His invitation, we pass that test.

RESPONDING TO PUZZLES

When we have a better explanation of Scripture, we test it. Pride cannot do this, only humility. Others' response matters for our new explanation. The body of Christ will begin affirming our explanation if from God.

Ultimately, believers in multiple cultures should agree that we've identified genuine puzzles. By definition, these are mysteries that are poorly explained by the present truth. Christians who agree to follow the Bible's puzzles can explore alternative interpretations. Together, we test the power of our alternative explanation to explain the mystery.

By nature, we resist seeing puzzles. When we avoid the Bible's challenging questions, we default to our existing understanding. That's why we have the saying, "Don't confuse me with the facts."

Our response to Scripture's puzzles is revealing. Its enigmas are God's carrot on a stick for us, to entice us "further in and further up" (C. S. Lewis, *The Last Battle*). But if the mysteries are unimportant, we miss His enticement. Instead, we settle, believing our present understanding is good enough.

Christians may be proud of their current interpretation. Alternative explanations feel like irritants at best, or heretical at worst. This is the historical pattern described previously, and is well documented in Dr. Bill Hamon's book, *The Eternal Church*. Have you experienced pushback from others as you pursued your puzzles? You are not strange; it is an age-old experience.

WHEN EXPLANATION MEETS BIBLE

The generally accepted explanation doesn't explain every Bible passage. By testing the power of our explanations, we identify the mysteries God still has for us in the Bible.

The traditional interpretation may require us to ignore the plain meaning of a verse or passage. These mismatches signal God's invitation to move from old to new. When the present truth leaves something in Scripture unexplained, we are called deeper into His Word, but we have a choice. We can do the work of updating our explanation. An opposite choice is even more work: the mental gyrations necessary to explain away the plain meaning and preserve our preferred explanation.

For example, let's use the widely accepted explanation that salvation is by faith in Jesus Christ alone. I firmly believe that is the gospel truth. But this same Jesus made many statements to the contrary. Their plain meaning says something different. To honor God's Word, we explore the mismatches. Are we saved by giving a prophet a cup of cold water? (Matthew 10:42) Are we saved by being poor in spirit? (5:3) Will visiting prisoners and the sick save us? (25:35–36) Or maybe faith in Christ requires a ritual, like communion (John 6:53). So are we saved by faith in Jesus? Or must we do these other behaviors as well? These force us to explore salvation by faith in Jesus.

Standard responses occur when our explanations meet the Bible's contrary statements. For one, we may ignore the verse. An example is Psalm 82. By exploring it, Dr. Michael Heiser made excellent discoveries in his book, *The Unseen Realm*. Verse 1 gives a window on the council of heaven, yet that verse laid unappreciated in the Scripture for twenty centuries prior to Dr. Heiser's book. No one could explain it, so they largely ignored it.

> God stands in the congregation of the mighty;
> He judges among the gods. (Psalm 82:1)

Jesus Himself used Psalm 82:6 to challenge the Pharisees' rigid loyalty to old interpretations. They could not rebut Him either.

> Jesus answered them, "Is it not written in your law, 'I said, "You are gods"'? (John 10:34, citing Psalm 82:6)

If we can't ignore a verse, then we explain away the plain meaning. A favorite way to dismiss a verse is calling it a metaphor or poetic description. Isaiah 55:12 begins with a promise. *"For you shall go out with joy, and be led out with peace."* Obviously we do not want to explain that away. But the next half usually is called metaphoric: *"The mountains and the hills shall break forth into singing before you, and all the trees of the field shall clap their hands."* This stretches our modern credulity: "Surely, this is poetic language."

But the eyewitness accounts of the 1811 New Madrid earthquake prove that trees can actually clap and ground can make sound. It's easy to imagine. When God's kingdom meets Creation, wouldn't such a response be appropriate? To explain such verses as metaphors could signal a resistance to its plain meaning. Why would we even want this to be a metaphor? How cool will it be when the earth breaks forth in singing about Jesus!

A mismatch between the Bible and the traditional explanation prompts some to appeal to the original languages. Appealing to the Greek and Hebrew is a tactic. By this method, few people can argue. When the plain meaning is downplayed by appeal to the original language, ask what alternative explanation is being ruled out. Often it is the plain meaning.

As discussed previously, such sermons begin like this: "What that word really means is..." When we hear that, we should ask why. Can only church elites who know Greek or Hebrew explain this verse? After all, God Himself conceived and bequeathed the translation process to us. Was He caught flat-footed because the English language can't carry His truth? Of course, knowledge of the original languages is valuable—but not as an excuse to explain away a verse's plain meaning.

And occasionally, someone will say candidly, "It can't mean that!"

Christians readily defer to these responses without contest or objection. We appreciate our leaders and respect their hard work and authority. We feel inadequate to dispute explanations by a knowledgeable person, such as our preacher or other Christian leader. And the penalty for upsetting apple carts intimidates us to keep our thoughts to ourselves. The Holy Spirit within us may also restrain us from vocalizing alternative interpretations.

At issue is whether we will casually disregard God's Word. He is the master of vocabulary. It was His choice to reveal Himself in Scripture's pages. With that choice, He subjected the revelation to the original languages and to the translation process.

When our present framework of beliefs does not adequately explain a Bible passage, we have two choices. Either we disregard the passage, or we use it as a shoehorn into a better understanding of God's revelation. Apostle Paul had to address this also in Romans 3:4 where he cited Psalm 51:4.

Indeed, let God be true but every man a liar. As it is written:

"That You may be justified in Your words,
And may overcome when You are judged."

TESTING NEW EXPLANATIONS

The cycle of old to new is well documented in history. It puts the question to us as individuals and as churches: are we curious? Are we willing to ask the Bible what it says about our questions? Do we really believe that the Holy Spirit of God lives in us? Can we really trust Him to guide us into all truth, as Jesus promised? When the answer is yes, we often come up with alternative explanations.

We do so under this standard of explanatory power, however. All human endeavor is subject to explanatory power. The *Unseen* series in particular must be tested by explanatory power. These nine books concern Earth's distant past and the unseen world. The reader of the nine-book *Unseen* series will perceive anew the unseen influence on our actions today.

This series develops a new and comprehensive explanation of reality. These topics are beyond the reach of scientific verification or lab experiments. For theories of reality, explanatory power is our only measuring tool. Does our comprehensive framework have more power to explain life? If so, it is an improved understanding of the Bible.

New solutions for Bible mysteries go on trial for a period. New explanations go on trial runs in life, in discussion, and in prayer. We must hold our alternative explanations lightly during that time. Love must govern debate. Apostle Paul admonished one church in 1 Thessalonians 5:21, *"Test all things; hold fast what is good." All things* is both rear-facing—tradition—and forward-facing—new ideas. All are scrutinized.

Our idea may be new, or long embraced by many. Neither popularity nor enduring acceptance excuses tradition from scrutiny. Tradition lasts long because it has acceptable explanatory power. Yet, a fertile Church periodically scrutinizes tradition. There is no basis for fear. Biblical truths that emerged from rigorous debates in centuries past can certainly endure our tests.

Examining alternative explanations of Scripture is how we grow. When healthy, the Church of Jesus recognizes there are gaps in our present understanding. We can trust the Spirit who inspired Scripture and indwells the Church. He arouses the curiosity that He wants to satisfy. The revealing Spirit elicits the questions He wants to answer.

The nine-book *Unseen* series explores many Bible puzzles. They are mysteries. By definition, the current theologies do not explain them adequately. I propose in this series a comprehensive point of view. It solves those Bible puzzles and releases Bible mysteries. Your present truth will be challenged by the enigmas and proposed solutions in the *Unseen* series. You can examine and test these solutions with others. If God validates this comprehensive point of view, you'll gladly adjust your current framework of reality. Besides enjoying His presence more readily, your spiritual gifts will explode in usefulness. The unsaved in your circle of life will have far less excuse to dismiss your gospel about salvation by faith in Jesus.

Yes, it is work—like updating your home. But it's the work of following Him. These habits of seeking the most explanatory power keep our spirits fresh. In the life of a growing Christian, this adventurous fertility compensates our sacrifices. We become intimate with Jesus.

LOVE WHILE TESTING

Adjusting our grid of interpretation is taxing. The new point of view affects our walk with God; adapting our behaviors takes time and effort. The way we pray, study the Bible—all altered. It is exceptionally rewarding and joyful, like no other work. But it's still work.

The Christians you respect don't immediately accept the discoveries that excite you. The solutions you'll find in this nine-book *Unseen* series may cause debate. That's good because any proposed interpretation requires scrutiny and testing.

Your Christian walk, education, and other qualifications give you the credibility to be heard, just like I am heard and my books are read. Yet, new insights must still be tried and proven—yours and mine both. People may agree because of their respect for us; this does not prove us correct. Nor can we demand agreement from them. The same Holy Spirit lives in you, me, and them. The responsibility for leading others into truth rests with Him—not you or me.

Most new explanations upset an apple cart somewhere. People find fault with new ideas. Additional puzzles arise as people weigh the suggested improvement. The present explanations for these new questions satisfy most Christians. Solving Bible mysteries is not an advancement to them. Others may oppose the new grid as complicating their Bible study. One group sees Bible puzzles and new explanations as more work on their plate.

Speaking the truth in love is God's command. The nature of vigorous discussion arouses passion. Heated arguments can ensue. Walking in love disarms hostility and insult, pride, and divisiveness. The burden of love and meekness is on the one with a better explanation of the Bible. You know from the outset that some will be defensive against alternative explanations.

The Spirit who leads us into all the truth is holy. Christlike conduct is His expectation when He releases a mystery from Scripture. During testing and debate, His care is our love, not our right. If we bully others with the interpretation He gives us, we will quickly be on our own. Bereft of His endorsement, our new idea will depend on our resources entirely. Will we manipulate others into agreeing with it?

I learned about tension over biblical explanations in 1997, as a respected founding elder of a church. We had to solve a very difficult church policy. I proposed we seek the Lord for the answer, relying on the promise in Proverbs 2:1–11, cited earlier. My specific suggestion was a dedicated hour of waiting on the Lord. The other elders paused. They looked at me like I was from another planet. After an awkward moment, the debate carried on, unaltered. It was as if I had said nothing at all. The pastor shrank from the tension, providing no leadership. I recognized the group's unspoken decision and deferred to it.

Unbeknownst to me, the groundwork of conflict was laid at that moment. Its eruption two years later revealed secret animosity toward my intimate walk with God. Separation from that church was the only remedy permitted to my wife and me. We have grown exponentially since then. I was an awkward kid in the spirit.

But my simple willingness to love evidently pleased God. I have been honored for my response. In contrast, those who harbored ill will have suffered a corrosive force from within. Jesus is adamant about love during debate. We dare not cross Him. He loves love.

> Behold, how good and how pleasant it is
> For brethren to dwell together in unity! (Psalm 133:1)

NON-NEGOTIABLES

Non-negotiable truths are plainly stated in the Bible. But not all our beliefs fall into that category. Some are implied by our non-negotiable truths. They are necessarily true, given the plainly stated truths. These implied truths are corollaries.

Reverse engineering from the Bible's direct statements produces these corollaries. If the plain statements of the Bible are true, then these unstated things must also be true. The Bible does not explicitly state the implied corollaries.

An example is the Trinity. Scripture is plain that God is one. It is also plain that Jesus was the Son of God, and that the Holy Spirit is God. By implication, God must be a triune unity. It comes from three non-negotiable, plainly stated Bible truths. 1. The Scripture is God's inspired Word. 2. Jesus' atonement on the cross fully satisfied God's wrath against our sin. 3. God is one, from the *Shema* in Deuteronomy 6:4.

> Hear, O Israel: The LORD our God, the LORD is one! You shall love the LORD your God with all your heart, with all your soul, and with all your strength.

The Trinity is not stated in Scripture, but it is implied and referenced. The early church resolved these questions in a three-century process, and it is orthodox Christianity ever since. Over the centuries, some standard alternative explanations arise periodically among some Christians. These non-Trinitarian concepts have been thoroughly debated and their proponents scrutinized. Yet no better explanation for the clearly stated biblical truths has been proven or gained acceptance. The orthodox explanation stands: God is a triune unity.

Debates about truth can cause factions. Almost all Christians have yielded to the explanatory power of the Trinity. Those who refused it fell on the ash heap of history, with their dearly held interpretations lying long forgotten. Paul listed party spirit or dissensions as a work of the flesh in Galatians 5:20, followed by the outcome in 6:7.

> Do not be deceived, God is not mocked; for whatever a man sows, that he will also reap.

The early Church had several complex considerations to identify the corollary truths of our faith. The kingdom of darkness used them as a door for confusion. Book Seven, *Nobody Sees This Church: Resisting Darkness,* describes this and other strategies in more depth.

THE NEW OLD STANDARD

We have reintroduced a major standard. New interpretations must explain the Scripture better.

Their proponents must observe the six boundaries above, which God has set for new ideas. We recognize new questions will result from better explanations. However, if the explanation is true, it will endure our debate and survive our scrutiny. After that process, the new framework will leave fewer puzzles unsolved, and will unlock more Bible mysteries.

This standard is Explanatory Power. We will rely heavily upon it in the books that follow.

CHAPTER TEN

Puzzles and Mysteries

We conclude Book Two with a formal invitation. Mysteries await you in the remaining seven books of the *Unseen* series.

ADMITTING DEFICIENCY

Puzzles are our personal invitation into God's mysteries. By accepting the Bible's puzzles, we admit deficiency in our current explanation. Not everyone can do that easily. Shortcomings in our beliefs are hard to admit. When we admit this lack, we can be a pariah to others.

Puzzles and mysteries can inspire a knee-jerk response: "We don't go there." It is an unworthy fear. If our present explanations of the Bible are inadequate, do we not want to improve them? Why is this a threat?

There is a worthy alternative to the fear: passionate love for God. We welcome His Spirit's guidance into all truth. Yes, there's a cost to seeing the puzzles. It's a cost of discipleship. We have to dig into Scripture anew and discuss it together. Aw, shucks!

Individual Christians can chafe under this standard of explanatory power. Group consensus tamps it down. Updating our present truth is work. Our practices and programs can be affected. Aren't the present explanations good enough? After all, "if it ain't broke, don't fix it."

Remember, our spirits live in the unseen realm, seated in the heavens with Jesus. When you propose a new understanding of Scripture, His Spirit is doing unseen work. Those who hear you may be under the Spirit's conviction. Your life may challenge their humility or their hunger for the Bible. You and your curiosity may be God's shaking to awaken them. Be God's partner in love.

THE COST OF DEFICIENCY

I believe Christian spirits always hear the Lord's whispers. He is not the variable; we are. The live issue is whether we respond as disciples. All of us can prefer our existing outlook over His invitations. The flesh and the spirit are at war. The flesh may be satisfied with what we know already, but our spirit inwardly knows we are resisting. Our flesh fears that the emperor (our preferred explanatory framework) has no clothes (is inadequate).

Therefore, you take a risk to admit deficient explanations in Christian groups. You may be marginalized, if not ostracized. Your pastor, priest, mentors, and elders may turn away at your approach. Church responsibilities can squeeze out vigilance to their own discipleship. They can unwittingly act as the very interlopers Jesus warned against. When leaders require your deference to their Bible explanation, it is a red flag. All these have happened to my wife and me in our lifetimes.

Your puzzles and answers may better explain the Scripture. Sadly, that is not the standard for many Christians and churches. Doctrines are very important; traditions provide stability. But when maintaining the *status quo* matters more to Christians and their leaders, they can actually oppose the Scripture. Jesus repeatedly used a phrase with the Bible-loving Jewish sects, the Pharisees, and the scribes: *"Have you never read...?"* Of course they had read it; He knew that. His phrase exposed that they had skipped over it or didn't like it.

In the same way, seeing the Bible's puzzles disturbs so many people. Your church may set you aside for trying to better explain the Bible.

Leaders don't like upsetting the apple cart. Your leaders may be unaware that darkness is feeding their fears. Various motives stimulate resistance to better explanations. Christian leaders easily suffer the pressure to be right. Another is pride and the related urge to control. Control is more delicate when a church has a large budget or physical plant. Pastors are sensitive about alienating big donors, who have their own preconceived notions.

All this inertial resistance to Bible puzzles can be intimidating. We can disdain the Lord's whispers because we fear the response of others. Yet our inadequacy is a great asset. Apostle Paul defended himself to the

Corinthian church with his inadequacy. He admitted deficiency for God's truths, as a jar of clay, in 2 Corinthians 4:7. Let us have the same attitude.

> We have this treasure in earthen vessels, that the excellence of the power may be of God and not of us.

TO UPDATE OR NOT

Christians, by default, preserve the good and the bad alike. But the standard of explanatory power does not relent. We are the only people on earth filled with the Holy Spirit. He can be trusted to lead us in the way everlasting. When He releases new understanding of the Bible, fear is unneeded.

> When He, the Spirit of truth, has come, He will guide you into all truth. (John 16:13)

> You have an anointing from the Holy One, and you know all things.... But the anointing which you have received from Him abides in you, and you do not need that anyone teach you. (1 John 2:20, 27)

We can huddle in supposed safety, with our accepted explanation of Scripture. "If it ain't broke, don't fix it." But then we're like those who don't paint the walls. Our explanation of reality looks dilapidated while our society advances. No one wants to visit the old church with its dilapidated theology. So society marginalizes us. And right there alongside to help: the kingdom of darkness. Thus, mainline churches decline today in part because they still fight the battles of past centuries and refuse to update. If we want to relate, we must update.

In contrast, the puzzles and solutions in the *Unseen* series deliver new effectiveness for our present times. The war of light and dark intensifies on the Earth today. Christians who follow the Holy Spirit deeper into the Bible and its mysteries will be ready. We are His army of living human spirits. His rule on earth awaits our maturity. If Apostle Paul was correct in Ephesians 6:12, we need much more effectiveness than we see presently among us.

> For we do not wrestle against flesh and blood, but against principalities, against powers, against the rulers of the darkness of this age, against spiritual hosts of wickedness in the heavenly places.

FIND AND FOLLOW THE PUZZLES

In Scripture, there are always puzzles. It is a gift from God because they prevent stagnation and irrelevance in His Church.

We think we know what God says in His Word. But then life happens. Experience argues with our interpretation. Will we accept God's gift and explore the Bible for alternative explanations? Having an open mind doesn't mean it is open at both ends. We have defined beliefs that are long proven, *and* we are open-minded.

Or Christians can dig their heels in and argue that our experience must be wrong—like Job's three friends argued. To unbelievers, that appears close-minded and dogmatic. In response they might argue for a different interpretation. It's more likely they will disdain our Scripture. Rebutting them doesn't require us to be right on all points. Instead, it requires love.

The kingdom of darkness encourages the pressure to be right. How do we disarm it? We freely admit inadequate understanding of the Bible. The pressure to be right is thoroughly considered in Book Seven of the *Unseen* series, *Nobody Sees This Church: Resisting Darkness.*

Christians were "consensus movers" for two thousand years. We pioneered every conceivable advancement: science, philosophy, economics, literature. Why were we the leaders? Because intimacy with God Almighty means we have the mind of Christ. We Christians are the only living human spirits on Earth. His inventiveness flows into His Church; it is not limited to our categories of religion and morality. It is Christians' birthright to lead humanity in discovery and advancement as we fulfill our Creation mandate (Genesis 1:26ff).

This birthright for our living spirits has awe-inspiring privileges. The Holy Spirit blesses our excellence in curiosity. He teaches us about the seen and unseen worlds alike. Nothing is beyond sharing it with us. I describe this intimate knowledge-sharing in Book One of the *Unseen* series, *Nobody Sees This You: How to Live as a Spirit in the Unseen Realm.*

The standard of explanatory power applies to seen and unseen—and unites them. I titled Book Three *Nobody Sees This Creation: The Origin of the Devil and His Replacements.* God created the firmament and the lesser light in Genesis 1. We read them as sky and moon, but nothing matches their description. The sky isn't firm, and the moon does not rule the night. A better explanation is needed.

This puzzle is a gift from God. He created these two objects and revealed them in Genesis 1. Therefore, a sensible explanation beckons us, both for the seen and the unseen world. We can't be correct in one realm, but not in the other. The *Unseen* series solves this and many other puzzles. Solving the firmament and the lesser light explains the geological prehistory of Earth. This single puzzle also explains behaviors of the kingdom of darkness. When our explanations improve, the marks of darkness become far more identifiable in the seen world.

Explanatory power must work in both the visible and the unseen. There are many puzzles regarding demons in the Bible. If you may never have noticed them, you'll enjoy both puzzle and solution. Book Four identifies the origin of demons and explains their methods. It's titled, *Nobody Sees These Enemies: How to Discern and Disarm Unseen Tempters.*

Puzzles about the Bible can threaten people. Preconceived notions are their protection—no puzzles welcome. But without mysteries, we miss out on Bible revelation. Seeing puzzles is a valuable sign: you are growing in your relationship with God.

SELF-DENIAL FOR PUZZLES

If you don't see puzzles, maybe you have resisted them. Don't be afraid! God blesses us when we admit our spiritual poverty. We mourn, and meekly hunger and thirst for Him. Jesus said ours is the kingdom, and promised we will be comforted and satisfied. He taught these Beatitude qualities in Matthew 5. The revealing Spirit of God lives in Beatitude people, and magnetizes us to the enigmas He planted in Scripture.

Jesus made exacting demands in Luke 9:23. When we attempt them, this blessed meekness grows in us. Denying ourselves includes following His leadership in Bible study.

If anyone desires to come after Me, let him deny himself, and take up his cross daily, and follow Me.

We follow Him, not those who could penalize us. King Saul differed from David in this way. Saul feared people's response more than he feared disobeying God. Like him, we can fear paying a price for following Jesus Christ. King Saul confessed his sin in 1 Samuel 15:24.

I have sinned, for I have transgressed the commandment of the LORD and your words, because I feared the people and obeyed their voice.

The parents of the healed blind man in John 9:22 are another example. They were more afraid of being penalized, than happy their son could see—the very picture of "no joy."

> His parents said these things because they feared the Jews, for the Jews had agreed already that if anyone confessed that He was Christ, he would be put out of the synagogue.

The Bible's mysteries entice us to deny ourselves, strengthening our will and weakening our fears. Self-denial overcomes the blindness of our preconceived notions. The cost of following Bible clues is real and requires sacrifice. To follow Jesus deeper into His Word requires self-denial. That's the way He set it up.

With a habit of self-denial, you can submit your existing beliefs to the Bible anew. Its mysteries beckon you. You can ask and wait on the Holy Spirit for leadership. Sooner or later, your curiosity grows, your passion for Scripture mounts. You become a detective with enigmatic clues, and seek the best explanation. Bible mysteries can be a thriller!

In my daily Bible study, I sit before God. He hid treasure for me in the passage. I let the passage tumble-dry in my mind all day. Like chewing long-lasting bubble gum, like a cow chewing the cud, I chew on the passage at hand. Often the first thing is not more answers, but more questions! Those curiosities are God's bait. He answers my prayer to know Him. My part is waiting and listening.

Sometimes the events of the day shed light on the passage. Ordinary conversations may help solve the puzzles, but not always. I've also returned to a Scripture I thought I understood, only to see more puzzles. The Reader Resources in the back of this book contain some images from my own Bible study, to demonstrate the result when we ruminate for days on one passage.

God leads you further in with a trail of cookie crumbs. But unlike Hansel and Gretel, what awaits you is no fairy tale woman wanting to cook you and eat you. If your present interpretation doesn't satisfy the puzzles, welcome the opportunity. If you do, you will grow. God loves for us to search out His mysteries.

> It is the glory of God to conceal a matter,
> But the glory of kings is to search out a matter. (Proverbs 25:2)

YOU, THE UNSEEN SERIES, AND THE BIBLE

What we are doing in the *Unseen* series is not conjecture. The Bible gives the complete information needed—but in code. It awaits our maturity in meekness. God entrusts the meek with full discovery in Scripture.

> Christ Jesus came into the world to save sinners, of whom I am chief. However, for this reason I obtained mercy, that in me first Jesus Christ might show all longsuffering, as a pattern to those who are going to believe on Him for everlasting life. (1 Timothy 1:15–16)

I believe in the authority and power of the Bible as God's Word. The *Unseen* series is committed to it. The nine-book series explains away nothing found in the Bible. Instead, we will seek the most effective and plausible explanation of the most puzzles. To facilitate that, there is a readers' only discussion forum at ParadigmLighthouse.com. (Visit the site to request credentials.) Together, we can discuss and yield to the complete information God gives in Scripture.

As you progress in the series, many questions about Scripture may be solved for you. More work to understand Scripture may beckon you. More adventure in Christ will certainly delight you.

RESOURCES

About The *Unseen* Series

PARADIGM LIGHTHOUSE

The *Unseen* Series comes to you through the ministry of Paul and Diane Renfroe, named Paradigm Lighthouse. Their calling is to help you mature as a living human spirit—but what does that look like?

The undeniable fact is this: between you and God is an inexpressibly enormous difference in scale, being, and quality. He is an eternal Spirit who is both perfect love and perfect rightness—a severe contrast to us.

Yet for all this gap, He can adopt you as His intimate child, born as a spirit. The *Lighthouse* name expresses the explosion of lighthearted safety that His peace implants into every such person. He fills you with His Holy Spirit, repeatedly, more and more.

This event and process pulls your thinking and beliefs into agreement with Him. The *Paradigm* name identifies this process as profound, life-changing paradigm shifts. One perception of reality supersedes another, as He blows your mind with the unseen things He reveals.

Further in and further up to our Father God is a lifelong process, and well worth every sacrifice known to mankind. This experience of large-scale paradigm shifts has also characterized the history of His Church, a core observation of the Present Truth movement.

The nine numbered books in this series are sequential. However, each contains the following series orientation and a summary of the preceding books, so any book is a beneficial starting point. For your full benefit, read each book for its unique contribution to your paradigm of reality.

Each book of the series is available where you purchased this one, and if not, you may visit ParadigmLighthouse.com. There you can also contact us to receive ministry directly, both public and private.

YOU

A burgeoning number of people worldwide are perceiving unseen realities today. The gap between seen and unseen, between natural and spirit, is narrowing. You were magnetized to this book and the *Unseen* series, and you are not alone. I wrote this series to equip you and your friends for holy perception of the Unseen Realm.

Questions are normal:

- How can you interpret what you are faintly perceiving? Are there rules or guidelines?
- What's causing your growing awareness of the hidden world? Why you?
- Where do the Bible and your church fit in? Why isn't everyone receptive?
- Can you make your perception clearer? Can you make it stop?

The words *dread* and *terror* are often used because the unseen threatens us with loss of control. Its spirits which are holy can, if fully unveiled, intimidate, and reduce us to quivering. Those which are unholy can trick us and take advantage of us.

We know ourselves terribly ill-equipped for the invisible world of spirit, and gravely unprepared for the accountability of perceiving it. As mere human beings, we are poor in spirit. We can go through our entire lives without noticing they are pulling our string and jerking our chain. But we came by that ignorance honestly: mankind's default is to control that perception—or prevent it altogether.

The unseen world is now rapping harder and faster on the windows of our souls.

RESPONDING TO THE SPIRIT WORLD

There are two extremes we use to control our interface with the invisible world of spirit. The low intensity method is to control the unseen by ignoring it. The high intensity method is to manipulate the unseen and its spirits, long named sorcery.

Between these two extremes, people use the spirit world for gain. Religion, for instance, is a tit-for-tat effort to secure favor from God and obligate Him to us. When we complain about God's unfairness, we reveal the religion in us.

People use the unseen for gain in the seen world, and not just with religion. The list includes business, family, education, and government. Deeds can be beneficial and character admirable, all the while treating the unseen as a mere tool for the natural world.

Today, the spirit world is becoming harder to ignore, manipulate, and use. There are many ways we try to limit it. All of them express our default reaction: "Stay in the place we assign you!"

But in our days, the unseen is refusing to stay there.

THE BEST RESPONSE

You can receive a welcome into the spirit world. God, a Spirit, revealed a specific protocol. No one can be a spirit without following it. The results are very desirable.

It begins simply but its results defy imagination: you admit to God your poverty for His world of spirit. This admission brings an inward mourning over your poverty as a spirit. You recognize how distant you are from the true God, a Spirit. Drastically lower expectations follow as meekness arises within you. You mercifully respond to others after facing your own poverty.

Simultaneously, you have a growing hunger and thirst for the good that God intends. As you mature, old values become replaced with what God wants, and you are purified. You gain new abilities to create peace in relationships, both with God and among people. And you become loyal to God at any cost.

This summarizes nine qualities God likes to bless, which Jesus of Nazareth listed in the first book of the Bible's New Testament, Matthew chapters 5 through 7, together with the specific blessings God places on each quality. Their lasting name is the Beatitudes.

So how do you gain these desirable qualities? You become a living spirit with the following protocol.

THE PROTOCOL TO BECOME A SPIRIT

For anyone poor in spirit to become a spirit requires help—the help of the Head Spirit, God. He wants you to become a living spirit with Him! He has revealed the protocol so you can.

1. Admit that you are spiritually poor. You do not have what it takes to relate to God, who is a spirit, and holy. The lasting word for this situation is sin.

2. Admit the dire consequences of that spiritual poverty. These are distance between you and the God who would be your Father, slowness to honor and obey Him, damage to yourself and those around you, and hindrance to His good desires for mankind. The lasting word for this step is confession.

3. Admit that He solved this spirit gap. Jesus proclaimed that His death on the cross fully satisfied God in the spirit world, where we are so poverty-stricken. When you believe this and follow Jesus, God the Father gives you birth as a spirit. Immediately, God adopts you as His own child, just as Jesus was. The lasting word is faith, because your adoption is unsee-able, and is perceived by trusting the truthfulness of what God's revealing.

4. Admit those three things directly to Him. Here's one way to express it to Him.

God, I admit You deserve much, yet I can only give so little. I want to follow Jesus so His death solves the spirit gap I have with You. So I ask you to forgive me. I put my trust in Jesus, that His death enables You to adopt me as your child. I don't know what to expect, but when You show me and help me, I will respond to You as my Father, with the best of my ability.

THE PROTOCOL TO STAY A SPIRIT

After you admit these facts, the spirit world tests your genuine intent. Did you mean it? Will you really maintain your new relationship with God?

The host of heaven observes your persistent commitments in this seen world. This includes angels who serve us, sent by God. Also included: spirits who hate people, including you. These evil spirits try to imprison your spirit. If they cannot, then these destroyers try to disrupt, discourage, dissuade, or deceive you.

Jesus knew this would happen and provided in the Bible a protocol for you to stay a living spirit.

1. Jesus started a protective group for people born as spirits after these admissions. Its lasting name is The Church, uppercase. Now it is globally huge, full of many churches, lowercase, in different forms. Not everyone in a church is the same. One quality is common:

180

poverty of spirit and dependence upon God. In church, God trains and tests everyone born in spirit to grow our ability to love others graciously.

2. There is a book He provided to everyone born as spirits; that book is the Bible, the subject of Book Two. Jesus rose from the dead and could still be here, but He did not remain physically in the seen world. His preferred method was to fill us with His Spirit and give us a Bible.

    To see and hear Him with our spirit's "eyes" and "ears," He endorsed an authoritative collection of writings—our Bible. It holds many yesterdays, written over 1,500 years and compiled in 397 AD. There are many translations available from its original, well-known languages. In it, you will find God and He will reveal the invisible to you. The Bible is an ancient book written by forty people distant in time and culture, both from each other and from us. That's why effort is required to understand it.

    This book, *Nobody Sees This Unseen Realm: How to Unlock Bible Mysteries,* describes that effort in detail. The effort is amply rewarded because the Bible is a proven book which also trains and proves your spirit. God uses His Word to grow your spirit for effective activity in both the seen and the unseen worlds.

3. Other commitments—not mere behaviors—help us grow as spirits. One example is self-sacrificing thoughts and deeds, such as service to others. Another is giving money as tithes to our particular church group and offerings to others. Obedience to God's explicit commands governs all our commitments. Submission to the leaders He provides us trains us to lead others as well.

THE EVENT OF YOUR SPIRIT'S BIRTH

The above admissions cause an unseeable event: you are born as a spirit into the unseen world. Anyone who sincerely follows the above protocol becomes a newborn spirit. Jesus described it to someone in the fourth book of the New Testament, John chapter 3 verse 6: "*That which is born of the flesh is flesh, and that which is born of the Spirit is spirit.*"

When we are born in this seen world, that's the limit of our being; we cannot participate in the spirit world. The Bible's word for this is the flesh. Every person is born in the flesh. But when we believe Jesus and follow Him, we are born into the unseen world. The Bible's word for that is the spirit. Only followers of Jesus are born in spirit.

THE MATURING

Your spirit begins as an immature spirit, just as your body was born immature. Likewise, either you feed it or it withers unnourished. Either you mature as a spirit, or you atrophy.

Church, the Bible, prayer, and obedience are good ways to nourish your spirit. Denying the cravings of the flesh strengthens your spirit, just as weight training strengthens your muscles. As your spirit matures, your spirit asserts its dominion over your natural self, as it should.

This Book Two of the *Unseen* Series is foundational because it equips you to study God's Bible for yourself. Maturity means that you are not dependent on others for your study of the Bible.

Maturing as a spirit is impossible without God's Spirit within, and we ask God's Spirit to fill us more every day. Holy is the adjective used to describe Him, so His lasting name is the Holy Spirit.

Some ask insincerely or without holiness. Some try to limit the spirit and control the unseen. As your spirit matures, you may feel the pain and desperation in their futile effort. Yet upon them we always have mercy and desire their best; God is patient with us all.

YOUR UNSEEN SPIRIT

As a newborn spirit, the world of spirits immediately recognizes you as an active participant. They see you as a spirit born of God's own doing. The unseen spirits who are holy are angels who rejoice as God assigns them to help you mature. Unholy spirits, including demons, are assigned to deter you by their chief, the devil.

The *Unseen* Series is a guide for every born as a spirit by following Jesus Christ. You have entered this very active but unseeable world. Being a spirit being raises many questions we'll investigate in this series. How do you act? What actually are you capable of, as a spirit? As a spirit, do you hear, like you do in your body? See? Feel? Smell? Taste? Do you talk as a spirit?

How do you distinguish between your unseen spirit and the more immediate parts of yourself? How do you identify and respond to the spirits you encounter?

If you are adopted by God as your Father, how does that interaction occur? Surely you talk together—but how? How does He speak in the Bible? In your prayers? In your dreams? What does He do, and what's your part? Do you have to forget old things? What new do you need to learn?

Take heart: Your Father will not leave you hanging. He may test your persistence. He may prove your sincerity by requiring patience—but you can count on Him.

THE FORGETTING

Even as a living spirit, everyone has some baggage from the old days. Parents and predecessors hand it down to us. Some baggage is from living by our own wits without full access to God's help and protection. There is also baggage that evil spirits tricked us into carrying. A constant experience of maturing spirits is shedding such baggage. Forgetting these hindrances is a welcome process.

That baggage includes our definition of impossible. When your spirit grows, you constantly see the falsity of limits which you once accepted without question. Forgetting these limits signals your growing intimacy with your Father.

A regular habit is to break agreements with old beliefs and habits in favor of what God reveals to us. Bible study is one cause of this action: His Word performs its discovery process in our hearts. Our area of agreement with God expands when we relinquish our newly discovered agreements with the kingdom of darkness, while the dominance of the seen world wanes.

THE LEARNING

The Father of your spirit, God Himself, desires intimacy with you. It is a process over time; there is much to learn about one another. He packaged His revelation in a book for us, and it simply takes effort and time to find Him in it. This is one reason He puts His Spirit into us, so we can understand His thoughts. Apostle John, one of Jesus' first four followers, described it in his first letter, chapter 2 verse 27: "*The anointing which you have received from Him abides in you [and] teaches you concerning all things.*"

THE PAYOFF

This forgetting and learning process requires outside help. The guidance of mentors and leaders is indispensable; God will lead you to the right ones.

Most important is God's active, vocal presence within your skin. This occurs by the repeated filling of the Holy Spirit, more and more very time. Reliance upon His Word is a constant need—as it should be for a meek, poor in spirit person.

God is a Spirit, and He will teach you to use your spirit senses. With His life inside you, you will be alive beyond imagination. You will surpass the discoveries of the *Unseen* Series. Your participation in the unseen world of spirit can only become more effective.

Welcome to the world of the spirit-born.

Works Referenced

1. C.S. Lewis. *The Lion, the Witch & The Wardrobe*. New York, NY: HarperCollins, 1994.
2. C.S. Lewis. *The Last Battle*. New York, NY: HarperCollins, 1994.
3. Steven Hawkings. *The Theory of Everything*. Mumbai, India: Jaico Publishing House, 2006.
4. James W. Sire. *How to Read Slowly: Reading for Comprehension*. Downers Grove, IL: InterVarsity Press, 1989.
5. Henry M. Roberts, Daniel Honemann, et al. *Robert's Rules of Order; Newly Revised 12th Edition*. Robert's Rules Association, 2020.
6. George Orwell. *1984*. San Jose, CA: Maple Press, 1949.
7. Helen Lemmell. *Turn Your Eyes Upon Jesus*. Anderson, SC: New Spring, 1922.

Topical Listing
of Books for Your Spirit

TOPIC	TITLE	AUTHOR	WHERE
Living as a born-again spirit	*Nobody Sees This You: How to Live as a Spirit in the Unseen World*	Paul Renfroe	ParadigmLighthouse.com
Becoming like Jesus	*You Can Be Just Like Jesus*	Luke Armstrong	Amazon
Building your local church	*Building Strong*	Robert Gay	highpraisepc.com
Checking with a Bible scholar	*Supernatural*	Dr. Michael S. Heiser	theunseenrealm.com
Cooperating with miracles	*Miracles Now! And Financial Miracles Now!*	Gale Sheehan	christianinternational.com
Finding your place in church	*I Belong*	Robert Gay	highpraisepc.com
Healing emotional hurts	*Restore My Soul: A 90 Devotional*	Kathleen Tolleson	kingdomlifenow.com
Healing sexual hurts	*Restoring Sexuality*	Kathleen Tolleson	kingdomlifenow.com
Hearing God's voice confidently	*God Speaks and You Can Hear Him*	Edgar Iraheta	christianinternational.com
Identifying globalism	*Globalists on Trial*	Sally Saxon	Amazon
Identifying spirits	*Discernment*	Jane A. Hamon	tomandjanehamon.com
Improving relationships	*Uprighting Relationships*	Linda Roeder	dave-linda.com
Interpreting dreams	*Dreams & Visions*	Jane A. Hamon	tomandjanehamon.com

TOPIC	TITLE	AUTHOR	WHERE
Leading as a woman	*Deborah Company*	Jane A. Hamon	tomandjanehamon.com
Mental health and hearing God	*But Deliver Me From Crazy*	Katie Dale	Amazon
Receiving deliverance from oppression	*Passport to Freedom*	Sharon Parkes	christianinternational.com
Serving others spiritually	*How to Reach Your Highest Level*	Jimmy Kellet	christianinternational.com
Speaking what God says to others	*Prophetic Divergence*	Robert Paul	kaiembassy.com
Transforming your community	*7 Anointings for Kingdom Transformation*	Tom Hamon	tomandjanehamon.com
Updating worship	*The Tabernacle of God*	Dean Mitchum	christianinternational.com
Verbalizing victory	*Declarations & Decrees of a Warrior*	Marlene Babb	Amazon

BOOKS ABOUT BIBLICAL PROPHECY BY DR. BILL HAMON, BISHOP OF CHRISTIAN INTERNATIONAL

Prophets & Personal Prophecy
Prophets & the Prophetic Movement
Prophets, Pitfalls, & Principles
Apostles/Prophets & the Coming Moves of God
Available from https://shop.christianinternational.com/

Following are the key resources in my library for my own Inductive Bible Study. I have never studied Hebrew or Aramaic (the languages of the Old Testament) therefore all the following pertain to my exploration of Greek words' meaning in the Bible.

Important Note: One boundary that God has placed upon us is to respect our elders. This includes not only our face-to-face leaders but also the ones we will never meet, such as Bible translators whose entire lives are devoted to accurately rendering the Bible languages. Meekness before God does not permit us to override their qualified judgments about the best translation of the original languages and words. The following resources are provided to you to enhance your application of the Bible. Vigilance to avoid presumptuous pride is an important preventive. Only in that way can the Scripture work to our good rather than our condemnation.

BibleGateway.com	A searchable Bible website and Bible app for phones at no expense, which quickly permits copying verses and passages into your own digital formats while taking notes of sermons, etc.
Netbible.org/Bible/	A more advanced online Bible study tool for researching words, phrases and cross-references, with available translation footnotes and commentaries.
The Septuagint with Apocrypha: Greek and English	By Sir Lancelot Brenton and originally published in 1851, this has the Greek text and KJV translation side by side.
The New Analytical Greek Lexicon	Edited by Wesley Perschbacher and published in 1990 by Hendrickson Publishers, this is the single most used tool in my library. It is organized alphabetically by first letter. The author catalogues every Greek word used in the NT with every word ending, tells the number/person and other details of declension, the root word and the places it is used in the NT. This helps identify the nuances and connotations associated with a word in its declensions that may not be present in its stem. Its Greek language refresher is also invaluable for the occasional student of Greek.
A Reader's Greek-English Lexicon of the New Testament	First published in 1975 by author Sakae Kubo by Zondervan, this lexicon is organized sequentially, as Greek words appear in the NT. The user can identify Greek words used in sequence with the English text of the NT.
Vine's Complete Expository Dictionary of Old and New Testament Words	William E. Vine published this work in 1940, most recently available through Thomas Nelson Publishers of Nashville. It is the granddaddy of Inductive Bible Study resources for word study. It is organized alphabetically by the English word in the Bible, and each original language root word is given for it with nuances of meaning.
Greek-English Lexicon of the New Testament, being Grimm's Wilke's Clavis *Novi Testamenti*, translated by Joseph Henry Thayer	Betraying again my preference for classic resources, this 1885 translation by Thayer of the original lexicon by Wilke (1851) and Grimm (1868) provides a fuller description of each Greek word present in the NT. It is organized alphabetically. Also provided are the variants present in multiple antique Bibles and codexes used in translation, as well as individual words' use by ancient authors.

READER ENGAGEMENT RESOURCES

OBTAINING CREDENTIALS FOR THE ONLINE DISCUSSION GROUP

As an owner of a book in the *Unseen* Series, you can request login credentials for a secure online discussion group at ParadigmLighthouse.com, to share your meditations and your progress. The group is limited to readers of the *Unseen* Series. There, you can share your reflections and discoveries. I am growing also and treasure your discoveries as you walk through this book and meditate on the scriptural principles.

With the correspondence and reflections our readers share there, we can all see how God is speaking to us, His body, about our spirits. I'm sure we will find patterns in God's speech to us. Doubtless we can use this book from our discoveries together.

To obtain your log-in username and password, please visit ParadigmLighthouse.com and follow the instructions you see after clicking *Request Log-in Credentials*.

REVIEWS ON AMAZON

Every single review left by a reader helps someone else see and benefit from this Book Two of the *Unseen* Series. Your review can help others unlock Bible mysteries. As you know from your own online shopping, the number of reviews for a book matters—whether the reviewer agrees or not. Short or long, general or specific, your review will make a positive impact.

Please visit Amazon.com to leave your review for *Nobody Sees This Unseen Realm: How to Unlock Bible Mysteries* .

SOCIAL MEDIA

Neither the author nor publisher utilize social media. If you do, please mention the book by its title, *Nobody Sees This Unseen Realm: How to Unlock Bible Mysteries*. Our ranking on Amazon is affected by people searching for the book by name.

You may also like to share the ParadigmLighthouse.com link, where people can purchase the books as well.

ESTHER

How can a regular person unlock Bible mysteries?

This sample study of Esther demonstrates the techniques and attitudes explained in this Book Two of the *Unseen* Series. You can apply these to any portion of the Bible.

Our goal is to hear and be submissive to what God is saying. We want to firmly establish our walk with God. We want to check and confirm that it is the real Jesus we are following.

We want to be Christians who are biblically based and biblically accurate. We want no foreign elements in our thoughts about God. Meekness demands that we check ourselves periodically: "is my theological framework truly biblical?" We can assume it is—or we can return to Scripture hungrily. We desire, rather than evade, our accountability to His revealed truth.

Why the book of Esther? Esther is the one Bible book in which God's name does not appear. Its author instead chose to put God's fingerprints all over the events it relates. Esther will equip us to recognize His "coincidences."

Esther's brevity makes it conducive to a four week time frame. Its content is 100% narrative (compared to Ezra's and Nehemiah's mixed styles). You will sharpen inductive Bible study skills and be equipped for any book of the Bible. Best of all, the book of Esther will strengthen our confidence that we know the true God and hear Him truly.

How is Persian courtroom intrigue 2,500 years ago relevant to us? This book tells how God led two people who loved Him. Through Esther, He spoke to its first readers—likewise, He speaks to us in the present. The term, "Present Truth Bible Study," uses Apostle Peter's assumption in 2 Peter 1:12.

The Present Truth Movement recognizes that Bible truths long-ignored are being restored to the Church at an accelerating pace. As a theological framework, Present Truth has the most explanatory power for what happens today, in the world at large, in our churches, and in our spirits. The word "theology" is not intimidating. It simply means *words about God.* But like the air we breathe, there can be foreign elements in our thoughts about God.

We want to *own* the book of Esther. By recognizing His patterns in their circumstances, we protect ourselves from any pretend God in our own times. We want to digest Esther so that we honor the voice of our Lord Jesus, and not a foreign pretender from the unseen kingdom of darkness.

This study is designed as a series of four overviews. Rather than verse by verse, you will read the entire book of Esther at one time in several sittings. Verse numbers are replaced by line numbers for reference. Traditional Bible paragraphing isn't used; the text is double spaced allowing plenty of room for your marks.

At first, it might feel odd not having a traditional verse, paragraph, and chapter organization. Esther is a short story; read it as you would read any short story—all at once, with full comprehension. With practice, you'll find this natural. Give yourself several days to chew on each overview reading of Esther. Interlacing the daily events of your own life with your overviews will help you understand Esther better each time.

Some alerts:

1. *Translation*
   In order to facilitate group conversation, it's helpful to use one common translation. The New King James is used in the following images; an unmarked original of Esther is available for download at ParadigmLighthouse.com. You can use any translation you like.

2. *Avoid Premature Outside Input*
   Study notes, commentaries, and other such resources are valuable but only after your own series of overview readings. The opinions of outside "scholars" may be qualified, but can precondition you. You can actually miss the plain meaning of the text itself.

3. *Speak Up*
   If used in a group study, no one person should dominate, especially not the leader. The open-ended design lets mutual discussion fill the room.

4. *Format*

   Chapter and verse numbers were added centuries afterward by others. To help discussion, the nine-chapter division is retained for this study of Esther. Instead of verse numbers, this study uses line numbers.

5. *Mark It Up*

   Some can feel that respect for the Scripture prohibits marking in it. Others want to make their Bible last a long time. That's another reason for the double spaced presentation following: so you feel free to mark it up! Here are some things I use:

   – triangles

   – rectangles

   – squares

   – circles

   – colors of ink

   – squiggly lines

   – exclamation marks

   – letter codes

   – symbols of all kinds

6. *The Wisdom*

   Esther is in the Scripture, the Word of God—but doesn't even mention God's name. The Holy Spirit of God wanted Esther in the Bible—but why? What is the unique contribution that the book of Esther makes to our walk with Jesus? Our fellowship? Our citizenship? We are studying **Esther**—and we want to *own* its wisdom, so that it echoes throughout our lives.

7. *Style*

   Using our overview methods, we'll observe that the book of Esther has a style all its own—and a very dramatic style it is. In fact, the style of writing will help us understand the wisdom God has for us.

8. *Inductive Study And The Courtroom Comparison*

   In a jury trial, there are attorneys who represent either the plaintiff or the defendant. There is a jury. How do their jobs differ? The attorneys start with their conclusion—and they align and present all the facts in a way that supports their conclusion. This is deductive reasoning. It has plagued the Church for centuries because people use Scripture to support their preferred conclusions and sacred cows.

Our privilege is like that of the jury: to listen to the Holy Spirit and let Him reveal facts to us in Esther. This is inductive reasoning, because we start with the facts and we follow them. Regardless of the conclusion they may lead to, we yield to the facts. We weigh the facts, deliberate with others about them, and submit ourselves to the conclusions we reach.

9. *Apply These Techniques And Attitudes To Every Bible Passage*
   We are accountable to use what God has made available to us. This Book Two in the *Unseen* Series has equipped you to understand God's Word and unlock His mysteries. But will you use this equipment? James 1:22-25 warns us to be doers of the word, and not hearers only. 2 Peter 1:5-10 tells us twice, *make every effort.* By adopting the attitudes described in this book, you will be in sync with His work on the earth today.

OVERARCHING IMPRESSIONS:

ESTHER

READING **ONE**:

A. What are your general impressions of Esther as a whole?

B. Write a dramatic summary.

C. If one of today's journalists were the recorder of Chapter 1, why would they have written it with so much detail? What motives would today's court recorder possibly have for including all the details you find? What questions would they be trying to answer for their viewer, readers, listeners?

D. What's your favorite part, and why?

READING **TWO**:

A. While reading all 9 chapters, identify the following using the marks suggested:
   - physical locations, # (pound sign)
   - king's responses, K
   - coincidences, C
   - rhythmic language or idioms, P (for "Persian")

B. What do you notice? What's meaningful to you?

C. How would you describe the style of the book?

READING **THREE**:

A. While reading the entire book, try giving a title to each chapter.

B. As if each chapter were a person, ask each one "What is your individual purpose? What do you contribute to this story? What would be absent if you were not here?"

C. How is the story of Purim augmented by each successive section? What is in each section, that was not in the previous one? Or undergirds the following one?

D. If you want to practice a new study skill, try creating some paragraph divisions. Indicate your paragraph division like this:... *went there.* ⌐ *After these things, the....*

READING **FOUR**:

A. Why did the Holy Spirit want this book in the Word of God?

B. What delighted you most to see? What affirms your walk with God? What challenges your walk with God?

C. What's in this book for *our church*?

D. After all that the Holy Spirit has shown me in Esther, what does He expect of me? Is He reinforcing something good in me? Maybe He's filling a gap in my life with something new. Consider these questions with the following list.
  • Attitudes
  • Habits
  • Ways I show His love
  • Pressure, calamity and stress
  • Response to others, high and low
  • Life as an unseen spirit in an unseen world

Reign of Ahasuerus = 486-465 BC
(aka Xerxes I)

Esther born @ 505 BC

Mordecai her uncle born @ 525 bc

Therefore:

486 34 Esther age 19 when Ahasuerus crowned

483 42   age 22 when Vashti lost her
                            throne (A's 3rd yr 1:3)
481 44   age 24 when virgins summoned (1:12)
479 46   age 26 when taken to A in
                            7th yr (2:16)

↑
Mordecai age

Esther queened 479 = 116 years after 595
                              destruction of Jerusalem
                        = 56 years after return
                        =

she was part of the group that stayed &
did not return   WAS GOD STILL WITH THEM?
The dominant target is that the Jews
could be wiped out, everywhere. It's
made more threatening because it was
God's severe judgement that put them
there. Was He still working to wipe
them out?
  Because this was a live question, Mordecai
          advised her to keep her secret.

1 ESTHER New King James Version. 363,392,404, 425,431 *inspiring love & fear*

distinguishing him as the greatest of the 2 rival kings

2 CHAPTER ONE
A vacuum created

(27)

3 Now it came to pass in the days of Ahasuerus (this *was* the Ahasuerus

4 who reigned over one hundred and twenty-seven provinces, from India

5 to Ethiopia), in those days when King Ahasuerus sat on the throne of

6 his kingdom, which *was* in Shushan the citadel, *that* in the third year of
   Venus Persepolis

7 his reign he made a feast for all his officials and servants—the powers

8 of Persia and Media, the nobles, and the princes of the

9 provinces *being* before him— when he showed the riches of his
   consolidating power? The Lord is

10 glorious kingdom and the splendor of his excellent majesty for many

187 total

11 days, one hundred and eighty days *in all.* And when these days were

12 completed, the king made a feast lasting seven days for all the people
   i.e. important moment too possibly women including

13 who were present in Shushan the citadel, from great to small, in the

one of these people wrote this

14 court of the garden of the king's palace. *There were* white and blue
   very detailed description including the materials - would be of interest to one who dug it? l.110 & guide servants

15 linen *curtains* fastened with cords of fine linen and purple on silver rods

16 and marble pillars; *and the* couches *were* of gold and silver on

17 a *mosaic* pavement of alabaster, turquoise, and white and black

18 marble. And they served drinks in golden vessels, each vessel being

19 different from the other, with royal wine in abundance, according to the

i.e. you didn't have to act a certain way to pay your head!

20 generosity of the king. In accordance with the law, the drinking was not
   this generosity foretold in Is 13.17 it's attitude of liberty - versus Gen. 15-8

21 compulsory; for so the king had ordered all the officers of his
   & not servants

22 household, that they should do according to each man's pleasure.

23 Queen Vashti also made a feast for the women *in the* royal palace *women only*
   of Susa, line 12-13

24 which *belonged to* King Ahasuerus. On the seventh day, when the heart

25 of the king was merry with wine, he commanded Mehuman, Biztha, *the eunuchs*

26 Harbona, Bigtha, Abagtha, Zethar, and Carcas, seven eunuchs who *named*

27 served in the presence of King Ahasuerus, to bring Queen Vashti *before the advisors*

K = Ahaseurus. E = Esther. H = Haman. M= Mordecai. V = Vashti.

1 ESTHER New King James Version.

2 CHAPTER ONE

3 Now it came to pass in the days

These events occurred beginning 486 BC. Ahasuerus (Xerxes I) reigned until 465 BC. The kingdom was that of Persia, founded by Cyrus the Great in 559 BC. Ahasuerus was the fifth in line, a line that endured until 1979.

4 of Ahasuerus (this *was* the

5 Ahasuerus who reigned over one hundred and twenty-seven provinces, from India to

6 Ethiopia),

7 in those

Why this identifier? What readers' question was the writer answering? That there was another Ahasuerus, and this is the one he is writing about.

8 days when King Ahasuerus sat on the throne of his kingdom, which *was* in Shushan the

Why this location statement? The Persians didn't have capitals in our manner—only one. They had at least two and for some time four, each with a different purpose. The Persian Empire consisted of four of what we would call states, and each state's capital served unique imperial functions. Whichever capital the king made his seat had special prominence. The writer is including this information assuming the reader knows this, and is wondering where the king's capital was.

9 citadel, *that* in the third year of his reign he 485 BC made a feast for all his officials

10 and servants—the powers of Persia and Media, the nobles, and the princes of the

11 provinces *being* before him— when he showed the riches of his glorious kingdom and the

12 splendor of his excellent majesty for many days, one

13 hundred and eighty days *in all*. And when these

14 days were completed, the king made a feast lasting

15 seven days for all the people who were present in

16 Shushan the citadel, from great to small, in the court

This and subsequent statements alert the reader that K strove to maintain a celebratory atmosphere. We may infer that his manner of coping with kingly pressures was to eliminate stressful people & surround himself with those who made him feel good. This set him up for H's deception.

17

18

19

20

Descriptions of the finery occur repeatedly in the book. Why? At least they show the writer was a direct witness to the events. But why the importance to include them? Ancient writers would not be writing to address modern authorship skepticism.

of the garden of the king's palace. *There*

were white and blue linen *curtains* fastened with

cords of fine linen and purple on silver rods and

marble pillars; *and the* couches *were* of gold and

21 silver on a *mosaic* pavement of alabaster, turquoise, and white and black marble. And they

22 served drinks in golden vessels, each vessel being different from the other, with royal wine

23 in abundance, according to the generosity of the

24 king. In accordance with the law, the drinking was

25 not compulsory; for so the king had ordered all the

> The description even of the drinking vessels, the uniqueness of each one, and the freedom of each person, conveys the wonder that the event inspired among its participants, and suggests that even the writer was there.

26

27

> This, the declaration concerning V, and the treatment of M suggests that K followed a policy of making all his male subjects under him feel kingly themselves.

officers of his household, that they should

do according to each man's pleasure.

28 Queen Vashti also made a feast for the women *in* the royal palace which *belonged* to King

29 Ahasuerus. On the seventh day, when the heart of the king was merry with wine, he

30 commanded

31 Mehuman, Biztha,

32 Harbona, Bigtha,

33 Abagtha, Zethar, and

> Why are the eunuchs named? At the least it again affirms the intimate knowledge the writer had of this king's court—very intimate. We might suspect E herself to be the author, who would certainly know these names, or at least the source of them. We might also suspect that their naming here is a form of honoring tribute, as if they had a significant role in subsequent events.

34 Carcas, seven eunuchs who served in the presence of King Ahasuerus, to bring Queen

35 Vashti before the king, *wearing* her royal crown, in order to show her beauty to the people

36 and the officials, for she *was* beautiful to behold. But Queen Vashti refused to come at the

37 king's command *brought* by *his* eunuchs; therefore the king was furious, and his anger

> The interplay of K & V is multi-layered. On one level, K is using these banquets to consolidate his three-year-old reign. By the display of his opulence, including his wife's beauty, he is exemplifying to his subjects the kingliness he welcomes all o them to manifest in their own homes—a stated objective in his coming decree about V. On another, V is serving as a foil for E. K calls V & she refuses. E risks her life to go to K, & he accepts. E approaches K quite humbly, assuming nothing. V thinks more highly of herself

38 burned within him. Then the king said to the wise men who understood the times (for

39 this *was* the king's manner toward all who knew law and justice, those closest to him *being*

40 Carshena, Shethar, Admatha, Tarshish, Meres, Marsena, and Memucan, the seven

41 princes of Persia and Media, who had access to the king's presence, *and* who ranked

42 highest in the

> Not only is intimate knowledge of the court evidenced by this list, and who was in ("closest") but also of the king's habitual attitude toward law & justice—based on "understanding the times." Thus we see K's considers law to be situational, not transcendent. Among the situational concerns are the precedents, namely, a king's decree may not be revoked—significant later.

28   before the king, *wearing* her royal crown, in order to show her beauty to

29   the people and the officials, for she *was* beautiful to behold. But Queen

30   Vashti refused to come at the king's command *brought by his* eunuchs;

31   therefore the king was furious, and his anger burned within him. Then

32   the king said to the wise men who understood the times (for

33   this *was* the king's manner toward all who knew law and justice, those

34   closest to him *being* Carshena, Shethar, Admatha, Tarshish, Meres,

35   Marsena, and Memucan, the seven princes of Persia and Media, who

36   had access to the king's presence, *and* who ranked highest in the

37   kingdom): "What *shall we* do to Queen Vashti, according to law,

38   because she did not obey the command of King Ahasuerus *brought to*

39   *her* by the eunuchs?" And Memucan answered before the king and the

40   princes: "Queen Vashti has not only wronged the king, but also all the

41   princes, and all the people who *are* in all the provinces of King

42   Ahasuerus. For the queen's behavior will become known to all women,

43   so that they will despise their husbands in their eyes, when they report,

44   'King Ahasuerus commanded Queen Vashti to be brought in before

45   him, but she did not come.' This very day the *noble* ladies of Persia and

46   Media will say to all the king's officials that they have heard of the

47   behavior of the queen. Thus *there will be* excessive contempt and

48   wrath. If it pleases the king, let a royal decree go out from him, and let it

49   be recorded in the laws of the Persians and the Medes, so that it will

50   not be altered, that Vashti shall come no more before King Ahasuerus;

51   and let the king give her royal position to another who is better than

52   she. When the king's decree which he will make is proclaimed

53   throughout all his empire (for it is great), all wives will honor their

54   husbands, both great and small." And the reply pleased the king and

Handwritten annotations:

- image the women, "why pa my egged heroe, should he be slave to these men?"
- dramatic mood change from p. 1 & 2 25
- PRIVATE
- His anger spurred him to seek advice, not to retaliate.
- what was? i.e., to seek advice & not act out of anger.
- He valued being just & lawful.
- none of these mentioned again
- not everyone. The K's presence governed by U. 193-197, cf. 256.
- the Scope of her offense
- who were at her party — the consequence of her offense.
- our media — fanning flames, sowing discord, opposing authority
- the solution for her offense.
- she wasn't executed
- they were wiser than us

the K's flaring again

the king not too proud

55 the princes, and the king did according to the word of Memucan. Then

56 he sent letters to all the king's provinces, to each province in its own *p*

57 script, and to every people in their own language, that each man should

58 be master in his own house, and speak in the language of his own

59 people. *this was extra, not in Memucan's advice. But shows a recognition/ acceptance of linguistic identity*

Beautification, or

60 CHAPTER TWO *E+ more positioned + keep each entity segregated*

61 After these things, when the wrath of King Ahasuerus subsided, he

62 remembered Vashti, what she had done, and what had been decreed *maybe he was brooding*

63 against her. Then the king's servants who attended him said: "Let ~~THE SECRET SAUCE~~

64 beautiful young virgins be sought for the king; and let the king appoint *127 candidates.*

65 officers in all the *127* provinces of his kingdom, that they may gather all the *E was there as*

66 beautiful young virgins to Shushan the citadel, into the women's *the most beautiful in Susa.*

67 quarters, under the custody of Hegai the king's eunuch, custodian of *See Herodotus*

68 the women. And let beauty preparations be given *them.* Then let the

69 young woman who pleases the king be queen instead of Vashti." This

70 thing pleased the king, and he did so. In Shushan the citadel there was

a specific lineage

71 a certain Jew whose name *was* Mordecai the son of Jair, the son of

72 Shimei, the son of Kish, a Benjamite. *Kish* had been carried away from *Whoever wrote this knew M's*

73 Jerusalem with the captives who had been captured with Jeconiah king *genealogy*

74 of Judah, whom Nebuchadnezzar the king of Babylon had carried

75 away. And *Mordecai* had brought up Hadassah, that *is,* Esther, his

why 2? *his cousin* *ABIHAIL, her mother & father, c. 4.28*

76 *lovely* uncle's daughter, for she had neither father nor mother. The young

includes

within 77 woman *was* lovely and beautiful. When her father and mother died, *violent*

they died young, close together *accident*

78 Mordecai took her as his own daughter. So it was, when the king's *disease*

PRIVATE

79 command and decree were heard, and when many young women were

not previously named

80 gathered at Shushan the citadel, *under* the custody of Hegai, that

81 Esther also was taken to the king's palace, into the care of Hegai the

110 years (480 BC) after being exiled here *She submits*

same offense as in Braveheart

H's approach is to use your power, at encouragement of 3 his wife + his wise men. Lk 22: 24-25

M + E's approach is not to use your power, + to defer with respect to proper authority Lk 22 26-30
with them were the maids, the eunuchs, the king's servants & the scribes.

✳

In our lives & society, unseen rulers promote undeserving, pompous, & self-absorbed priorities and command us to bow & pay homage. Yet they must be recognized as enemies, and we must not bow & pay homage to them. And whatever intensified persecution it promotes, we must not bow, and leave it to God to work out the circumstances as he sees fit.

82 custodian of the women. Now the young woman pleased him, and she   *favor*

83 obtained his favor; so he readily gave beauty preparations to her,

84 besides her allowance. Then seven choice maidservants were provided   *3 signs*

85 for her from the king's palace, and he moved her and her maidservants   *of favor.*

86 to the best place in the house of the women. Esther had not revealed   *private* *one private thing*

87 her people or family, for Mordecai had charged her not to reveal *it.* And   *would + he have*

    she submitted   *given her identity away &*

88 every day Mordecai paced in front of the court of the women's quarters,   *this!*

from whom?

The king's servants who see a family bond that's unique + strong + maybe unusual

89 to learn of Esther's welfare and what was happening to her. Each

90 young woman's turn came to go in to King Ahasuerus after she had

91 completed twelve months' preparation, according to the regulations for

92 the women, for thus were the days of their preparation apportioned: six

93 months with oil of myrrh, and six months with perfumes and

94 preparations for beautifying women. Thus *prepared, each* young

95 woman went to the king, and she was given whatever she desired to   *not excessively named*

96 take with her from the women's quarters to the king's palace. In the

97 evening she went, and in the morning she returned to the second

98 house of the women, to the custody of Shaashgaz, the king's eunuch   *Contrast: desires.*

99 who kept the concubines. She would not go in to the king again unless   *Nowhere do we see it as a woman*

100 the king delighted in her and called for her by name. Now when the turn   *dominated by desire! unlike*

why is the r'ship repeated? b/c it's valued

101 came for Esther the daughter of Abihail the uncle of Mordecai, who had   *others?*

102 taken her as his daughter, to go in to the king, she requested nothing   *humble*

    she submits

"Tevet"

103 but what Hegai the king's eunuch, the custodian of the women,   *intelligence*

Heb or Persian

104 advised. And Esther obtained favor in the sight of all who saw her. So   *the talk of the palace - no criticism heard -*

105 Esther was taken to King Ahasuerus, into his royal palace, in the tenth

106 month, which *is* the month of Tebeth, in the seventh year of his   *#7 (4 yrs after V)*

107 reign. The king loved Esther more than all the *other* women, and she   *favor* *I hope it's her!"*

108 obtained grace and favor in his sight more than all the virgins; so he set

Hegai the custodian of the women 3 x

her deferential character made her the anti-Vashti

The Feast of Esther

109 the royal crown upon her head and made her queen instead of

110 Vashti. Then the king made a great feast (the Feast of Esther) for all his — *he included the servants! a la*

111 officials and servants; and he proclaimed a holiday in the provinces and

112 gave gifts according to the generosity of a king. When virgins were — *he gave gifts to honor himself? this generosity*

for what?

113 gathered together a second time, Mordecai sat within the king's — *i.e. m had*

114 gate. Now Esther had not revealed her family and her people, just as *become one of the K's officials* PRIVATE

115 Mordecai had charged her, for Esther obeyed the command of *so who is the real king.*

116 Mordecai as when she was brought up by him. In those days, while

117 Mordecai sat within the king's gate, two of the king's eunuchs, Bigthan

118 and Teresh, doorkeepers, became furious and sought to lay hands on

119 King Ahasuerus. So the matter became known to Mordecai, who told — *she didn't seek a reward for it,*

120 Queen Esther, and Esther informed the king in Mordecai's name. And — *either for honor her, setting up*

121 when an inquiry was made into the matter, it was confirmed, and both — *her, setting up*

122 were hanged on a gallows; and it was written in the book of the — *U. 270-273. Neither*

123 chronicles in the presence of the king. *a servant was — E nor m would have here writing it down — requested such a reward. And then*

DEATH DECREE

124 CHAPTER THREE *0-d-4 ways to exalt H — EoM's rise is b but not H's — example of not seeking*

Aging one of EX 17 Amalekites

125 After these things King Ahasuerus promoted Haman, the son of *unilateral/sudden — reward War followed by few's in 398 etal*

also in I Sam 15 in 1100 BC + Hermon in 479 BC

126 Hammedatha the Agagite, and advanced him and set his seat above all *This is in here to set up*

127 the princes who were with him. And all the king's servants *M's difference, but is there a — those in Ull. 34-33*

128 who were within the king's gate bowed and paid homage to Haman, for *subtle it they wouldn't have done*

129 so the king had commanded concerning him. But Mordecai would not *it except by K's — but not the orig 7 to bow? where did this come from? (really from*

130 bow or pay homage. Then the king's servants who were within the *command?*

the story never gives an answer

131 king's gate said to Mordecai, "Why do you transgress the king's — *their focus is on*

132 command?" Now it happened, when they spoke to him daily and he *K's command - not H's qualities!*

133 would not listen to them, that they told it to Haman, to see whether *Not what he told Esther*

134 Mordecai's words would stand; for Mordecai had told them that he was a *i.e. they tell H M was a Jew*

135 Jew. When Haman saw that Mordecai did not bow or pay him homage, *knowing H was sensitive*

was it a command like De 190-193, which H himself created - Ull. 234-231

→ Mordecai's words are not recorded!

bow & pay homage 3 x   M needed,   synonyms, or 2 separate acts?   no such decree   Uu 367-372

keep his duplicitous character — it may have part to him anonymous jews

about it - did H know I am a Jew?

136 Haman was filled with wrath. But he disdained to lay hands on

137 Mordecai alone, for they had told him of the people of Mordecai.

138 Instead, Haman sought to destroy all the Jews who *were* throughout   *he didn't 'throw it*

139 the whole kingdom of Ahasuerus—the people of Mordecai. In the first   *was Esther's too!*

140 month, which is the month of Nisan, in the twelfth year of King   *E now @ 5 years*

141 Ahasuerus, they cast Pur (that *is*, the lot), before Haman to determine

142 the day and the month, until *it fell on the* twelfth *month*, which *is* the   *Haman + friends*

143 month of Adar. Then Haman said to King Ahasuerus, "There is a   *the Jews had gone*

144 certain people scattered and dispersed among the people in all the   *everywhere that did not*
                                                                              return to Israel.

145 provinces of your kingdom; their laws *are* different from   *a lie. from the I to the many*

146 all *other* people's, and they do not keep the king's laws. Therefore

147 it *is* not fitting for the king to let them remain. If it pleases the king, let *a*

148 *decree* be written that they be destroyed, and I will pay ten thousand   *Haman's generosity*
                                                                              to the king impressed
149 talents of silver into the hands of those who do the work, to bring *it* into   *him.*

150 the king's treasuries." So the king took his signet ring from his hand and

151 gave it to Haman, the son of Hammedatha the Agagite, the enemy of

152 the Jews. And the king said to Haman, "The money and the   *K seems to differ too*
                                                                    readily w/o considering
153 people *are* given to you, to do with them as seems good to you." Then   *the consequences.*

154 the king's scribes were called on the thirteenth day of the first month,

155 and *a decree* was written according to all that Haman commanded—to

156 the king's satraps, to the governors who *were* over each province, to

157 the officials of all people, to every province according to its script, and

158 to every people in their language. In the name of King Ahasuerus it was

159 written, and sealed with the king's signet ring. And the letters were sent

160 by couriers into all the king's provinces, to destroy, to kill, and to

161 annihilate all the Jews, both young and old, little children and women, in

162 one day, on the thirteenth *day* of the twelfth month, which *is* the month

Hebrew month

source of feast of name

H's decree had a motive or bribe of punishment for those who obeyed

163 of Adar, and to plunder their possessions. A copy of the document was

164 to be issued as law in every province, being published for all people,

165 that they should be ready for that day. The couriers went out, hastened

166 by the king's command; and the decree was proclaimed in Shushan the

167 citadel. So the king and Haman sat down to drink, but the city of *like D.C., mostly*

168 Shushan was perplexed. *Foreshadowing* *fed ee's like the king's servants*

169 CHAPTER FOUR *Esther Decides to Risk*

170 When Mordecai learned all that had happened, he tore his clothes and *SO PUBLIC*

171 put on sackcloth and ashes, and went out into the midst of the city. He *Mordecai conducted himself publicly +*

172 cried out with a loud and bitter cry. He went as far as the front of the *not withdrawn.*

173 king's gate, for no one *might* enter the king's gate clothed with

174 sackcloth. And in every province where the king's command and

175 decree arrived, *there was* great mourning among the Jews, with fasting,

176 weeping, and wailing; and many lay in sackcloth and ashes. So

177 Esther's maids and eunuchs came and told her, and the queen was *Esther's company*

178 deeply distressed. Then she sent garments to clothe Mordecai and take

179 his sackcloth away from him, but he would not accept *them*. Then

180 Esther called Hathach, *one* of the king's eunuchs whom he had *not previously named*

181 appointed to attend her, and she gave him a command concerning

182 Mordecai, to learn what and why this *was*. So Hathach went out to

183 Mordecai in the city square that *was* in front of the king's gate. And

184 Mordecai told him all that had happened to him, and the sum of money *how did he know this? He*

185 that Haman had promised to pay into the king's treasuries to destroy *has his ear to the*

186 the Jews. He also gave him a copy of the written decree for their *ground + some of the servants*

187 destruction, which was given at Shushan, that he might show it to *present knew it.*

188 Esther and explain it to her, and that he might command her to go in to *+ favored M.*

189 the king to make supplication to him and plead before him for her

190 people. So Hathach returned and told Esther the words of Mordecai.

191 Then Esther spoke to Hathach, and gave him a command for

192 Mordecai: "All the king's servants and the people of the king's provinces

193 know that any man or woman who goes into the inner court to the king,

194 who has not been called, *he has* but one law: put *all* to death, except the

195 one to whom the king holds out the golden scepter, that he may live.

196 Yet I myself have not been called to go in to the king these thirty

197 days." So they told Mordecai Esther's words. And Mordecai told *them* to

198 answer Esther: "Do not think in your heart that you will escape in the

199 king's palace any more than all the other Jews. For if you remain

200 completely silent at this time, relief and deliverance will arise for the

201 Jews from another place, but you and your father's house will perish.

202 Yet who knows whether you have come to the kingdom for *such* a time

203 as this?" Then Esther told *them* to reply to Mordecai: "Go, gather all the

204 Jews who are present in Shushan, and fast for me; neither eat nor drink

205 for three days, night or day. My maids and I will fast likewise. And so I

206 will go to the king, which *is* against the law; and if I perish, I perish!" So

207 Mordecai went his way and did according to all that Esther commanded

208 him.

209 CHAPTER FIVE

210 Now it happened on the third day that Esther put on *her* royal *robes* and

211 stood in the inner court of the king's palace, across from the king's

212 house, while the king sat on his royal throne in the royal house, facing

213 the entrance of the house. So it was, when the king saw Queen Esther

214 standing in the court, *that* she found favor in his sight, and the king held

215 out to Esther the golden scepter that *was* in his hand. Then Esther went

216 near and touched the top of the scepter. And the king said to her, "What

217   do you wish, Queen Esther? What *is* your request? It shall be given to

218   you—up to half the kingdom!" So Esther answered, "If it pleases the   *she didn't presume upon his invitation*

219   king, let the king and Haman come today to the banquet that I have   *she did it before he*

220   prepared for him." Then the king said, "Bring Haman quickly, that he   *agreed. It was*

221   may do as Esther has said." So the king and Haman went to the   *ready when he arrived.*

222   banquet that Esther had prepared. At the banquet of wine the king said

223   to Esther, "What *is* your petition? It shall be granted you. What *is* your

224   request, up to half the kingdom? It shall be done!" Then Esther

225   answered and said, "My petition and request *is this:* If I have found   *she didn't presume.*

226   favor in the sight of the king, and if it pleases the king to grant my   *did she lose her*

227   petition and fulfill my request, then let the king and Haman come to the   *nerve? change in*

228   banquet which I will prepare for them, and tomorrow I will do as the king   *midstream? or*

229   has said." So Haman went out that day joyful and with a glad heart; but   *perceive the time wasn't right.*

230   when Haman saw Mordecai in the king's gate, and that he did not stand

231   or tremble before him, he was filled with indignation against

232   Mordecai. Nevertheless Haman restrained himself and went home, and

233   he sent and called for his friends and his wife Zeresh. Then Haman told

234   them of his great riches, the multitude of his children, everything in

235   which the king had promoted him, and how he had advanced him) *ee126-129*   *all this,*

236   above the officials and servants of the king. Moreover Haman said,   *honor doesn*

237   "Besides, Queen Esther invited no one but me to come in with the king   *satisfy Me he*

238   to the banquet that she prepared; and tomorrow I am again invited by   *needs them— they*

239   her, along with the king. Yet all this avails me nothing, so long as I see   *he just couldn't*

240   Mordecai the Jew sitting at the king's gate." Then his wife Zeresh and   *leave well enough*

241   all his friends said to him, "Let a gallows be made, fifty cubits high, and   *alone*

242   in the morning suggest to the king that Mordecai be hanged on it; then

243   go merrily with the king to the banquet." And the thing pleased Haman;   *neither E nor k knew this during next banquet!*

244   so he had the gallows made.

245   **CHAPTER SIX**

246   That night the king could not sleep. So one was commanded to bring

247   the book of the records of the chronicles: and they were read before the

248   king. And it was found written that Mordecai had told of Bigthana and

249   Teresh, two of the king's eunuchs, the doorkeepers who had sought to

250   lay hands on King Ahasuerus. Then the king said, "What honor or

251   dignity has been bestowed on Mordecai for this?" And the king's

252   servants who attended him said, "Nothing has been done for him." So

253   the king said, "Who *is* in the court?" Now Haman had *just* entered the

254   outer court of the king's palace to suggest that the king hang Mordecai

255   on the gallows that he had prepared for him. The king's servants said to

256   him, "Haman is there, standing in the court." And the king said, "Let him

257   come in." So Haman came in, and the king asked him, "What shall be

258   done for the man whom the king delights to honor?" Now Haman

259   thought in his heart, "Whom would the king delight to honor more than

260   me?" And Haman answered the king, "*For* the man whom the king

261   delights to honor, let a royal robe be brought which the king has worn,

262   and a horse on which the king has ridden, which has a royal crest

263   placed on its head. Then let this robe and horse be delivered to the

264   hand of one of the king's most noble princes, that he may array the

265   man whom the king delights to honor. Then parade him on horseback

266   through the city square, and proclaim before him: 'Thus shall it be done

267   to the man whom the king delights to honor!'" Then the king said to

268   Haman, "Hurry, take the robe and the horse, as you have suggested,

269   and do so for Mordecai the Jew who sits within the king's gate! Leave

270   nothing undone of all that you have spoken." So Haman took the robe

271 and the horse, arrayed Mordecai and led him on horseback through the

272 city square, and proclaimed before him, "Thus shall it be done to the

273 man whom the king delights to honor!" Afterward Mordecai went back

274 to the king's gate. But Haman hurried to his house, mourning and with

275 his head covered. When Haman told his wife Zeresh and all his friends

276 everything that had happened to him, his wise men and his wife Zeresh

277 said to him, "If Mordecai, before whom you have begun to fall, is of

278 Jewish descent, you will not prevail against him but will surely fall

279 before him." While they *were* still talking with him, the king's eunuchs

280 came, and hastened to bring Haman to the banquet which Esther had

281 prepared.

282 CHAPTER SEVEN

283 So the king and Haman went to dine with Queen Esther. And on the

284 second day, at the banquet of wine, the king again said to Esther,

285 "What *is* your petition, Queen Esther? It shall be granted you. And

286 what *is* your request, up to half the kingdom? It shall be done!" Then

287 Queen Esther answered and said, "If I have found favor in your sight, O

288 king, and if it pleases the king, let my life be given me at my petition,

289 and my people at my request. For we have been sold, my people and I,

290 to be destroyed, to be killed, and to be annihilated. Had we been sold

291 as male and female slaves, I would have held my tongue, although the

292 enemy could never compensate for the king's loss." So King Ahasuerus

293 answered and said to Queen Esther, "Who is he, and where is he, who

294 would dare presume in his heart to do such a thing?" And Esther said,

295 "The adversary and enemy *is* this wicked Haman!" So Haman was

296 terrified before the king and queen. Then the king arose in his wrath

297 from the banquet of wine *and went* into the palace garden; but Haman

298   stood before Queen Esther, pleading for his life, for he saw that evil

299   was determined against him by the king. When the king returned from

300   the palace garden to the place of the banquet of wine, Haman had

301   fallen across the couch where Esther *was*. Then the king said, "Will he

302   also assault the queen while I *am* in the house?" As the word left the

303   king's mouth, they covered Haman's face. Now Harbonah, one of the   *v. 26*

304   eunuchs, said to the king, "Look! The gallows, fifty cubits high, which   *how handy!*

305   Haman made for Mordecai, who spoke good on the king's behalf, is

306   standing at the house of Haman." Then the king said, "Hang him on it!"

307   So they hanged Haman on the gallows that he had prepared for

308   Mordecai. Then the king's wrath subsided.

309   *CHAPTER EIGHT E's COUNTER DEGREE OF LIFE*

310   On that day King Ahasuerus gave Queen Esther the house of Haman,

311   the enemy of the Jews. And Mordecai came before the king, for Esther   *the k now realized*

312   had told how he *was related* to her. So the king took off his signet ring *how little they had*

313   which he had taken from Haman, and gave it to Mordecai; and Esther *used their position*

314   appointed Mordecai over the house of Haman. Now Esther spoke again *for their benefit*

315   to the king, fell down at his feet, and implored him with tears to

316   counteract the evil of Haman the Agagite, and the scheme which he

317   had devised against the Jews. And the king held out the golden scepter

318   toward Esther. So Esther arose and stood before the king, and said, "If *she never presumes*

319   it pleases the king, and if I have found favor in his sight and the

320   thing *seems* right to the king and I am pleasing in his eyes, let it be

321   written to revoke the letters devised by Haman, the son of

322   Hammedatha the Agagite, which he wrote to annihilate the Jews

323   who *are* in all the king's provinces. For how can I endure to see the evil

324   that will come to my people? Or how can I endure to see the

325   destruction of my countrymen?" Then King Ahasuerus said to Queen

326   Esther and Mordecai the Jew, "Indeed, I have given Esther the house

327   of Haman, and they have hanged him on the gallows because he *tried*

328   *to* lay his hand on the Jews. You yourselves write *a decree*concerning

329   the Jews, as you please, in the king's name, and seal *it* with the king's

330   signet ring; for whatever is written in the king's name and sealed with

331   the king's signet ring no one can revoke." So the king's scribes were

332   called at that time, in the third month, which *is* the month of Sivan, on

333   the twenty-third *day;* and it was written, according to all that Mordecai

334   commanded, to the Jews, the satraps, the governors, and the princes

335   of the provinces from India to Ethiopia, one hundred and twenty-seven

336   provinces *in all*, to every province in its own script, to every people in

337   their own language, and to the Jews in their own script and

338   language. And he wrote in the name of King Ahasuerus, sealed *it* with

339   the king's signet ring, and sent letters by couriers on horseback, riding

340   on royal horses bred from swift steeds. By these letters the king

341   permitted the Jews who *were* in every city to gather together and

342   protect their lives—to destroy, kill, and annihilate all the forces of any

343   people or province that would assault them, *both* little children and

344   women, and to plunder their possessions, on one day in all the

345   provinces of King Ahasuerus, on the thirteenth *day* of the twelfth month,

346   which *is* the month of Adar. A copy of the document was to be issued

347   as a decree in every province and published for all people, so that the

348   Jews would be ready on that day to avenge themselves on their

349   enemies. The couriers who rode on royal horses went out, hastened

350   and pressed on by the king's command. And the decree was issued in

351   Shushan the citadel. So Mordecai went out from the presence of the

352   king in royal apparel of blue and white, with a great crown of gold and a

353   garment of fine linen and purple; and the city of Shushan rejoiced and

354   was glad. The Jews had light and gladness, joy and honor. And in

355   every province and city, wherever the king's command and decree

356   came, the Jews had joy and gladness, a feast and a holiday. Then

357   many of the people of the land became Jews, because fear of the Jews

358   fell upon them.

detail
public favor for m

interesting adjective series

l.277

359   CHAPTER NINE   *VICTORY & ITS REPEAT*

360   Now in the twelfth month, that *is*, the month of Adar, on the thirteenth

361   day, *the time* came for the king's command and his decree to be

362   executed. On the day that the enemies of the Jews had hoped to

363   overpower them, the opposite occurred, in that the Jews themselves

364   overpowered those who hated them. The Jews gathered together in

365   their cities throughout all the provinces of King Ahasuerus to lay hands

366   on those who sought their harm. And no one could withstand them,

367   because fear of them fell upon all people. And all the officials of the

368   provinces, the satraps, the governors, and all those doing the king's

369   work, helped the Jews, because the fear of Mordecai fell upon

370   them. For Mordecai *was* great in the king's palace, and his fame spread

371   throughout all the provinces; for this man Mordecai became

372   increasingly prominent. Thus the Jews defeated all their enemies with

373   the stroke of the sword, with slaughter and destruction, and did what

374   they pleased with those who hated them. And in Shushan the citadel

375   the Jews killed and destroyed five hundred men. Also Parshandatha,

376   Dalphon, Aspatha, Poratha, Adalia, Aridatha, Parmashta, Arisai, Aridai,

377   and Vajezatha— the ten sons of Haman the son of Hammedatha, the

378   enemy of the Jews—they killed; but they did not lay a hand on the

enemies' plan BACK FIRES

mordecai's rise — & unlike Haman, he was feared w/o a command of K to bow

they had a right to plunder, they didn't exercise

379 plunder. On that day the number of those who were killed in Shushan

380 the citadel was brought to the king. And the king said to Queen Esther, *the K got a report*

381 "The Jews have killed and destroyed five hundred men in Shushan the

382 citadel, and the ten sons of Haman. What have they done in the rest of

383 the king's provinces? Now what *is* your petition? It shall be granted to *P*

384 you. Or what *is* your further request? It shall be done." Then Esther

385 said, "If it pleases the king, let it be granted to the Jews who *are* in

386 Shushan to do again tomorrow according to today's decree, and let

387 Haman's ten sons be hanged on the gallows." So the king commanded

388 this to be done; the decree was issued in Shushan, and they hanged

389 Haman's ten sons. And the Jews who *were* in Shushan gathered

390 together again on the fourteenth day of the month of Adar and killed

391 three hundred men at Shushan; but they did not lay a hand on the *all tho entitled.*

392 plunder. The remainder of the Jews in the king's provinces gathered

393 together and protected their lives, had rest from their enemies, and *75,000*

394 killed seventy-five thousand of their enemies; but they did not lay a *all tho entitled*

395 hand on the plunder. *This was* on the thirteenth day of the month of

396 Adar. And on the fourteenth of *the month* they rested and made it a day

397 of feasting and gladness. But the Jews who *were* at Shushan

398 assembled together on the thirteenth *day*, as well as on the fourteenth;

399 and on the fifteenth of *the month* they rested, and made it a day of

400 feasting and gladness. Therefore the Jews of the villages who dwelt in

401 the unwalled towns celebrated the fourteenth day of the month of

402 Adar with gladness and feasting, as a holiday, and for sending presents

403 to one another. And Mordecai wrote these things and sent letters to all *Letters #1*

404 the Jews, near and far, who *were* in all the provinces of King

405 Ahasuerus, to establish among them that they should celebrate yearly

406   the fourteenth and fifteenth days of the month of Adar, as the days on

407   which the Jews had rest from their enemies, as the month which was

408   turned from sorrow to joy for them, and from mourning to a holiday; that

409   they should make them days of feasting and joy, of sending presents to

410   one another and gifts to the poor. So the Jews accepted the custom

411   which they had begun, as Mordecai had written to them, because

in his letter #1

412   Haman, the son of Hammedatha the Agagite, the enemy of all the   *Summary*

413   Jews, had plotted against the Jews to annihilate them, and had cast

414   Pur (that *is*, the lot), to consume them and destroy them; but

namely the k

415   when *Esther* came before the king, he commanded by letter that

416   this wicked plot which *Haman* had devised against the Jews should

417   return on his own head, and that he and his sons should be hanged on

418   the gallows. So they called these days Purim, after the name Pur.

419   Therefore, because of all the words of this letter, what they had seen

M's letter #1

420   concerning this matter, and what had happened to them, the Jews

421   established and imposed it upon themselves and their descendants and

422   all who would join them, that without fail they should celebrate these

423   two days every year, according to the written *instructions* and according

M's letter #1

424   to the *prescribed* time, *that* these days *should be* remembered and kept

425   throughout every generation, every family, every province, and every) *comprehensive*

426   city, that these days of Purim should not fail *to be observed* among the

427   Jews, and *that* the memory of them should not perish among their

428   descendants. Then Queen Esther, the daughter of Abihail, with

429   Mordecai the Jew, wrote with full authority to confirm this second letter

430   about Purim. And *Mordecai* sent letters to all the Jews, to the one   *127*

431   hundred and twenty-seven provinces of the kingdom of

432   Ahasuerus, *with* words of peace and truth, to confirm these days of

433   Purim at their *appointed* time, as Mordecai the Jew and Queen Esther

434   had prescribed for them, and as they had decreed for themselves and

435   their descendants concerning matters of their fasting and lamenting. So

436   the decree of Esther confirmed these matters of Purim, and it was

437   written in the book.

interesting final phrase

Note what the book includes as "a matter of Purim:"
1) Vashti's sin allows E to rise up
   + K's sexual needs
2) Court intrigue allows M to rise up

I left off Ch 10
greatness
of Mordecai

And King Ahasuerus imposed tribute on the land and *on* the islands of the sea. 2 Now all the acts of his power and his might, and the account of the greatness of Mordecai, to which the king advanced him, *are* they not written in the book of the chronicles of the kings of Media and Persia? 3 For Mordecai the Jew *was* second to King Ahasuerus, and was great among the Jews and well received by the multitude of his brethren, seeking the good of his people and speaking peace to all his countrymen.[a]

This is the exclamation mark!
It builds faith: Follow me. This is
K decided M was better than H,
& K prospered more w/ M than w/ H.